NEW TECHNOLOGIES, ARTIFICIAL INTELLIGENCE AND SHIPPING LAW IN THE 21ST CENTURY

MARITIME AND TRANSPORT LAW LIBRARY

MARITIME AND TRANSPORT LAW LIBRARY

Offshore Contracts and Liabilities
Barış Soyer and Andrew Tettenborn

*International Maritime Conventions
Volume Two*
Navigation, Securities, Limitation of Liability
and Jurisdiction
Francesco Berlingieri

*International Maritime Conventions
Volume Three*
Protection of the Marine Environment
Francesco Berlingieri

Ship Building, Sale and Finance
Edited by Barış Soyer and Andrew Tettenborn

*The Modern Law of Marine Insurance
Volume 4*
Edited by D. Rhidian Thomas

Air Cargo Insurance
Malcom A. Clarke and George Leloudas

Offshore Oil and Gas Installations Security
An International Perspective
Mikhail Kashubsky

International Trade and Carriage of Goods
Edited by Barış Soyer and Andrew Tettenborn

Maritime Law and Practice in China
Liang Zhao and Lianjun Li

Maritime Law
Fourth Edition
Edited by Yvonne Baatz

Maritime Cross-Border Insolvency
Lia Athanassiou

The Law of Yachts and Yachting
Second Edition
Edited by Filippo Lorenzon and Richard Coles

*Maritime Liabilities in a Global and Regional
Context*
Edited by Barış Soyer and Andrew Tettenborn

New Technologies, Artificial Intelligence and Shipping Law in the 21st Century
Edited by Barış Soyer and Andrew Tettenborn

NEW TECHNOLOGIES, ARTIFICIAL INTELLIGENCE AND SHIPPING LAW IN THE 21ST CENTURY

EDITED BY

BARIŞ SOYER

ANDREW TETTENBORN

LONDON AND NEW YORK

First published 2020 by Informa Law from Routledge

2 Park Square, Milton Park, Abingdon, Oxon, OX14 4RN
605 Third Avenue, New York, NY 10017

Routledge is an imprint of the Taylor & Francis Group, an informa business

First issued in paperback 2020

Copyright © 2020 selection and editorial matter, Barış Soyer and Andrew Tettenborn; individual chapters, the contributors

The right of Barış Soyer and Andrew Tettenborn to be identified as the authors of the editorial material, and of the authors for their individual chapters, has been asserted in accordance with sections 77 and 78 of the Copyright, Designs and Patents Act 1988.

All rights reserved. No part of this book may be reprinted or reproduced or utilised in any form or by any electronic, mechanical, or other means, now known or hereafter invented, including photocopying and recording, or in any information storage or retrieval system, without permission in writing from the publishers.

Notice:
Product or corporate names may be trademarks or registered trademarks, and are used only for identification and explanation without intent to infringe.

British Library Cataloguing-in-Publication Data
A catalogue record for this book is available from the British Library

Library of Congress Cataloging-in-Publication Data
Names: Soyer, Barış. | Tettenborn, Andrew.
Title: New technologies, artificial intelligence and shipping law in the 21st century / Edited by Barış Soyer and Andrew Tettenborn.
Description: New York, NY : Routledge, 2019. | Series: Maritime and transport law library | Includes bibliographical references and index.
Identifiers: LCCN 2019020544| ISBN 9780367139179 (hardback) | ISBN 9780429029172 (ebook)
Subjects: LCSH: Maritime law. | Contracts, Maritime. | Transportation–Law and legislation. | Artificial intelligence. | Technological innovations.
Classification: LCC K1155 .N49 2019 | DDC 343.09/6–dc23
LC record available at https://lccn.loc.gov/2019020544

ISBN: 978-0-367-13917-9 (hbk)
ISBN: 978-0-367-77792-0 (pbk)

Typeset in Times New Roman
by Swales & Willis, Exeter, Devon, UK

Dedicated to Dr Theodora Nikaki, the heart and soul of the Institute of International Shipping and Trade Law, whom we lost to a cruel and swift illness on 11 April 2018.

CONTENTS

Notes on editors and contributors	ix
Foreword	xv
Preface	xvii
Table of cases	xix
Table of legislation	xxiii

	PART 1 EFFECT OF NEW TECHNOLOGIES ON CONTRACTING IN SHIPPING PRACTICE	1
1	Blockchain and smart contracts in shipping and transport: a legal revolution is about to arrive? *Professor Francesco Munari*	3
2	Smart contracts: the BIMCO experience *Grant Hunter*	17
3	Can commercial law accommodate new technologies in international shipping? *Professor Michael F. Sturley*	22
4	Electronic signatures in shipping practice *Professor Erik Røsæg*	36
5	Pinning down delivery: *Glencore v MSC* and the use of PIN codes to effect delivery *Simon Rainey QC*	47

	PART 2 ARTIFICIAL INTELLIGENCE AND SHIPPING	65
6	Autonomous shipping and maritime law *Paul Dean and Henry Clack*	67
7	Botport law – the regulatory agenda for the transition to smart ports *Professor Dr Eric Van Hooydonk*	90

8   Autonomous vessels and third-party liabilities: the elephant
    in the room   105
    Professor Barış Soyer

9   Shipping: product liability goes high-tech   116
    Professor Andrew Tettenborn

10 Who is the master now? Regulatory and contractual challenges of
    unmanned vessels   129
    Professor Simon Baughen

11 Carrier liability for unmanned ships: goodbye crew, hello liability?   148
    Dr Frank Stevens

PART 3 LEGAL TECH AND ITS IMPACT ON SHIPPING AND INSURANCE   163

12 Impact of technology on disclosure in shipping litigation   165
    Peter MacDonald Eggers QC

13 Insurance and artificial intelligence: underwriting,
    claims and litigation   178
    Simon Cooper

Index   191

NOTES ON EDITORS AND CONTRIBUTORS

EDITORS

Professor Barış Soyer
Professor of Commercial and Maritime Law
Director of the Institute of International Shipping and Trade Law
Swansea University

Professor Soyer directs the Institute of International Shipping and Trade Law at Swansea University and is a member of the British Maritime Law Association and British Insurance Law Association. He is the author of *Warranties in Marine Insurance* (2001), *Marine Insurance Fraud* (2014) and many articles published in journals such as *Cambridge Law Journal, Law Quarterly Review, Edinburg Law Review, Lloyd's Maritime & Commercial Law Quarterly*, the *Journal of Business Law*, the *Torts Law Journal* and the *Journal of Contract Law*. *Warranties in Marine Insurance* won the Cavendish Book Prize 2001, and was awarded the British Insurance Law Association Charitable Trust Book Prize in 2002 for its contribution to insurance literature. *Marine Insurance Fraud* also won the latter prize in 2015. He has also edited large numbers of collections of essays on commercial, maritime and insurance law. In addition, he sits on the editorial boards of the *Journal of International Maritime Law, Shipping and Trade Law* and editorial committee of the *Lloyd's Maritime and Commercial Law Quarterly* (*International Maritime and Commercial Law Yearbook*). Professor Soyer currently teaches Admiralty Law, Charterparties: Law and Practice and Marine Insurance on the LLM Programme at Swansea.

Professor Andrew Tettenborn
Professor of Commercial Law
Institute of International Shipping and Trade Law
Swansea University

Andrew Tettenborn has been attached to the IISTL at Swansea Law School since 2010; he has also taught at the universities of Cambridge, Exeter and Geneva and held visiting positions in Europe, Australia and the US. Professor Tettenborn is author or co-author of books on torts, damages and maritime law, has written extensively on widespread aspects of private, shipping and commercial law, sits on the editorial board of *Lloyd's Maritime & Commercial Law Quarterly* and the *Journal of*

International Maritime Law. In addition, he is the editor of the leading student commercial law text. *Sealy and Hooley's Text and Materials on Commercial Law*.

CONTRIBUTORS

Professor Simon Baughen
Professor of Law
Institute of International Shipping and Trade Law
Swansea University

Professor Baughen joined Swansea in 2013 from Bristol Law School as Professor of Shipping Law, having previously practised as a shipping lawyer in the London P&I Club and later as a solicitor with Horrocks & Co. He is a leading expert on shipping law; his book on the subject, simply called *Shipping Law*, has run to six editions and is well-known to academics and students alike as by far the most learned and approachable work on the subject. In addition, he is now the author of the very well-established practitioner's work *Summerskill on Laytime*, the sixth edition of which was published in 2017. In addition to shipping law, he is also a leading writer on the regulation of multinational corporations in the developing world, having authored *International Trade and the Protection of the Environment* and *Holding Corporations to Account: Closing the Governance Gap*. His teaching includes trust law, shipping law, carriage of goods, charterparties and international corporate governance.

Henry Clack
Associate
Holman Fenwick Willan LLP, London

Henry specialises in international commercial dispute resolution, with a particular focus on both "wet" and "dry" shipping issues. He has experience representing shipowners, P&I Clubs, commodity traders, brokers and logistics companies. He has worked on disputes arising from collisions, groundings, cargo contamination, charter parties, bills of lading, pipeline and other offshore installations and commodity supply contracts.

Henry has represented clients in both English High Court proceedings and international arbitration under LMAA and LCIA rules. During his training contract, Henry was seconded to the firm's Geneva office where he worked on a broad range of commodity disputes including Taurus Petroleum Limited v State Oil Marketing Company of the Ministry of Oil, Republic of Iraq [2017] UKSC 64 before the Supreme Court. The case dealt with the situs of a debt owed under a letter of credit. He also spent time in the firm's transactional shipping and contentious insurance teams.

Simon Cooper
Partner
Ince & Co LLP, London

Simon is a partner in the insurance & reinsurance group of Ince & Co LLP having joined from another International law firm in 2011. He has more than 30 years' experience of advising clients in the London and international insurance and reinsurance markets and has extensive experience of all forms of dispute resolution both in England and in a number of overseas jurisdictions. Many of these disputes have involved multiple parties and complex issues of fact and law. His practice focuses on commercial dispute resolution, insurance and reinsurance and he heads the cyber group at Ince in Europe. He is experienced in working with lawyers in many jurisdictions and coordinating multi jurisdictional projects on clients' behalf, besides also being a member of the IUA Clauses Subcommittee and also edited the second edition of *Reinsurance Practice & the Law* as well as writing and lecturing frequently.

In addition, Simon is a past winner of the UK Leading Insurance & Reinsurance Lawyer of the Year award from ACQ Magazine, and of the International Law Office Client Choice Award for Insurance/Reinsurance.

Paul Dean
Partner and Head of Global Maritime Operations
Holman Fenwick Willan LLP, London

Paul is head of HFW's Autonomous Vessel Group. He focuses mainly on dispute resolution and advisory work involving offshore vessels and rigs including contractual disputes and drafting, collisions, fire and explosion, total loss, towage, seismic and limitation.

He regularly speaks at and chairs offshore vessel conferences and is on the BIMCO panel for their "Using Supplytime" course. Experience gained working for an International Group P&I club specialising in offshore vessels, enables Paul to combine practical understanding with the legal role and he is identified in the Legal Directories as one of the leading individuals in his fields. He has produced a much-praised contribution to the most recent edition of the leading textbook on offshore contracts by Simon Rainey QC.

Peter MacDonald Eggers QC
Barrister
7 King's Bench Walk, London

Peter MacDonald Eggers QC is a successful commercial silk specialising in all aspects of commercial law, with a particular focus on insurance and reinsurance, shipping and transport, energy, commodities and international trade. He also regularly acts as an arbitrator. Some of his recent cases include *Cultural Foundation v Beazley Furlonge Ltd* (on professional indemnity insurance), *Aspen Underwriting v Kairos Shipping* (on insurance settlement and jurisdiction, a case arising from the *Atlantik Confidence* saga) and *The Cape Bari* (on limitation). In May 2017 he was appointed a Deputy Judge of the High Court.

Peter is a Visiting Fellow at the Institute of International Shipping and Trade Law at Swansea and is a contributing editor of *Chitty on Contracts*, co-author of *Carver on Charterparties* and is the author of *Good Faith and Insurance Contracts, Deceit: The Lie of the Law* and *The Vitiation of Contractual Consent*.

NOTES ON EDITORS AND CONTRIBUTORS

Professor Dr Eric Van Hooydonk
Research Professor
Maritime Institute
University of Ghent

Professor Eric Van Hooydonk is a professor of law at Ghent University. His research fields and main areas of practice are maritime law, international law of the sea and seaport law. From 2000 to 2010, he chaired the European Institute of Maritime and Transport Law. In 2007, he was appointed Chairman of the Royal Commission for the Reform of Belgian Maritime Law which prepares, on his initiative, a new Maritime Code for Belgium. In 2009, he founded Portius, an international and EU port law centre, which is hosted by the University of Ghent and the College of Europe at Bruges and Warsaw. Prof. Van Hooydonk is a Titulary Member of the Comité Maritime International (CMI). In 2014, he was appointed chairman of an International Working Group of the Comité Maritime International which will restate the general principles of the maritime law or "lex maritima". Prof. Van Hooydonk has run a niche law firm in Antwerp since 1995.

Grant Hunter
Head of Contracts and Clauses
BIMCO, Denmark

Grant Hunter is BIMCO's Head of Contracts and Clauses, responsible for overseeing the development, revision and promotion of BIMCO's wide range of internationally used standard contracts and clauses. He has worked in the shipping industry for 40 years, having begun in 1978 as a deck cadet with Ben Line, followed by eight years working ashore in the commercial and operations department of P&O Bulk Shipping in London. He has worked for BIMCO since 1997.

Professor Francesco Munari
Professor in Law
University of Genoa

Professor Munari's interests focus on EU law, maritime and transportation law, law of the sea, antitrust and regulated markets and environmental law. He has been awarded research projects by Italian and EU institutions inter alia on transport and maritime law, EU law, competition law and environmental law. In addition, he has a legal practice, being partner in and co-founder of MGMP & Associati, a law firm with offices in Genoa and Milan.

As well as this he is the chairman of the Interuniversity Centre on Law concerning International Economic Organizations), and a board member of the European Maritime Law Organization and the Italian Association of Maritime Law.

His academic work includes the co-directorship of the journal *Diritto del commercio internazionale*, and membership of the editorial boards of *Diritto dell'Unione europea* and *Diritto marittimo*.

Simon Rainey QC
Barrister
Quadrant Chambers, London

Simon Rainey is one of the best-known practitioners at the Commercial Bar with a broad commercial advisory and advocacy practice spanning substantial commercial contractual disputes, international trade and commodities, shipping and maritime law in all its aspects and energy and insurance. He also has extensive experience of international arbitration, both as advocate and arbitrator, and regularly sits as a Recorder and Deputy High Court Judge.

His recent high-profile cases include *Volcafe v Compania Sud Americana de Vapores SA* in 2018; *NYK Bulkship (Atlantic) NV v Cargill International SA (The Global Santosh)* in 2016; and *Bunge v Nidera* in 2015.

Professor Erik Røsæg
Scandinavian Institute of Maritime Law
University of Oslo

Professor Røsæg was formerly the Director of the Scandinavian Institute of Maritime Law, University of Oslo. He is now at UiO PluriCourts, the Centre for the Study of the Legitimate Roles of the Judiciary in the Global Order. He teaches and writes in the fields of law of the sea, maritime law and third party interests in commercial law.

He has been much involved in the negotiations of liability Conventions in the IMO, chairs the Norwegian Maritime Law Commission and has chaired other committees preparing draft legislation. He has published extensively in national and international journals and books, and he has been a speaker and consultant in a number of jurisdictions. He is currently involved in the Oslo Law of the Sea Forum.

Dr Frank Stevens
Associate Professor in Law
Erasmus University

Frank Stevens holds a law degree from the University of Leuven in 1991, an LL.M. in Admiralty from Tulane, a "Special Degree in Maritime Sciences" from the University of Antwerp (1993) and a Doctorate from the University of Ghent. He joined the Antwerp Bar in 1993, and has been practising transport and maritime law since then. Since 2016, he has been an Assistant Professor at the Erasmus School of Law in Rotterdam, and also an adviser to Roosendaal Keyzer, one of the leading maritime law firms in Antwerp.

Mr. Stevens is the author of textbooks on carriage by sea and limitation of liability, and regularly publishes and speaks on many issues of transport and maritime law. He is the Editor-in-Chief of *Tijdschrift voor Internationale Handel en Transport* (Journal of International Trade and Transport Law) and is on the boards of two other legal journals.

Professor Michael F. Sturley
Chair in Law
University of Texas

Michael Sturley holds the Fannie Coplin Regents Chair in Law at the University of Texas Law School, where he teaches *inter alia* maritime law and commercial law courses and directs the Supreme Court Clinic.

Prof. Sturley is a Titulary Member of the Comité Maritime International (where he served as the Rapporteur for the International Sub-Committee on Issues of Transport Law and currently serves on the Standing Committee on the Carriage of Goods, the Planning Committee, and the International Working Group on the "lex maritima"); a proctor member of the Maritime Law Association of the United States (where he is active on several committees and chairs the Uniformity Committee); the Senior Advisor on the US Delegation to Working Group III (Transport Law) of the United Nations Commission on International Trade Law (UNCITRAL); a member of the UNCITRAL Experts' Group on Transport Law; a life member of the American Law Institute; and the Book Review Editor of *The Journal of Maritime Law and Commerce*. In 2008, American Maritime Cases dedicated its seventeenth Five-Year Digest to him.

Prof. Sturley has written extensively on maritime subjects; has lectured on maritime subjects at law schools and conferences in the United States and around the world; and has been consulted in maritime cases before the US Supreme Court, in many of the lower federal courts and in state and foreign courts.

FOREWORD

It is a pleasure and privilege to contribute the Foreword to this volume, containing the papers presented at the Fourteenth Annual International Colloquium of the Institute of International Shipping and Trade Law, Swansea University, "New Technologies and Shipping/Trade Law", held at Swansea on 10–11 September 2018

The purpose of commercial law is to facilitate commerce, as crisply observed by one of the Colloquium participants. To do so commercial law needs to inform itself of, and keep up to date with, commercial practice. As commerce adapts, so commercial law must adapt; that is indeed the common law method.

Commercial law cannot and must not ignore revolutionary developments in technology, affecting the shipping industry, including:

- Blockchain;
- Smart contracts;
- Autonomous ships;
- Autonomous ports;
- AI.

Each of these developments and, even more so, these developments cumulatively, will have an impact on international maritime conventions, the regulatory framework, traditional roles (by way of examples, masters, pilots and trade unions) the manning of ships (think of an autonomous ship and the *Marie Celeste* or even *The Flying Dutchman*), current business models and insurance. Commercial law will need to grapple with this rapidly changing landscape.

Lawyers and judges should not approach these changes defensively, as if legal professionals constituted an "endangered species". Instead, we should play our part in shaping the changes to come. Those changes will ultimately take effect in a manner we cannot yet predict. It is unlikely to be "all or nothing" across the board – so, smart contracts may work for some contractual situations but not all. Above all, changes cannot be left to the IT "gurus" alone – those with knowledge of the relevant commercial and legal contexts must be fully engaged. Indeed, ideally, they should be instrumental in the changes which come about.

Importantly, the technology bringing about these major changes is only one part of the jigsaw and cannot be considered in isolation. Thus:

- Are we substituting new risks for old? For example, will IT/cyber risks simply fill the gaps left by the elimination of human error?

- Where would these changes leave precautions against terrorism, fraud and cyber-crime?
- If a shore controller (who has, *ex hypothesi*, replaced the on-board master) is expected to have nautical experience or qualifications (cf., the position of a drone pilot), where will these be obtained if all ships become autonomous?
- What will be the liability/insurance regime?
- What will be the cost of introducing these changes? Are they worth it? Might there be different answers for different parts of the world?
- Will there be public acceptance? Consider Professor Soyer's example of the autonomous chemical tanker, whether at sea or entering a crowded port.

All these topics – and more – were comprehensively introduced and discussed at the Colloquium. The papers presented then are now collected here. This can only be the start of the debate – but the debate should not be delayed. A real "thank you" is due from the law and the industry to Professors Soyer and Tettenborn, together with their colleagues at the Institute, the Institute itself and the distinguished speakers (domestic and international) who participated.

Finally, that the papers are now available in this volume is due to the generosity of the Colloquium sponsors, Informa Law (Routledge) – generosity which is much appreciated.

Sir Peter Gross
May 2019.

PREFACE

The shipping sector is a profoundly conservative industry. Witness, for example, the fact that standard charterparty forms, devised in the 1940s or even earlier, are still very much favoured by parties even though numerous attempts may have been made to update them since then. Nothing demonstrates this conservatism better than the continuing scepticism about doing serious business through electronic means. Owners and charterers may communicate by email; they may order supplies and bunkers electronically without turning a hair; but charters, bills of lading and other significant documents remain resolutely paper-bound.

Admittedly this is sometimes understandable. Paper has a comforting feeling when, as so often in the shipping world, you are dealing with a counterparty you do not know and may not entirely trust. Furthermore, digitisation tends not to work without widespread take-up and standardisation across the world. This was one of the reasons why, for example, the 1990s BOLERO project turned out to be something of a damp squib. It still remains very much to be seen whether more recent plantings like essDOCS and e-title will fall on more fertile soil.

However, even in the shipping world the advance of technology is gradually challenging the traditional ways in which we do business, and this includes shipping law. It is pretty clear that at least some traditional legal principles dating from the last (or for that matter the nineteenth) century will have to adapt or mutate in order to deal with the issues raised by information technology. For example, it is doubtful whether current legal rules and principles can deal with, let alone facilitate, the burgeoning use of EDI and, in the not too distant future, blockchain technology in shipping practice. Equally, the development of autonomous craft and ports is likely to create new legal problems relating to liability that the current law is simply unfit to handle (for example, think for a moment: can you have a negligent computer?).

The main objective of this book is to provide a critical understanding of the main legal issues at stake and offer a few suggested solutions. It is our hope that we can contribute to the learning and understanding of new technologies used in maritime field and possibly even provoke further research.

To this end, this book is in three parts. Part I offers a detailed and critical analysis of issues emerging and likely to emerge from the use of advanced computer technology, particularly in connection with the process of contracting and in the context of issuing trading documents.

PREFACE

Part 2, focusing more particularly on artificial intelligence, discusses contemporary issues that will emerge once autonomous ships and similar craft start to regularly ply the world's oceans. It will also look at the sedentary side of things: once ports cease to bustle with noise and men and become humming hubs controlled by mobile machines and computer servers, what might be the legal impact?

Part 3 then looks at how the increasing use of digital technology is likely to change such traditionally paper-based matters as marine insurance, claims handling and shipping litigation generally. This is something which already takes up a great deal of the time of management throughout the business – or at least the management of those firms that wish to have a sporting chance of surviving in the long term.

We are enormously grateful to many people for making possible our 2018 Annual Colloquium (our fourteenth), out of which this book grew. The research assistants at the IISTL, Alicia McKenzie and Stella Kounakou, provided the essential unsung back-up without which these international events just cannot happen. Our publishers, Informa Law, again provided their unstinting support and encouragement, just as they have done with our previous events. We would like to take the opportunity to thank them and their entire editorial staff, but in particular Amy Jones and Caroline Church, for their assistance during the production of this book.

We would like to dedicate this book to the memory of our colleague and friend Dr Theodora Nikaki, whom we tragically lost in April 2018 to a swift and cruel illness. She had been with us since 2005, having previously worked in private practice. Her knowledge, particularly but not exclusively in the field of carriage law, was encyclopaedic; her patience with students unbounded; and her administrative flair impeccable. She is, and will always be, sorely missed by the academic and professional community alike.

B. Soyer and A. Tettenborn
March 2019
Swansea

TABLE OF CASES

UK

A v National Blood Authority [2001] 3 All E.R. 289; [2001] Lloyd's Rep Med 187 126
Albacora S.R.L. v Westcott & Laurence Line 1966 S.C. (H.L.) 19; [1966] 2 Lloyd's Rep. 53 156
Andrew Weir Shipping Ltd v Wartsila UK Ltd [2004] EWHC 1284 (Comm); [2004] 2 Lloyd's Rep 377 117
Re Atrium Training Services Ltd (In Liquidation) [2013] EWHC 2882 (Ch) 167
The Antonis P Lemos [1985] AC 711 119
The Arawa [1977] 2 Lloyd's Rep. 416 62
The Atlantik Confidence [2016] EWHC 2412 (Admlty); [2016] 2 Lloyd's Rep 525 76
Bailey v HSS Alarms Ltd, The Times, June 20, 2000 123
Baker v KTM Sportmotorcycle UK Ltd [2017] EWCA Civ 378; [2018] ECC 35 123
Barclays Bank Ltd v Commissioners of Customs and Excise [1963] 1 Lloyd's Rep 81 .... 52, 53
Barking & Dagenham LBC v GLS Educational Supplies Ltd [2015] EWHC 2050 (TCC) 123
Beta Computers (Europe) Ltd v Adobe Systems (Europe) Ltd [1996] CLC 821 128
Bilta (UK) Ltd v Nazir (No.2) [2015] UKSC 23; [2016] A.C. 1; [2015] 2 Lloyd's Rep. 61 50
The Bow Spring and The Manzanillo II [2004] EWCA Civ 1007; [2005] 1 Lloyd's Rep 1 113
Bow Valley Husky (Bermuda) Ltd v St John Shipbuilding Ltd [1997] 3 SCR 1210 117
BP Exploration Operating Co Ltd v. Chevron Shipping Co (The Chevron North America) [2001] UKHL 50; [2003] 1 AC 197 107
Brandt v. Liverpool, Brazil and River Plate Steam Navigation Co [1924] 1 KB 575 26
The British Aviator [1965] 1 Lloyd's Rep 271 (CA) 113
British Shipowners v Grimond (1876) 3 R. 968 55
Broome v. Cassell & Co Ltd [1972] AC 1027 110
Brown v BCA Trading Limited [2016] EWHC 1464 (Ch) 173
Carroll v Fearon [1998] PIQR P 416 123
CBS Butler Ltd v Brown [2013] EWHC 3944 (QB); [2013] Info TLR 263 172
Clifford v. Hunter (1827) 1 M & M 103 151
Colin & Shields Ltd v W Weddel & Co [1952] 2 All ER 337 57
Compagnie Financière du Pacifique v Peruvian Guano Co Ltd (1882) 11 QBD 55 166
Computer Associates UK Ltd v Software Incubator Ltd [2018] EWCA Civ 518; [2018] 1 Lloyd's Rep 613 .... 27, 128
Cremer v General Carriers SA [1974] 1 WLR 341 57
Dairy Containers Ltd v Tasman Orient CV [2004] UKPC 22; [2005] 1 W.L.R. 215; [2004] 2 Lloyd's Rep. 647 51
The Delfini [1990] 1 Lloyd's Rep. 252, 268 (Mustill, L.J.) 23

TABLE OF CASES

Digicel (St Lucia) Ltd v Cable & Wireless plc [2008] EWHC 2522 (Ch); [2009] 2 All ER 1094 .... 169, 170, 171, 172
Donoghue v Stevenson [1932] AC 562 .... 113, 117, 121, 122–3, 125, 128
Earles v Barclays Bank plc [2009] EWHC 2500 (QB); [2010] Bus LR 566 .... 167, 168, 172
The Empire Jamaica [1955] P. 259 (affirmed, [1957] A.C. 386) 150
The Esso Bernicia [1989] AC 643 .... 116, 121
The Eurasian Dream [2002] EWHC 118 (Comm); [2002] 1 Lloyd's Rep. 719 .... 150, 151, 153
Fairstar Heavy Transport NV v Adkins [2013] EWCA Civ 886; [2013] 2 CLC 272 176
Fiddes v Channel 4 TV Corporation [2010] EWCA Civ 516 169
The Flowergate [1967] 1 Lloyd's Rep 1 156
Gatoil International Inc v Tradax Petroleum Ltd [1985] 1 Lloyd's Rep 350 156
Glencore International AG v MSC Mediterranean Shipping Co SA (The Eugenia) [2015] EWHC 1989 (Comm); [2015] 2 Lloyd's Rep 508 and [2017] EWCA Civ 365; [2017] 2 Lloyd's Rep 186 .... 47–63, 118, 123, 176
Goodale v Ministry of Justice [2009] EWHC B41 (QB) 170–1
Grant v Australian Knitting Mills Ltd [1936] AC 85 117
Great Eastern Shipping Co Ltd v Far East Chartering Ltd (The Jag Ravi) [2012] EWCA Civ 180; [2012] 1 Lloyd's Rep. 637 .... 53, 54
Hamble Fisheries Ltd v Gardner & Sons Ltd [1999] 2 Lloyd's Rep1 .... 117, 123
The Happy Day [2002] 2 Lloyd's Rep. 487 62
Hindustan SS Co Ltd v Siemens Bros & Co Ltd [1955] 1 Lloyd's Rep 167 125
Homburg Houtimport BV v Agrosin Private Ltd (The Starsin) [2003] UKHL 12; [2004] 1 A.C. 715; [2003] 1 Lloyd's Rep. 571 .... 50, 51
Hongkong Fir Shipping Co. Ltd. v Kawasaki Kisen Kaisha Ltd. (The Hongkong Fir) [1962] 2 Q.B 26. .... 150, 151
Hourani v Harrison (1927) 28 Lloyd's L L R 120 124
Kairos Shipping Ltd v ENKA & Co LLC [2016] EWHC 2412 (Admlty); [2016] 2 Lloyd's Rep 525 176
Klausen & Co A/S v Mediterranean Shipping Co SA [2013] EWHC 3254 (Comm) 157
Leesh River Tea Co v British India SN Co [1967] 2 QB 250 124
Lickbarrow v. Mason (1787) 2 TR 63 26
Lisle-Mainwaring v Associated Newspapers Ltd [2018] EWCA Civ 1470; [2018] 1 WLR 4766 166
Macieo Shipping Ltd v Clipper Shipping Lines Ltd (The Clipper Sao Luis) [2001] C.L.C. 762 150
The Makedonia [1962] 1 Lloyd's Rep. 316, 336 .... 50, 151, 152
Manifest Shipping Co. Ltd. v Uni-Polaris Shipping Co Ltd (The Star Sea) [1997] 1 Lloyd's Rep. 360, 374 550
Merchants' Marine Insurqance Co. v North of England P&I Association (1926) 26 Ll L L Rep 201 83
Montpellier Estates Ltd v Leeds City Council [2012] EWHC 1343 (QB) 168
Mueller Europe Ltd v Central Roofing (South Wales) Ltd [2012] EWHC 3417 (TCC); [2013] TCLR 2 172
The Nicholas H. [1996] AC 211 .... 120–1, 124
The Nordic Ferry [1991] 2 Lloyd's Rep 591 113
Perks v Clark and Others [2001] EWCA Civ 1228; [2001] 2 Lloyd's Rep 431 70
Peter Cremer GmbH v General Carriers SA (The Dona Mari) [1973] 2 Lloyd's Rep. 366 59
Polpen Shipping Co Ltd v Commercial Union Insurance Co Ltd [1943] KB 161 70
Pyrrho Investments Limited v MWB Property Limited [2016] EWHC 256 (Ch) 170, 173

TABLE OF CASES

R. v. Lawrence (Stephen) [1981] 1 All ER 974.. 114
Renton (GH) & Co Ltd v Palmyra Trading Corp. of Panama [1957] AC 149, 166 156
Republic of Bolivia v. Indemnity Mutual Marine Assurance Co. Ltd., [1909] 1
  K.B. 785, 802 145
Rio Tinto Co. Ltd. v. Seed Shipping Co. (1926) 134 L.T. 764, (1926) 42 T.L.R. 381 151
Riverstone Meat Co Pty Ltd v Lancashire Shipping Co Ltd [1961] AC 807 .... 117, 119, 124
Simaan General Contracting Co v Pilkington Glass Ltd (No.2) [1988] QB 758 123
Smailes v McNally [2014] EWCA Civ 1299 .... 767, 169
Smallwood v Allied Van Lines, Inc, 660 F.3d 1115, 1120 n.5, 2012 AMC 370, 374
  n.5 (9th Cir. 2011) 28
Smith v Littlewoods Organisation Ltd [1987] AC 241 123
Southwark LBC v IBM UK Ltd [2011] EWHC 549 (TCC) 121
St Albans D.C. v. International Computers Ltd [1996] 4 All E.R. 481 .... 121, 127, 128
Standard Oil Co of New York v Clan Line Steamers Ltd (The Clan Gordon) [1924]
  A.C. 100 151
The Star Sea [1997] 1 Lloyd's Rep. 360 .... 151, 153
Taylor v. Rover Co Ltd [1966] 1 WLR 1491 113
The Tempus [1913] P 166 107
The *Rafaela S* [2005] UKHL 11, [2005] 2 AC 423 32
Triumph Controls UK Limited v Primus International Holding Co [2018] EWHC
  176 (TCC) 168
Ventouris v Mountain [1991] 1 WLR 607 166
Volcafe Ltd v Cia Sud Americana de Vapores SA (trading as CSAV) [2016] EWCA
  Civ 1103; [2017] Q.B. 915 156
Waren Import Gesellschaft Krohn & Co v Internationale Graanhandel Thegra NV [1975]
  1 Lloyd's Rep 146 .... 57, 58–59
Wilkes v Depuy International Ltd [2016] EWHC 3096 (QB); (2017) 153 BMLR 91 126
Woodland v Swimming Teachers Association [2013] UKSC 66; [2014] AC 537 124
Wrightson v Mcarthur & Hutchisons Ltd [1921] 2 K.B. 807 .... 54–5, 55
Your Response Ltd v Datateam Business Media Ltd [2014] EWCA Civ 281; [2015]
  QB 41 121

Australia
Sony Music Entertainment (Australia) Ltd v University of Tasmania [2003] FCA 532 167

Canada
JD Irving Ltd v. Siemens Canada Ltd (The SPM 125) 2016 FC 287 140

Belgium
CA Ghent 19 March 1998, [1998] E.T.L. 419 150
The City of Berytus CA Antwerp, 4th Section, 06.03.2017, Docket N° 2015/AR/19 157

Germany
BGH 26.10.2006 (I ZR 20/04), TranspR 2007, 36 151

Netherlands
Hoge Raad (Supreme Court), 28.03.2003, S&S 2005, 133 (ECLI:NL:HR:2003:AF2677)
  (Quo Vadis) 150

USA
CNA Insurance Co v Hyundai Merchant Marine Co, 747 F.3d 339, 2014 AMC 609
  (6th Cir. 2014) 28

TABLE OF CASES

Ferrostaal, Inc v M/V Sea Phoenix, 447 F.3d 212, 2006 AMC 1217 (3d Cir. 2006) 28
James N. Kirby Pty Ltd v Norfolk Southern Railway Co, 543 US 14, 2004 AMC 2705 (2004) 27, 27, 28
Kawasaki Kisen Kaisha Ltd v Regal-Beloit Corp, 561 US 89, 100, 2010 AMC 1521 (2010) 28
Lindsay v. McDonnell Douglas Aircraft Corp, 460 F2d 631 (8th Cir. 1972) 127
Lozman v City of Riviera Beach (2013) 133 S Ct 735; [2013] AMC 1 72
Pan-Alaska Fisheries, Inc. v. Marine Const. & Design Co., 565 F2d 1129 (1977) 127
Stewart v. Dutra Construction Co 543 U.S. 481, [2005] AMC 609 71

TABLE OF LEGISLATION

UK Cases
Automated and Electric Vehicles
  Act 2018 ....111, 189–90
Bills of Lading Act 1855 ....25, 26
Carriage of Goods by Sea
  Act 1992 .... 25, 26, 57, 58, 59, 144
Communications Act 2003 26
Companies (Consolidation)
  Act 1908 54
Companies Act 2006 39
Consumer Protection
  Act 1987 .... 126, 127
Data Protection Act 2018 186
Equality Act 2010 181
Food and Environmental Protection
  Act 1985 81
Harbours, Docks and Piers Clauses
  Act 1847 ....84, 107
Income and Corporation Taxes
  Act 1988 70
Insurance Act 2015 184
Merchant Shipping
  Act 1995 ..70–71, 75, 78, 79, 80, 81, 82,
  83, 89, 113, 119, 125, 126, 131, 136,
  139, 140, 145
Railways and Transport Safety
  Act 2003 71

UK Subordinate Legislation
Civil Procedure Rules 167
Merchant Shipping (Compulsory
  Insurance of Shipowners for Maritime
  Claims) Regulations 2012,
  SI 2012/2267 137
Merchant Shipping (Distress Signals
  and Prevention of Collisions)
  Regulations 1996 133

Merchant Shipping (Load Line)
  Regulations 1998/2241 80
Merchant Shipping (Oil Pollution)
  (Bunkers Convention)
  Regulations 2006/1244 82
Merchant Shipping (Prevention and
  Control of Pollution) Order
  1987/470 80
Merchant Shipping (Prevention of Oil
  Pollution) Regulations 1996 ....40n29
Merchant Shipping (Prevention of
  Pollution by Sewage and Garbage)
  Order 2006/2950 80
Merchant Shipping (Standards of
  Training Certification and
  Watchkeeping) Regulations 2015 ... 138
Merchant Shipping (Tonnage)
  Regulations 1997/1510 80

USA
Bills of Lading Act, 49 U.S.Code § 80101
  (Pomerene Act 1916) 85
Carriage of Goods by Sea Act, 46
  U.S.Code § 30701 28
Electronic Signatures in Global and
  National Commerce Act, 15 U.S.
  Code § 7001 36
Harter Act 1893, 27 Stat. 445 24
Rules of Construction Act, 1 U.S.
  Code § 3 ....71, 72

Other Countries
Sea-Carriage Documents Act 1997
  (N.S.W.) (Australia) 26
Bills of Lading Act, RSC 1985, c.
  B-5 (Canada) 25
Bills of Lading Act 1994 (Singapore) ...25

TABLE OF LEGISLATION

Civil Code (Netherlands) 71
Civil Law Act 1956 (Malaysia) 25
Code des Transports (France) 72
Maritime Code 1994 (Norway) 44
Torts Law 1969 (Norway) 45

EU

Charter of Fundamental Rights 187
Directive 85/374/EC
    (Product Liability) 116, 126
Directive 95/46/EC (General Data
    Protection) 12
Directive 1999/93/EC
    (eIDAS) 36, 41, 42, 43, 43, 44
Directive 2000/31/EC (Electronic
    Commerce) 16
Directive 2002/6/EC (Reporting
    Fomalities) 103
Directive 2002/59/EC (Community
    vessel traffic monitoring) 98
Directive 2005/65/EC (Port Security) ...97
Directive 2006/87/EC (Technical
    Requirements for Inland
    Waterway Vessels) 94
Directive 2009/20/EC (Insurance of
    Shipowners for Maritime
    Claims) 119, 137, 137, 140
Directive 2009/100/EC (Reciprocal
    Recognition of Navigability
    Licences) 94
Directive 2010/65/EU (Reporting
    Formalities) 103
Directive (EU) 2016/1629 (Technical
    Requirements for Inland Waterway
    Vessels) 94
Regulation (EC) 725/2004 (Ship and
    Port Facility Security) 97
Regulation (EC) 324/2008 (Revised
    Procedures for conducting
    Commission Inspections in the
    field of Maritime Security) 97
Regulation (EU) 1257/2013 (Ship
    Recycling) 7
Regulation (EU) 910/2014 (eIDAS) 36
Regulation (EU) 2016/679 (General
    Data Protection Regulation).. 12,
    180, 181, 184–186
Regulation (EU) 2017/352 (Port Services) 95
Treaty on the Functioning of the
    European Union (TFEU) 91

Conventions

Convention and Statute on the
    International Régime of Maritime
    Ports (Geneva 1923) 91
Convention concerning International
    Carriage by Rail (COTIF) 27
Convention concerning the Social
    Repercussions of New Methods of
    Cargo Handling in Docks
    (Geneva 1973) 102
Convention for the Protection of the
    Marine Environment of the North
    East
    (OSPAR) (Paris 1992) 1
Convention for the Suppression of
    Unlawful Acts of Violence against
    the Safety of Maritime Navigation
    (London 1988 and 2005) 81, 88, 137
Convention for the Unification of
    Certain Rules of Law with respect
    to Collisions between Vessels
    (Brussels 1910) 93, 125
Convention for the Unification of
    Certain Rules of Law
    respecting Assistance and
    Salvage at Sea (Brussels 1910) 136
Convention on the Contract for the Inter-
    national Carriage of Goods by
    Road (CMR) (Geneva 1956)..27, 155
Convention on Limitation of Liability
    for Maritime Claims (LLMC)
    (London 1976) 74–6, 75, 112, 114,
    119, 120, 139–140
Convention on Facilitation of
    International Maritime Traffic
    (London 1965) 88, 103, 137
Convention on the Prevention of Marine
    Pollution by Dumping of Wastes and
    Other Matter (London 1972
    and 1996) 81
Convention relating to the Carriage of
    Passengers and their Luggage by
    Sea (Athens 1974 and 2002) ..88, 114
International Convention for the
    Prevention of Pollution from Ships
    (MARPOL) (London 1973
    and1978) 80, 88, 137, 140
International Convention for the
    Safety of Life at Sea (SOLAS)
    (London 1974, 1978

TABLE OF LEGISLATION

and 1988) ..78–79, 87, 88, 92, 97, 98, 106, 130, 132–133, 136
International Convention for the Unification of Certain Rules of Law Relating to Bills of Lading (The Hague 1924 and Brussels 1968) 23, 24, 27, 28, 29, 32, 33, 62, 114, 119, 120, 124, 139, 144, 149, 152, 153–155, 156, 158–161
International Convention for the Unification of Certain Rules of Law relating to Maritime Liens and Mortgages (Brussels 1926) 84
International Convention for the Unification of Certain Rules relating to Maritime Liens and Mortgages (Brussels 1967) 84
International Convention on Civil Liability for Bunker Oil Pollution Damage (London 2001).......82, 88, 107, 125, 137
International Convention on Civil Liability for Oil Pollution Damage (Brussels 1969 and 1992) 82, 107, 111, 112, 125, 137, 139
International Convention on Liability and Compensation for Damage in connection with the Carriage of Hazardous and Noxious Substances by Sea (London 1996 and 2010) ..82, 125–6
International Convention on Load Lines (LLC) (London 1966) 80, 87, 130
International Convention on Maritime Liens and Mortgages (Brussels 1993) 84
International Convention on Maritime Search and Rescue (SAR) (Hamburg 1979) 88
International Convention on the Removal of Wrecks (Nairobi 2007) 82–83, 88, 137
International Convention on Salvage (London 1989) 83, 88, 136, 144
International Convention on Standards of Training, Certification and Watchkeeping for Seafarers (STCW Convention) (London

1978) 78, 87, 88, 89, 92, 137–138, 141, 146, 152
International Convention on Tonnage Measurement of Ships (TMC) (London 1969) 80, 87
International Convention relating to the Arrest of Seagoing Ships (Brussels 1952) 84
International Convention relating to Intervention on the High Seas in Cases of Oil Pollution Casualties (Brussels 1969 and 1973) 81–2
International Convention relating to the Limitation of the Liability of Owners of Sea-Going Ships (Brussels 1957) 75, 114
Maritime Labour Convention (Geneva 2006) 92, 138
MARPOL, see International Convention for the Prevention of Pollution from Ships
SOLAS, see International Convention for the Safety of Life at Sea
STCW convention, see International Convention on Standards of Training, Certification and Watchkeeping for Seafarers
SUAC, see Convention for the Suppression of Unlawful Acts of Violence against the Safety of Maritime Navigation
UN Convention on the Carriage of Goods by Sea (Hamburg 1978) ...24, 27, 29, 33, 149, 155, 159, 161
UN Convention on Contracts for the International Carriage of Goods Wholly or Partly by Sea (Rotterdam 2008)............28–34, 35, 40, 101, 119, 150, 153, 155, 159, 161
UN Convention on Conditions for Registration of Ships (Geneva 1986) 83–84
UN Convention on the Law of the Sea (UNCLOS) (Montego Bay 1982)................73–74, 87, 131–132, 135–136, 145
UN Convention on the Liability of Operators of Transport Terminals in International Trade (Vienna 1991) 01

PART 1

EFFECT OF NEW TECHNOLOGIES ON CONTRACTING IN SHIPPING PRACTICE

CHAPTER 1

Blockchain and smart contracts in shipping and transport
A legal revolution is about to arrive?

Professor Francesco Munari[*]

1 Introductory remarks

Blockchain technology is gradually shaping many sectors of business. In past years it was commonly associated with so-called cryptocurrencies; however, its uses are now growing, and it is studied in many other fields of business.

According to recent data,[1] at the end of 2017 about 60% of blockchain projects worldwide were still focussed on finance. Logistics was ranked third with 24 ongoing projects, representing almost 7.5% of the overall figures; second was the governmental sector with 30 ongoing projects).[2] But, significantly, blockchain projects in the logistics sector grew by 600% in the period 2016–2017 – much more than any other field of business.

As I hope to be able to explain later on, I believe that this is due to parallels that blockchain technology has with 'traditional' transport and logistics operations,[3] this being a strong stimulus for experts to consider the potentialities of blockchain in this area.

On the other hand, although some very interesting studies on this matter have recently been published,[4] experts point out that there are still substantial uncertainties and caveats concerning the application of blockchain to transport. They gave some indications of where policy-makers should start working (especially in urban and shared mobility for passengers),[5] but for the remaining areas of transport and logistics less clear indications can be envisaged.[6]

---

[*] Professor of EU Law, University of Genoa Law School. Adjunct Professor of EU Law and International and European Environmental Law at LUISS-Università Guido Carli, Rome; partner at Munari Giudici Maniglio Panfili & Associati, Genoa & Milan.

1 See www.blockchain4innovation.it/eventi-e-convegni/blockchain-business-revolution-la-blockchain-e-una-realta-concreta-ed-e-ora-di-studiarla-davvero/.

2 See e.g. European Parliament Research Services, *How blockchain technology could change our lives* (P. Boucher author), February 2017, at 14 (http://www.europarl.europa.eu/RegData/etudes/IDAN/2017/581,948/EPRS_IDA(2017)581948_EN.pdf), at 18.

3 See K. Takahashi, *Blockchain Technology and Electronic Bills of Lading* (2016), 22 *JIML*, 202.

4 Reference is made in particular to the Corporate Partnership Board Report *Blockchain and Beyond: Encoding 21st Century Transport* by the International Transport Forum at the OECD, in https://www.itf-oecd.org/blockchain-and-beyond.

5 W. Hofman, C. Brewster, *The Applicability of Blockchain Technology in the Mobility and Logistics Domain*, in Müller B., Meyer G. (eds), *Towards User-Centric Transport in Europe. Lecture Notes in Mobility* (Springer, Cham, 2018), 185.

6 See *Blockchain and Beyond* (above note 4), at 55 ff.

Smart contracts were conceived and experimented with long before the arrival of blockchain technology.[7] Their inventor was Nick Szabo, who defined these contracts as

> a set of promises, including protocols within which the parties perform other promises. The protocols are usually implemented with programs on a computer network, or in other forms of digital electronics, thus these contracts are "smarter" than the paper-based ancestors. No use of artificial intelligence is implied.[8]

However, it is blockchain technology which may cause them to burgeon in the coming years, as a sort of by-product of that technology.[9] As is commonly known, smart contracts have been defined since 1994 as a 'computerised transaction protocol that executes the terms of a contract',[10] *i.e.* a contract which is implemented through software algorithms (codes) stored in a blockchain and activated when certain conditions occur that are defined in the code. These contracts seem to have a future in the shipping, transport and logistics sectors. The purpose of this chapter is to shed some light on this.

The above comes, however, with a preliminary series of caveats. Firstly, as in many other areas of knowledge and science, lawyers do not seem equipped to avoid the necessity for a thorough cooperation (and sometimes confrontation) with engineers and IT experts, as the legal and technical languages in this matter are not easy and are still far from being mutually supportive.[11]

Secondly, the scope of this chapter will allow me only to sketch some profiles on possible developments in our legal fields of blockchain and smart contracts. The approach will be to mirror the (forthcoming) potentialities of blockchain and

---

7 See K. Werbacht, N. Cornell, *Contracts ex Machina* (2017) 67 *Duke L.J.*, 312; S. Tönnissen, F. Teuterberg, *Towards a Taxonomy for Smart Contracts*, Conference Proceedings of European Conference on Information Systems (ECIS), Portsmouth, UK, 2018, on file by the author; M. Bellini, *Blockchain Smart Contracts: che cosa sono, come funzionano quali sono gli ambiti applicativi*, https://www.blockchain4innovation.it/mercati/legal/smart-contract/blockchain-smart-contracts-cosa-funzionano-quali-gli-ambiti-applicativi/.

8 See N. Szabo, *Smart Contracts: Building Blocks for Digital Markets*, reprinted in http://www.fon.hum.uva.nl/rob/Courses/InformationInSpeech/CDROM/Literature/LOTwinterschool2006/szabo.best.vwh.net/smart_contracts_2.html. See also L.W. Cong, Z. He, *Blockchain Disruption and Smart Contracts*, available on https://papers.ssrn.com/sol3/papers.cfm?abstract_id=2,985,764, at 9 ff.

9 J. I.-H Siao, '*Smart' Contract on the Blockchain-Paradigm Shift for Contract Law?* (2017) 14 *US China Law Review*, 685; D. Di Sabato, *Gli* smart contracts: *robot che gestiscono il rischio contrattuale*, (2017) *Contratto e impresa*, 2, 378.

10 This the reference used also at by European institutions: see *How blockchain technology could change our lives* (above note 2).

11 See, T. Kiviat, *Beyond Bitcoin: Issues in Regulating Blockchain Transactions* (2015) 65 *Duke L.J.*, 569; P. Cuccurru, *Blockchain ed automazione contrattuale. Riflessioni sugli smart contract*, (2017) Nuova Giur. Civ., 1, 107, at 112, J.A. Bergstra, M. Burgess, *Blockchain Technology and Its Applications. A Promise Theory view – V0.11*, http://markburgess.org/BlockchPromises.pdf, published online, 23 May 2018; J. Goldenfein, A. Leiter, *Legal Engineering on the Blockchain: 'Smart Contracts' as Legal Conduct*, in *Law Critique*, https://doi.org/10.1007/s10978-018-9224-0, published online, 19 May 2018. An understanding of the above is provided by the reading of a very recent US patent application submitted by International Business Machines Corporation (inventors: Nicholas C.M. Fuller; Prabhakar Kudva; Deborah Ann Neumayer) concerning *Blockchain Ledgers of Material Spectral Signatures for Supply Chain Integrity Management* US Patent App. 2018/0276600 A1, Sept. 27, 2018 (https://patentimages.storage.googleapis.com/0d/e7/ec/672c2f52608e5d/US20180276600A1.pdf).

smart contracts with shipping and logistic practice. In so doing, the outcome, I fear, will be putting more questions to the reader than giving answers.

2 Is distributed ledger technology (DLT) a technological remake of the ancestors of the bill of lading?

One of the best known features of blockchain is that it works as a ledger, however, which is not centralised, but distributed among all persons belonging to the relevant network.[12] Such ledgers cannot be updated, managed, controlled or coordinated by one single entity, only by all actors participating in the network, each of whom is required to handle a given block of the network. This sort of shared database can be modified by each actor, but only provided all other actors consent to this. The block is thus constantly updated and each actor is provided with the latest entry which has been input by other actors. Each entry is not modifiable nor can it be deleted. This evolution especially avoids the need for persons to rely on 'authorities' (or third parties, including notaries and lawyers) to assess the truthfulness, trust, reliability, accountability and security of the information and data contained in the relevant entries of the block.

If we transpose this line of thought to maritime transport, then we find a *rationale* which is similar to the *cartolario* (*i.e.* a form of ledger) developed in the Middle Ages before the bill of lading was invented.[13] With the flourishing of commercial cities whose vessels ruled trade in the Mediterranean, goods were moved from port to port and the need arose to avoid disputes between shippers and ships' masters as to precisely what goods had been delivered on board. Accordingly, statutes were passed by many such cities insisting the master be accompanied by a clerk who, on oath of fidelity, was required in the presence of the master and a witness to enter a true record of the goods received on board in the *cartolario*. The clerk was a 'third party authority', agent of neither the shipper nor the master, and the contents of these 'books of lading' became evidence of the receipt of the goods. The next step was the passing of a statute, apparently in the Italian city of Ancona, requiring the clerk to give a copy of the register to persons entitled to demand it. In addition, for the purposes of allowing cargo insurance coverage which had also developed at that time, the clerk had to keep a safe copy of the register at the port of departure in order to secure evidence of the goods loaded in the event of loss of the vessel.[14] When this statute was adhered to, excerpts of

---

12 See e.g. B. Wigley, N. Cary (eds.), *The Future Is Decentralised. Block Chains, Distributed Ledgers, & the Future of Sustainable Development*, https://blog.blockchain.com/2018/03/05/future-is-decentralised/; M. Bellini, *Che cosa sono e come funzionano le Blockchain Distributed Ledgers Technology – DLT*, in *Blockchain4innovation*, https://www.blockchain4innovation.it/esperti/cosa-funzionano-le-blockchain-distributed-ledgers-technology-dlt/. For an easier understanding see also the video https://www.youtube.com/watch?v=_boyFStBuo4.

13 See R. Mancuso, *Polizza di carico*, in M. Deiana (ed.), *Diritto della navigazione* (Milan, Giuffrè, 2010), 305; B. McLaughlin, *The Evolution of the Ocean Bill of Lading* (1925) 35 *Yale L.J.*, 548, 550.

14 G.M. Boi, *La lettera di trasporto marittimo* (Milan, Giuffrè, 1995) 1; D.E. Murray, *History and Development of the Bill of Lading* (1983) 37 *University of Miami Law Review*, 689.

these 'books' were delivered to the shipper, then something similar to a bill of lading actually came into existence.[15]

If we apply the DLT allowed by the blockchain to a merchant vessel engaged in maritime transport, and each person interested in the transport is given access to a block in the relevant network, then in real time it is possible to add any new record to the blockchain. This represents each event occurring for this transport and keeps all parties informed about what is happening to the transport: e.g. the loading of a given good onboard in a given port, the departure of the vessel from such a port, its arrival at another port, the unloading of an item, or any other event occurring on the voyage.[16]

The above is a prospected blockchain application to a maritime transport. Easily enough, we can enlarge our view to the non-maritime leg of the transport and enhance the potentialities of the blockchain.

3 How do we translate this technology into a legal-contractual frame? A possible case for non-permissioned DLTs and registers of ships

Once this has been done we need to frame some rules on how this system should work, in order to have its functions properly performed as in a traditional sea carriage contract where bills of lading or charter-parties are issued. This bring us to the next step of our analysis, i.e. the selection of people who are entitled to organise the blockchain, and of those who are given access to it with their blocks.

Blockchain technology utilises two different methods for DLT: 'unpermissioned ledgers', where there is no owner nor 'godfather'; such DLTs are conceived for the purpose of being controlled only by the actors connected to the blockchain. At present the most famous unpermissioned ledger is probably Bitcoin. These ledgers can be utilised as global databases for all entries/transactions that need to be absolutely non-modifiable over time, unless a consensus has been given that updates take place with the highest security. In the legal arena, a good example can be the case for ledgers containing either lists of property or goods, or wills.

Yet ledgers of this kind may become useful in shipping as well. More precisely, they can be applied to ships, in particular concerning their ownership, any visit undergone by the vessel in any port of call, possible remarks issued by the competent port authorities or classification societies, and so on. Further information could be inserted in the blockchain concerning any ship, such as the compliance (i)

---

15 F. Munari, *Bill of lading* in *European Encyclopedia of Private International Law* (J. Basedow, G. Rühl, F. Ferrari and P. de Miguel Asensio, eds.), vol. I (Cheltenham Spa, Edward Elgar Publishing, 2017) 193, also for further references.

16 See P. Verhoeven, F. Sinn, T.T. Herden, *Examples from Blockchain Implementations in Logistics and Supply Chain Management: Exploring the Mindful Use of a New Technology* (2018) 2 *Logistics*, 20; for a diagram L.W. Cong, Z. He, Blockchain Disruption (above note 8), at 12. For a possible example of a system for tracking goods in real time and its benefits, see B. Rankin, *Tracking shipping using blockchain*, US Patent App. 15/818, 611, 2018, as well as the other patent application mentioned above at note 11.

with technical standards or measures, or (ii) with environmental standards (e.g. the implementation of ballast water treatment, relevant rules for future scrapping and recycling consistently with regulation (EU) no. 1257/2013, and the like).[17] Were such a blockchain to be constructed, keeping records of all merchant vessels and the events characterizing them 'from cradle to grave', this might mark a substantial change both in the enforcement and compliance of the applicable international conventions or regional rules, such as those adopted at EU level, and in the simplification of the access to information concerning each vessel by any potential, interested party. And needless to say, the whole area of transactions concerning sale and chartering of vessel would undergo substantial changes, in practice and as regards the role of intermediaries. There might be, indeed, problems of enforcement; on that I shall however try to deal with below.[18]

4 Permissioned ledgers and their potential applications to shipping and transport

If the ledgers outlined above may have a use for 'public' purposes, some even more interesting examples of the potential application of blockchain technology in our sector can be found if we turn to the 'permissioned ledgers'. These ledgers can be controlled and owned only by specified interested parties. More precisely, particular trusted actors may exclusively modify entries in them; other, non-trusted, people can have access to the ledgers, and can see whatever is occurring, but without being entitled to modify any records. Needless to say, the above should also function in connection with electronic signatures, a topic which will be dealt with elsewhere in this volume.[19] As a consequence, these ledgers make it possible to set governance rules and allocate rights and obligations concerning a transaction or a given series of transactions.

We might thus imagine a shipping company using its ledger, giving the master as well as its agents and suppliers trusted access to the blockchain to modify the ledger upon the occurrence of any new event concerning the transport. Clients might also be given access, potentially with different levels of authority: e.g. the task of signalling whether property on a given item of cargo in transit has passed to a new owner, or the right to become entitled as consignee to delivery of goods upon payment of the freight, in a situation in which the blockchain is reliable as to the safe arrival of goods at their final destination. Financial and insurance institutions may also be willing to be trusted clients, to secure transactions or payment of any insurance premium. They can also be appointed as 'oracles' (i.e. an agent that finds and verifies real-world occurrences and submits this information to a blockchain to be used by smart

---

17 The environmental positive impact of blockchain technology in the international transport industry is also stressed by N. Degnarain, *Supply Chain Management*, in *The Future Is Decentralised* (above note 11), at 23 ff. and K. Czachorowski, M. Solesvik, Y. Kondratenko, *The Application of Blockchain Technology in the Maritime Industry*, in Kharchenko V., Kondratenko Y., Kacprzyk J. (eds), *Green IT Engineering: Social, Business and Industrial Applications. Studies in Systems, Decision and Control*, (Springer, Cham, 2018), 561.
18 See § 9.
19 See the contribution by E. Røsaeg, *Electronic Signatures in Shipping Practice*, at 36.

contracts).[20] Finally, public authorities may also be granted access for the proper discharge of their duties: custom clearance of the goods before their arrival in the port once the blockchain has confirmed that they will be discharged there, payment of taxes and anchorage dues by vessels upon their arrival at a given port, and information concerning the necessity for the vessel to carry out specific activities normally governed at port-State level, from compliance with any port-State control measure to the embarking or disembarking of crew. A blockchain would quite probably allow a much more seamless and efficient discharge of many activities related to a transport of goods by sea. And as we shall see below, it may also substantially affect the number of intermediaries normally engaged in the transportation or logistical chain.

5 Issues of responsibility in the (maritime) transport industry

Other noteworthy legal implications stemming from the use of the blockchain technology applied to the shipping industry can certainly extend to liability rules.

An immediate, fully reliable and precise system detecting whatever events occur to goods, while moving from the place of origin to that of their final destination, seems capable of simplifying the individuation (a) of the responsible party for loss or damage to the good, and almost invariably (b) of the precise causes of such a loss or damage. It would also allow (c) the adoption of immediate measures to assess the quantification of damages, with potential costs and litigations savings.

In general terms, it is hardly contested that in digital markets liability rules can, and will, be seriously affected.[21] This being so, one can wonder whether such a technology might not eventually modify both well rooted rules on a carrier's liability, as established at international level by well-known conventions, as well as identically rooted commercial practices and contracts that are typical in our sector.

A few examples will suffice. Would it still be acceptable by the market to have reference to paramount clauses in a bill of lading or charter party when the whole set of information concerning the transport, previously unknown to a shipper, would be available in real time and utterly reliably? Would it still be sound to insert in a contract for transportation (especially multi-modal) a *Himalaya* clause whose rationale (i.e. the channelling of liability onto the maritime carrier) might have become obsolete in a case where a DLT system is capable of establishing precisely when an issue has arisen, and thus who should be held responsible for it? Would a bill of lading remain the fundamental contractual documents for the purposes of liner shipping?[22]

More generally, would stakeholders still consider the existing international conventions on the liability of maritime and multimodal carriers fit for market purposes? Or would the market forces adapt their commercial standards to these new technologies? Maybe a precise answer to such questions is premature, but I would not be surprised if, once blockchain technology were to develop in large scale in

---

20 See https://blockchainhub.net/blockchain-oracles/.
21 See e.g. R.H. Weber, *Liability in the Internet of Things* (2017) 6 *EuCML*, 207.
22 See on this question also the remarks made by R. Stahlbock, L. Heilig, S. Voß, *Blockchain in der maritimen Logistik*, published online by Springer.

our business, its legal consequences would determine substantial and radical changes in maritime law and its fundamental institutions which people have been studying and working on for many decades.

Such a conclusion seems strengthened by the strong interaction that blockchain technology and smart contracts may not only have at an inter-individual level of business, but more generally in the marketplace, also as a consequence of the widespread development of sharing economy.

This is the next topic on which I wish to sketch some ideas.

6 Blockchain as a tool to revolutionise transport markets

As anticipated earlier, at present the relationship between blockchain technology and transport has been deepened especially in connection with passenger transport and urban mobility:[23] these studies make clear the importance of transport sharing devices (and apps) that in the past years have boosted shared mobility. This having been said, however, analogies and implications are clear also in the transport of goods and outside urban areas.

The starting point of our reasoning stems from the fact that blockchain technology is a peer-to-peer system.[24]

In this system, a DLT capable of connecting demand and supply of transport of goods would immediately show any interested shipper the availability of transport suppliers from a given area to another one. Tellingly, it would also allow the former to be thoroughly informed about the characteristics of the available carriers, their past performances, their reliability, accountability and possibly their pricing policies.[25] Information asymmetries would be highly reduced, and rational choices would be available for customers and also for carriers. Generally, there are prospects for efficiency gains in the transportation industry, carrying with them advantages that should not be underestimated: for example, a blockchain system matching in real time demand and supply of transportation would reduce overcapacity and maximise the use of vessels and other transportation means, while at the same time potentially limiting GHG emissions.

Even more promising as an advantage of blockchain technology applied to transport and logistics is that it could prevent counterfeiting of goods and related frauds, guarantee the origins of goods and permit the operation of IOT solutions all along the supply chain,[26] while simultaneously cutting paperwork and its related costs.[27]

If this seems an ideal world, it has some applications already, albeit outside of shipping. A preliminary example is the start-up *Wave*, focussed on international

---

23 See in particular *Blockchain and Beyond* (above note 4).
24 See J.A. Bergstra, M. Burgess, *Blockchain Technology and Its Applications* (above note 11), at 6 ff. and the video https://www.youtube.com/watch?v=3xGLc-zz9cA.
25 See *Blockchain and Beyond* (above note 2), at 58.
26 See N. Hackius, M. Petersen, *Blockchain in Logistics and Supply Chain: Trick or Treat?* in Kersten W., Blecker T., Ringle C.M. (eds), *Digitalization in Supply Chain Management and Logistics*, e-published in October 2017 on https://tubdok.tub.tuhh.de/bitstream/11,420/1447/1/petersen_hackius_blockchain_in_scm_and_logistics_hicl_2017.pdf, at 7 ff.; R. Stahlbock, L. Heilig, S. Voß (above note 22).
27 See R. Stahlbock, L. Heilig, S. Voß (above note 22).

trade and supported by Barclays Bank Plc, whose aim is to reduce operators' costs in the management of their supply chain.[28] To take another, *Alibaba* has just announced that it will use blockchain technology for tracking the food it supplies to its customers.[29] Another instance is *Interfishmarket*, more focused on the road transport of one type of perishable goods (fish).[30] In this case, a marketplace has been created where the 'owner' of a permissioned DLT puts hauliers and sellers, interested in delivering their products in small quantities in a given place, in touch with each other. All these people become part of the blockchain and relevant transport transactions are governed by smart contracts.[31]

In container transport, initiatives are gaining momentum such as *300Cubits*.[32] An analogous idea has been proposed recently, to make the business process for less container load (LCL) transport industry more efficient, whereby producers can 'pool' through blockchain technology for their cargo for subsequent export. This proposed *LCL Export Platform* (LEP) would utilise blockchain technology to optimize the LCL operations for international trading, by integrating and sharing information among forwarder agencies and their clients.[33]

Even more recently, AP Møller-Mærsk has announced its platform *Tradelens*, which has been developed in partnership with IBM. *Tradelens* is a permissioned blockchain, presented as a 'neutral platform' using 'open standards' and capable of allowing all members of the blockchain to have relevant information concerning any moving cargo in real time.[34] On a larger scale, one might imagine similar platforms being organised for the liner transportation industry, or for bulk carriage of commodities. Especially in this latter market, which is much more fragmented than that of liner container shipping, both shipowners and shippers may be interested in participating to such a blockchain platform: the former to extend their reach to potential customers, and the latter to avoid the use of intermediaries (e.g. brokers) and connected transactional costs. At the same time, if adherence to the platform could also encompass a uniform, smart contractual regime for all transport transaction carried out within the platform, contractual implementation would be easier, the risks of litigation reduced and connected costs (including legal fees) diminished in regard to negotiating, drafting and concluding relevant contracts for carriage of goods.

Indeed, the same positive outcomes were promised by other much older projects using IT application for shipping. Reference is made, in particular, to the *Bolero*

---

28 See P. Rizzo, *Wave Brings Blockchain Trade Finance Trial to Barclays*, https://www.coindesk.com/wave-blockchain-trade-finance-barclays/.

29 *Alibaba Food Supply Chain Consortium Uses Blockchain*, https://www.porttechnology.org/news/alibaba_food_supply_chain_consortium_uses_blockchain.

30 See the platform Interfishmarket (www.interfishmarket.com).

31 Further examples are provided for by R. O'Shields, *Smart Contracts. Legal Agreements for the Blockchain* (2017) 21 *North Carolina Banking Institute*, 177, at 181 ff.

32 P. Verhoeven, F. Sinn, T.T. Herden (above note 16), at 9.

33 A.W. Kwan Tan, Y. Zhao, T. Halliday, *A Blockchain Model for Less Container Load Operations in China* (2018) 11 *International Journal of Information Systems and Supply Chain Management*, 2.

34 See www.tradelens.com.

project,[35] launched in 1999 and governed as well by a 'ledger', named the *Bolero Rulebook*, which in fact works also as a contractual regime among all participants to the *Bolero* network. Thus it obliges them to recognise *Bolero* digital messages with the same legal force as paper documents, creates a marketplace where participants may transfer rights and obligations relating to goods as well as giving instructions to carriers, and prohibits *Bolero* members from challenging the legitimacy of electronic messages encrypted by *Bolero*. The Rulebook refers also to English law and English jurisdiction, i.e. the topic concerning enforceability of 'agreements' among network members, a matter on which I shall try to provide some brief insights below. Apparently, the *Bolero* project has not been as successful as expected. Scholars believe that this reason may be the lack of support by large shipping carriers, by the banking and insurance systems and by the risks of not being enforceable outside of English jurisdiction, because the *Bolero Bill of Lading* (BBL) would not be recognised as falling within the legal notion of the bill of lading accepted at international level by the applicable conventions and domestic legislation.[36]

This example may signal a resistance of the 'classical' shipping stakeholders to cope with new technological solutions, and possibly their fear that IT may deprive them of market power – a role traditionally enjoyed in this sector. And yet, it is difficult to foresee whether the sudden changes in the economy, generally brought by technology, internet and the 'new economy', will eventually bend the traditional stakeholders to the new reality. After all, the Rotterdam Rules have opened the path to negotiable electronic transport documents already.[37]

7 Other legal concerns: antitrust, data protection and security

Needless to say, a platform like the one we have imagined would not exist in a legal vacuum, and should comply with other rules and principles applicable to phenomena like the one we are dealing with.

For instance, the availability of all information concerning a given number of carriers might be capable of generating anti-competitive effects, in so far as sensitive information (e.g. pricing terms) could become available among competitors.[38] This obstacle needs to be considered,[39] but should not be insurmountable: indeed,

---

35 Bolero (www.bolero.net) is a trading platform, yet it does not use blockchain technology. On Bolero see D.A. Bury, *Electronic Bills of Lading: A Never-Ending Story?* (2016) 41 *Tulane Maritime Law Journal*, 196, at 218–222.

36 D.A. Bury, *Electronic Bills of Lading* (above note 34), at 221–222.

37 M. Alba, *The Use of Electronic Records as Collateral in the Rotterdam Rules; Future Solutions and Present Needs* (2009) 14 *Uniform Law Review*, 801 ff.

38 An interesting analysis on competition and smart contracts is offered by L.W. Cong, Z. He, *Blockchain disruption* (above note 8), 23 ff., in which the reverse side of the coin is also examined (see especially at 32 ff.), *i.e.* how competition authorities might be advantaged to discover collusive behaviours if they were granted access to a blockchain ledger where firms operate.

39 See L. Calzolari, *La collusione fra algoritmi nell'era dei big data: l'imputabilità alle imprese delle 'intese 4.0' ai sensi dell'art. 101 TFUE* (2018) 2 *Medialaws – Rivista del diritto dei media*, 3, at http://www.medialaws.eu/rivista/la-collusione-fra-algoritmi-nellera-dei-big-data-limputabilita-alle-imprese-delle-intese-4-0-ai-sensi-dellart-101-tfue/.

experts have already considered the idea of 'hybrid' blockchain systems, where the existing information in the relevant DLT is not made available to all members. Hence, at least in theory, only the purchasers of transport services, and not the providers, might have access to sensitive data in order to avoid distortions of competition among carriers.

Similarly delicate matters might be issues concerning data protection and security. An analysis of this matter would clearly go beyond the scope of this paper;[40] however, at least some hints can be provided. Information which is in the blockchain is *per se* transparent and accessible, but will remain forever available and accessible, and should not therefore contain personal or sensitive data. At least as regards the EU legal system, the GDPR,[41] recently coming into force, which introduces severe limitations to the permissible storage of data, and obliges data managers to comply with strict provisions, including restrictions of processing, or the right to be forgotten. It does not explicitly deal with blockchain, but it would seem that permissioned ledgers are consistent with the duty to minimise data processing and management.[42] Thus, it may be possible to segregate some data and avoid making it generally available to the participants of a ledger. Furthermore, as has been persuasively pointed out, there may be a substantial difference between the cases where the trusted 'manager' of a DLT is a State and where it is a private firm offering 'state-line' blockchain services.[43] Moreover, the 'right to be forgotten', which is enshrined in article 17 GDPR, is not absolute and encounters some limitations, inter alia 'for archiving purposes in the public interest, … in so far as the right referred to in paragraph 1 is likely to render impossible or seriously impair the achievement of the objectives of that processing'.

One might assume that, in the shipping and transport industry, the transmission or uploading of personal or sensitive data concerning the individual would not be very frequent. On the other hand, security issues might more frequently come into play and would again require particular attention by legislators and policy-makers.[44]

8 The issue of smart contracts: would they fit in the shipping and logistics industry?

It seems undisputable that blockchain technology applied to shipping or logistics may provide substantial advantages to business.[45] With that said, problems seem to arise when trying to 'import' the blockchain system into legal terms. This technology should be accompanied by smart contracts, that should eventually replace – or

---

40 For more information, please refer again to *Blockchain and Beyond* (above note 2), at 42. A short analysis on cybersecurity issues is provided also by R. Stahlbock, L. Heilig, S. Voß (above note 22).

41 Regulation (EU) 2016/679 of the European Parliament and of the Council of 27 April 2016 on the protection of natural persons with regard to the processing of personal data and on the free movement of such data and repealing Directive 95/46/EC (General Data Protection Regulation), *O.J.* L 119/2016, 1.

42 See e.g. recital 26 and article 3, let. e) GDPR.

43 See *How blockchain technology could change our lives* (above note 2), at 19.

44 See R. O'Shields, *Smart Contracts* (above note 31), at 184 ff.

45 This is generally accepted by legal scholars (see K. Werbacht, N. Cornell, *Contracts ex Machina* (above note 7), 317 ff).

maybe initially accompany – the traditional contracts we are used to in our sector: movement of the goods should be checked, tracked and followed in the blockchain, and the legal consequences progressively arising out of such movement (e.g. their preparing for transport, loading, moving, unloading and so on) should be accompanied by relevant payments made by clients to suppliers. And in this vein, 'clients' and 'suppliers' clearly include all firms active in the supply chain, or else all agents of the maritime carrier, if such a carrier is the 'main' supplier of the transport service, or potentially the vendor of the goods, who may eventually consider the maritime carrier as one of its servants.[46]

Commentators have stressed the idea of smart contracts as IT tools capable of eliminating intermediaries, lawyers included, and as a way to obtain certainty of execution through digitization. As it has been persuasively pointed out,

> using computer [sic], the parties are using an ex ante method to guarantee contractual compliance, and explicitly forbearing in accepting the occasional incorrect automated assessment for the sake of efficiency and certainty.... By using smart contracts, the parties are actually changing the paradigm of contract practice from ex post authoritative judgment to ex ante automated assessments. Parties are into smart contract [sic] because they believe that the ex ante automate results will only infrequently diverge from an authoritative decision maker such as a judge. In this way, the parties deliberately forbear of ex-post corrections for the sake of ex ante efficiency.[47]

Other scholars believe that, once encoded in a smart contract, the possibilities of breaching the same become impossible for the parties, since the contract is self-executing without further possibilities for them to change their will and behaviours as agreed. In this situation, the main advantages of smart contracts would be an increase in efficiency, the reduction of negotiating costs and a curtailed risk of contractual pathologies.[48]

Needless to say, this might be sad news for many of us. Yet some *caveats* are worth noting. Firstly, smart contracts will not replace contract law, which is remedial and, unlike smart contracts, not, focused to ensure performance *ex ante*.[49] Secondly, not all intermediaries can be excluded, because clients and suppliers must appoint IT managers to insert the relevant algorithmic rules into codes that can be processed in a computer system. This, it has been maintained, can itself turn out into a problem, because of the difficulties in understanding whether the 'legal' clauses inserted into the code actually correspond to the will of the parties. In this sense – at least until computers shall have become so user-friendly as to allow normal people and businessmen to encode relevant instruction into a smart contract – IT managers would possibly replace lawyers, and their presence would always be indispensable, while this is not the case for traditional contracts, many of which are not negotiated with the assistance of a lawyer, and in fact only

---

46 See also below, § 8, last part.
47 J.I.-H. Hsiao, *'Smart' contract* (above note 9), at 690. Almost identically also K. Werbacht, N. Cornell, *Contracts ex Machina* (above note 7), 318.
48 P. Cuccurru, *Blockchain ed automazione contrattuale* (above note 11), at 3.
49 K. Werbacht, N. Cornell, *Contracts ex Machina* (above note 7), 318.

a limited portion of them involve legal 'intermediaries'.[50] Thirdly, some scholars doubt that computer codes or 'orders' can cope with complex issues that are at the core of legal work, i.e. interpretation of contracts and assessment of unforeseen situations that may arise during contractual performance. Thus, they argue, the inherent 'rigidity' of algorithms and computer science is at odds with the much more nuanced approach lawyers and businessmen tend to apply.

In this vein, it is generally believed that smart contracts are fit for 'simple' situations, where almost invariably performance is easy and secure (this being in our sector the case of urban mobility and passenger transportation), whereas for complex transactions such as many of those concerning shipping or movement of goods (also) by sea, smart contracts are in general depicted as premature.[51]

However, I tend to believe that the eventual capacity of such *caveats* to delay or hamper smart contracts in shipping should be considered at least doubtful. Firstly, shipping is well acquainted with detailed contracts that are *de facto* issued by one party and accepted by the other parties, such as bills of lading. And when charter-parties are used, their sophistication has not prevented the diffusion of standards that are used worldwide, and might be written into computer codes too.

Furthermore, the digital economy and e-commerce have profoundly changed the patterns of transport. Moreover, one potentially paramount driver for change should not be underestimated. This is the appearance in the market of huge shippers (e.g. Amazon) capable of dispatching an enormous volume of differentiated goods for many millions of customers and organising all information concerning them and their final purchasers with big data and real time characteristics.

The probable effects of these changes have not been totally understood yet. However, studies suggest that smart contracts work well when the number of parties involved is high,[52] including the case of a business-to-consumer framework.[53] Moreover, large vendors are considering whether to directly manage the transportation and delivery of the goods worldwide (projects to use drones are already under way, and the purchase of dedicated (unmanned) ships also appears to be under way). In this situation, one cannot exclude the possibility that such vendors may be interested in organising their supply chain using this new technology and thus standardising millions of sales worldwide under more efficient patterns because of the high grade of trust between all the parties which characterises

---

50 *Id.*, at 4.

51 This is the general view expressed by the scholars (e.g. those mentioned in the preceding notes), but also by the European Parliament (*How blockchain technology could change our lives*, above note 2, at 16 ff.):

> At this stage, smart contracts still require some initial effort and expense to set up, so they are better suited to repetitive agreements rather than one-off contracts. Given their predetermined nature, they are not well suited to situations that are subject to substantial change during the contract period. Indeed, the level of legal uncertainty would make it prudent to restrict smart contracts to relatively consensual relationships and agreements that are unlikely to be disputed by either party. Finally, since they react to digital stimuli and trigger further digital processes, they are most effective where the various clauses' conditions and consequences are also of a digital nature, and are thus well-suited to digital automation.

52 See *Blockchain and Beyond* (above note 2), at 38.
53 S. Tönnissen, F. Teuterberg (above note 7).

a blockchain system.[54] Furthermore, the combination of permissioned and hybrid ledgers may at least induce these large vendors to carry out their sales and related logistic chain through sophisticated smart contracts, because the advantages they would have in 'capturing' the logistic chain would increase their market power *vis-à-vis* traditional carriers; besides, in the end, the latter may be seen as any other 'intermediary' between sellers and purchasers of goods.

These advantages would push them to abandon the handling of 'difficult' contractual situations (for which smart contracts may be sub-optimal) in favour of a speedier, seamless and costless logistic chain. Such a trade-off, if applied, would boost smart contracts in the transportation of goods, and would also probably have substantial effects at market level in the shipping industry.

9 Issues of dispute resolution

With that said, as lawyers, we cannot overlook the legal environment where these contracts are located, as well as the potential remedies in case contractual relationships become pathological, that is, how smart contracts in our sector may be managed when their implementation encounters problems.

Scholars have deeply studied the issues of enforceability of international contracts in the internet age,[55] and some of these studies are exclusively focussed on smart contracts.[56] For the purposes of this paper, for example, among the instructions to be encoded in a smart contract, one could easily insert a choice of law and choice of forum clause, as is already frequently done in transport and shipping, and indeed in most international contracts. This would probably avoid complicated issues on jurisdiction and applicable law, which might be particularly awkward given the (numerous) entities managing the nodes of a blockchain and the difficulties in individuating, locating and maybe assessing their contractual performance.[57]

The trusted 'managers' of such contracts would decide the legal (domestic or conventional) framework under which the contract would be interpreted in case of a dispute and the place (court or arbitrators) where such a dispute would be settled.

Of course, once convened before a human judge, the parties and their counsels should undergo a reverse-engineering from algorithms and computer codes to 'natural' language, in case evidence is required to assess whether the 'natural language'

---

54 See T. Locker, S. Obermeier, Y.-A. Pignolet, *When can a Distributed Ledger Replace a Trusted Third Party?*, published at *IEEE Blockchain 2018*, 28 June 2018, available online at https://arxiv.org/abs/1806.10929v1. Interestingly enough, blockchain may be also used to enhance pooper people having no bank account to participate to the global economy simply recording their financial transactions in a credit history, to give them a baseline, and provide them the opportunity to leverage financial services. This is, e.g., the scope and purpose of the *BanQu* platform, which is recalled by P. Verhoeven, F. Sinn, T.T. Herden (above note 16), at 10–11.

55 See the classical work by D.J.B. Svantesson, *Private International Law and the Internet*, 3rd ed. (2016) Alphen aan den Rijn, Wolters Kluwer.

56 See S. Bourque and S.F.L. Tsui, *A Lawyer's Introduction to Smart Contracts* (2014), *Scientia Nobilitat. Review of Legal Studies*, 4 (https://documen.site/download/document-2551827_pdf), as well as the authors quoted respectively in notes 7, 9, 11, 21 and 31, also for further references.

57 R. O'Shields, *Smart Contracts* (above note 31), at 191.

agreed between the parties actually corresponds to the computer codes used to write the relevant contractual regime.

It is highly likely that, with smart contracts, the number of disputes would decrease as a consequence of it being impossible for one party to run afoul of its contractual obligations. And this, *per se*, will diminish the incidence of pathological situations. Once potential variables occurring during implementation of a shipping contract have been properly identified and transformed into computer codes, the fears expressed by non-shipping scholars concerning the difficulties of using smart contracts for complex situations might actually vanish.

A different evaluation can be forecast in case the smart contract does not contain choice of law and forum clauses, or if their validity is challenged (e.g. because they breach mandatory provisions existing in a given legal system). In these cases, issues of jurisdiction and enforceability might actually prevent the seamless implementation of the contract. To prevent this, however, the use of the 'intermediate' lawyers might still be required, e.g. to provide the parties (and in particular the party *de facto* governing the transaction, *i.e.* the trusted person governing the ledger) with the correct advice on how to avoid these potential obstacles.

On the other hand, smart contracts do not exist in a legal vacuum, since they can be considered as a form of e-contracts, something that is already known to courts and legislators. Aside from other legal systems,[58] in the EU, for instance, reference can be done to directive 2000/31 on electronic commerce.[59] Such a directive might be in need of rejigging in case smart contracts increase in popularity;[60] but this phenomenon is no different from the constant updating of the law to the needs of the society and commerce.

It may only be a matter of time, but I have little doubts that a sharp change will be brought about by IT to shipping law and practice.

---

58 On which see e.g. R. O'Shields, *Smart Contracts* (above note 31), at 187 ff.

59 Directive 2000/31/EC of the European Parliament and of the Council of 8 June 2000 on certain legal aspects of information society services, in particular electronic commerce, in the Internal Market (O.J. L 178, 1).

60 In fact, attempts have been made by the Commission since 2015 to amend the digital commerce directive, so far unsuccessfully, and further studies are under way (see, for further references, https://ec.europa.eu/digital-single-market/en/platforms-to-business-trading-practices).

CHAPTER 2

Smart contracts

The BIMCO experience

*Grant Hunter**

1 Introduction

Businesses may talk about the importance of trust in building strong commercial relationships, but essentially modern enterprise is based on the principle of mutual distrust. In the global marketplace we buy goods we have never physically seen from people we do not know and may never meet. When we are unable to do business "face to face" we introduce uncertainty into the transaction. How can the buyer know for sure that the goods he has ordered from someone on the other side of the planet will actually be delivered? And how can the seller know for sure that he will receive the money for the goods? To help manage this mistrust and uncertainty we use "middlemen", institutions like banks that both parties can trust.

In the 1980s the development of the internet helped create a global "digital" market place where new "middlemen" like Amazon now play a dominant role in the digital economy. The use of "middlemen" depends on centralised processing of transactions. A bank will hold records of customers and transactions in a database, but this data will be independent of any similar data held by other banks or institutions. Centralised data systems are vulnerable because it is possible that the single source of data may become corrupted or be tampered with. Can banks always be trusted? History might suggest otherwise. And, of course, banks provide these services at a cost.

New technologies have emerged that have the potential to radically change the way business is done in our digital economy. The most talked about of these current new technologies is blockchain. The word "blockchain" gives little away about what the technology is or what it can do. It was developed ten years ago (quite a long time in technology terms) by Satoshi Nakamoto – a mysterious figure who has since disappeared without trace.[1]

Blockchain was created to provide a secure platform for transactions using digital currency without involving banks – a peer to peer cash system. It provides a means of preventing double-spending of digital currencies like Bitcoin (meaning you cannot simply copy a "Bitcoin") – there are a limited number of them and

---

* Head of Contracts & Clauses at BIMCO.
1 The idea was first introduced in an article published under the same name: https://bitcoin.org/bitcoin.pdf (last tested 31 January 2019).

each one has a unique identity. Blockchain maintains a fully transparent and unchangeable audit trail of each transaction. It is essentially a database. What makes blockchain different from existing transactional technologies is that it does not reside on one single computer. The blockchain database is distributed across tens of thousands of computers worldwide, each of which participates in verifying every transaction and then adding a new "block" of that recorded transaction to the chain of transactions for each Bitcoin. A block cannot be deleted from the blockchain, it is a permanent record. To change any information in a blockchain would require that data be changed in every single computer comprising the blockchain. This makes the technology highly secure.

Within the last few years technologists have realised that blockchain technology can be developed for many other uses than just managing crypto currencies. One of the main focus areas is supply chain logistics and business transactions. In the logistics world blockchain can be used as an easily accessible single global network to record every movement of goods from origin to destination – a permanent record of where an item has been and where it is currently located. Blockchain avoids the need to reconcile data between different systems, it reduces duplication of data, and provides authentication of records and a permanent audit trail.

There is a growing interest in the use of blockchain technology to develop applications for self-executing contracts, known as "smart contracts". Using this technology all or part of a conventional "written" commercial contract is transposed into computer code. A smart contract sits on the blockchain network and responds automatically to certain "trigger" events. This means that smart contracts not only set out the terms and conditions of an agreement in the same way as a traditional contract, but also automatically enforces those obligations.

Understandably, the concept of a self-executing contract might give rise to anxiety. In its simplest form a smart contract works much like a vending machine – you make your selection, put in your money and out pops your chosen item – no middleman involved. But what happens in a more complex contract like a charter party which is often subject to negotiation and amendment? One of the main strengths of blockchain is its certainty and security because its records are immutable. But in the contractual world this means that it may not be possible to modify or cancel a contract. Producing a smart contract is a two-step process; first you draft the contract in the conventional way and then you convert it to computer code. But if every negotiated charter party is slightly different then you would need to compile new code for every transaction.

Blockchain has been described as a network. The internet is a decentralised network of computer networks that has revolutionised the way we communicate. It cannot be switched off and cannot be owned by a single entity. In many ways blockchain may be the foundation of a new digital revolution – a decentralised network for business transactions. But unlike the internet, there can be many blockchain networks. Some will be public blockchains like Bitcoin which are not "owned" by any single entity; others will be private, or "permissive" like those built by IBM. This creates issues of interoperability – a current lack of standards means that it may not be possible for one blockchain network to communicate with another.

Blockchain technology is developing rapidly and becoming ever more sophisticated. Although there have been many useful experiments using the technology, we are yet to see the development of any mainstream applications. It seems likely that much more research and pilot studies will need to be conducted before this technology can be fully evaluated.

2 The BIMCO perspective

BIMCO can only guess what the future holds for charter parties and other shipping industry contracts. Unless, of course, we decide to take matters into our own hands and help shape the future ourselves.

It is easy to get swept along with the latest technological advances, each offering the "ultimate" solution to problems we sometimes did not know we had. Which is the right technology to invest in? Will new technology bring the promised benefits of transparency and efficiency, or are there hidden pitfalls awaiting us?

BIMCO occupies a unique position in the shipping industry. It is an organisation with a long history. It was born in the early 20th century out of a desire by a group of shipowners to bring stability and sustainability to the Baltic timber trade where freight rates were in freefall. By creating a freight "conference" in which shipowners would all agree not to fix voyages below a certain freight rate, they hoped to control the market. They failed.[2]

But out of their failure came a realisation that there was little point in forcing charterers to agree a minimum freight rate if the charterers simply clawed the money back through charter parties highly favourable to themselves. So, the answer was to create standard terms and conditions that were fair and acceptable to both parties. This may not seem part of a technological "revolution" as such, but the importance of this event is that it established the concept of a "standard" charter party. And as we know, the key to technological success is the acceptance of a standard way of doing things which is widely accepted. Microsoft Windows is a classic example of global standardisation. You can walk in to almost any office in the world and sit down and know how to use their computers because most of them run the same Windows operating system as you have on your own computer.

BIMCO's charter parties are designed with a similar philosophy in mind: pursuing global familiarity and widespread use. The GENCON voyage charter party is perhaps in many respects the BIMCO equivalent of Microsoft Windows! Computer operating systems are a means of helping you to do your daily work more easily – they facilitate tasks but contain no actual content. BIMCO contracts, on the other hand, are all about content. The standard terms and conditions they provide will certainly make the task of contracting easier, but they are essentially an inanimate body of words.

Until the advent of the personal computer in the 1980s, charter parties were amended by hand. This could be as basic as using a pen and ruler to strike out text and add handwritten amendments, or it could involve the use of a typewriter. Either way it was a laborious job. The difficulty in making changes to a standard charter

---

2 For a historical account of BIMCO, see, www.maritime-executive.com/magazine/bimco (last tested on 31 January 2019).

party probably meant that people were less inclined to make amendments. Which, for an organisation like BIMCO that promotes the use of "standardised" terms and conditions, was a good thing!

But then came along one of the biggest technological advances of our time – the desktop computer followed shortly thereafter by the internet. Shipowners and charterers now wanted to edit their charter parties on their computers. The typewriter was to be consigned to history as a new breed of one-fingered typists took control of editing charter parties.

How did BIMCO react to these developments? When the people who used BIMCO charter parties asked for electronic copies that they could use on their new desktop computers, we said "no". This may seem an ill-judged reaction of a luddite organisation shying away from the reality of the digital age. But this was far from the truth. Our concern was that giving users free reign to make whatever changes they wanted to Word copies of our charter parties would result in uncertainty – you would not easily be able to see the authentic original wording of the standard form.

To counter this threat, in 2001 we built our own online charter party editing system, IDEA. This provided a "walled garden" in which secure copies of BIMCO contracts could be edited and amended, but always clearly showing those changes.

In 2018 we launched a new product called SmartCon[3] which uses the very latest technology to do something that we previously thought was not possible. We can now distribute Word copies of all our contracts in a format that allows people to edit them on their own computers without the need for any special "charter party editor" software. What SmartCon does is control the way these Word documents are used, even when the user is offline. Track changes is permanently locked on and a full audit trail of amendments is preserved. SmartCon documents can be opened and edited on any copy of Microsoft Word – software that is standard on almost every office computer in the world.

SmartCon has given BIMCO the opportunity to re-think the way its documents are used. One low tech solution to help users is to give every BIMCO contract the same look and feel. Gone are the two column documents with tiny print!

One of the drivers behind the development of SmartCon has been the ambition to increase the distribution and use of BIMCO contracts. A SmartCon document can be sent to anyone as an email attachment or stored on a shared filing system. You cannot open the document until you have registered as a user and you can only open other people's SmartCon documents if they give you permission. But this gives you security as well as certainty.

SmartCon is the start of a process by BIMCO to investigate how charter parties and other maritime contracts might be used in the future. Making sure that people can easily obtain authentic copies of BIMCO contracts is one important aspect. We have built a free authenticator-check on our website where people can quickly check that their BIMCO contract is genuine, before they start negotiations.

---

3 For more information on SmartCon, please visit: www.bimco.org/contracts-and-clauses/create-a-contract/smartcon (last tested on 31 January 2019).

Looking further forward, we are working together with technology partners in a feasibility study into so-called blockchain "smart contracts" – self-executing contracts that are encoded as computer programmes. We do not necessarily think at this stage that blockchain smart contracts are "the way forward" – it may well be that other emerging technologies offer better solutions, or perhaps a combination of new technologies. We do not want to be reactive to technological innovation, we want to be part of the process if the use of contracts is to change radically in the future.

But which BIMCO contract to pick for the smart contract prototype? A conventional charter party poses a lot of challenges in terms of a self-executing contract. How would you deal with a provision that is triggered by weather conditions or is subject to the discretion of the master? Such a contract would be dependent on the input of a large amount of reliable and trusted data.

We decided to go for a simpler transaction model – our newly published BIMCO Bunker Terms 2018 standard bunker contract. Buying marine fuel is a regular activity for ship owners and operators and there may be some benefit in automating some of the more repetitive or laborious tasks involved in this process.

The prototype smart contract for bunker purchases will not cover the entire agreement. We will select certain clauses within the contract that we feel lend themselves to the concept of "self-execution". BIMCO fully appreciates the importance of being able to break out of a smart contract and revert to the written copy if needs be. Work is at a very preliminary stage and the prototype will need to be rigorously tested. But perhaps the greatest test of all will not be to determine if it can be done technologically, but whether there is likely to be a demand for a smart contract in our conservative industry – even if it offers increased efficiencies. Is our industry ready and willing to contemplate handing over control to a computer – and what happens if things go wrong? From a legal perspective there will be new challenges – are the parties bound by the terms and conditions of the written contract, or the encoded "smart contract" version? Once the contract has been encoded, how do you amend it and what are the consequences for other "smart contracts" using the same code that are already active? Will we need a new breed of lawyers familiar with coding to help prepare smart contract and provide guidance when things go wrong?

3 Conclusion

Although there are challenges ahead, BIMCO can foresee one immediate benefit of smart contracts – and that is "standardisation" of terms and conditions. It would benefit the shipping industry to go through the exercise of rationalising contracts to weed out duplicate and conflicting provisions from charter parties – to have consistency between contracts of the same type. This is a task for which BIMCO is eminently suited – to provide harmonised contract standards that can be adapted to meet the future technological needs of the industry.

CHAPTER 3

Can commercial law accommodate new technologies in international shipping?

Professor Michael F. Sturley*

1 Introduction

When I started teaching commercial law 34 years ago, Elizabeth Warren was my colleague and a mentor. She has since moved on to more prominent pursuits.[1] Before she left the University of Texas, however, I learned a few things about her approach to teaching the subject. In her introductory class, she discussed with the students the fundamental purpose of commercial law. Why do we have commercial law? What do we as a society seek to accomplish with commercial law? How should we evaluate how well commercial law achieves its goals? The short answer was that the purpose of commercial law is to facilitate commerce. That pithy summary of purpose has since become one of the themes that informs my course each time that I teach the subject.

During this colloquium, we have heard and will hear a lot about new technologies (such as blockchain) and how they have the potential to usher in the most profound changes that the shipping industry has seen since the container revolution.[2] The industry is actively pursuing those possibilities on many fronts. The question that we as lawyers and legal academics need to face is whether commercial law is keeping pace. Will the legal system continue to facilitate commerce in the electronic age? Or will commercial law fail in its fundamental purpose, instead serving as a barrier to progress and making it impractical for the industry to adopt new technologies?

---

* Fannie Coplin Regents Chair in Law, University of Texas at Austin; B.A., J.D., Yale; M.A. (Jurisprudence) Oxford. I served as the Senior Adviser on the United States Delegation to Working Group III (Transport Law) of the United Nations Commission on International Trade Law (UNCITRAL), which negotiated the Rotterdam Rules; as a member of the UNCITRAL Secretariat's Expert Group on Transport Law; and as the Rapporteur for the International Sub-Committee on Issues of Transport Law of the Comité Maritime International (CMI) and for the CMI's associated Working Group, which prepared the initial draft for UNCITRAL's consideration. But I write here solely in my academic capacity and the views I express are my own. They do not necessarily represent the views of, and they have not been endorsed or approved by, any of the groups or organizations (or any of the individual members) with which (and with whom) I have served.

1 *See, e.g.*, A. Burns and J. Martin, "Warren Is Warming Up for 2020. So Are Many Other Democrats" *NY Times* 15 July 2018, at A1 (describing Sen. Elizabeth Warren as a leading contender for the Democratic Party's nomination to run for President of the United States).

2 See generally, e.g., M. Levinson, *The Box: How the Shipping Container Made the World Smaller and the World Economy Bigger* (Princeton: Princeton UP, 2006) (documenting the early history of the container revolution); B. Cudahy, *Box Boats: How Container Ships Changed the World* (New York: Fordham UP, 2006) (same).

In this chapter, I examine the role that commercial law plays in facilitating or hindering the adoption of new technologies in one important context—regulating relationships among the principal stakeholders in a contract for the carriage of goods by sea. For centuries, contracts evidenced by paper documents have governed the relationship between shippers (or those who succeed to shippers' rights) on the one hand and carriers (or those who do the carriers' work as agents or sub-contractors) on the other hand. Particularly when shippers transfer their rights to third parties, the negotiable bill of lading has been the proverbial "key to the warehouse."[3] But paper documents are relatively expensive. In my own conversations with shipping executives, I have heard that 5 to 10% of the cost of a shipment can be attributed to the expenses associated with preparing and issuing physical documents.[4] Some estimates are significantly higher.[5] Thus the industry has long explored ways in which electronic records could replace documents such as the bill of lading.[6] Unfortunately, the current legal regimes make it impractical for carriers to abandon paper documents. At least in this respect, commercial law today is not facilitating commerce as it should.

2 The current legal regimes

In today's legal environment, international shipments under a bill of lading are subject to a mosaic of legal regimes established by international conventions, domestic statutes, common-law doctrines, and customary trade practices. To understand why current law is inadequate to deal with new technologies such as blockchain—at least in the context of regulating relationships among the principal stakeholders in a contract for the carriage of goods by sea—it will be helpful to review the range of current regimes.

2.1 The international conventions governing the carriage of goods by sea

The first international convention governing the carriage of goods by sea, popularly known as the Hague Rules,[7] was signed almost 95 years ago, but its principles had

---

3 E.g., *The Delfini* [1990] 1 Lloyd's Rep. 252, 268 (Mustill, L.J.).

4 When the International Air Transport Association (IATA) eliminated paper tickets in 2008, industry experts estimated that the cost of processing a single airline ticket would drop from US$10 to US$1, which was expected to save the industry over US$3 billion annually. See *Industry Bids Farewell to Paper Ticket*, IATA Press Release No. 25 (31 May 2008), available at <www.iata.org/pressroom/pr/Pages/2008-31-05-01.aspx> accessed November 2018. Of course the documentation associated with an international ocean shipment is much more complicated than a simple airline ticket (and the costs have presumably risen in the last decade), so the savings for the shipping industry presumably would be much greater.

5 See, e.g., "Thinking outside the box", *The Economist* (London, 28 April 2018), at 21, col. 3 (reporting "that putting all the Asia-Pacific region's trade-related paperwork online could ... cut the cost of [exporting goods] by up to 31%").

6 *See, e.g.*, "Ocean Bills of Lading: Traditional Forms, Substitutes, and EDI Systems" (Int'l Academy of Comparative Law, 14th Int'l Congress of Comparative Law) (A.N. Yiannopoulos ed. 1995).

7 International Convention for the Unification of Certain Rules of Law Relating to Bills of Lading, Aug. 25, 1924, 120 LNTS 155 [hereinafter Hague Rules].

previously been enacted as domestic legislation in the United States' 1893 Harter Act[8] and Harter-inspired domestic legislation in other countries.[9] Following the central compromise first adopted in 1893 and carried forward to the present day, the Hague Rules allocate responsibility for cargo loss or damage between carriers and cargo interests.

A 1968 protocol amended the Hague Rules to produce the Hague-Visby Rules,[10] but the fundamental structure of the amended regime remained the same. The protocol simply revised a handful of provisions that were considered problematic. The protocol was widely adopted, and the Hague-Visby Rules are now the most popular regime to address liability for cargo loss or damage during international ocean shipments.

Ten years after the Visby Protocol, the United Nations adopted a new convention, popularly known as the Hamburg Rules,[11] which was intended to supersede the Hague and Hague-Visby Rules. The Hamburg Rules are widely perceived as being more generous to cargo interests than the Hague or Hague-Visby Rules, but it is remarkable how similar they are to the prior regimes. All three allocate the risk of cargo loss or damage between a carrier and cargo interests on the basis of the carrier's presumed fault with a reversed burden of proof, meaning that the carrier is presumptively liable for any loss or damage unless it can establish a defense. All three regimes permit the carrier to limit its liability at specified levels. And all three regimes focus almost exclusively on liability.

It is not surprising that none of the existing international conventions adequately address electronic substitutes for the traditional paper bill of lading. In the 1920s, when the Hague Rules were negotiated, none of the negotiators would have dreamed that electronic substitutes might someday exist. And we have no reason to think that anyone involved in negotiating the Visby Protocol thought about the possibility either. The closest that the Hamburg Rules came to addressing the issue was to recognize that telegrams and telexes should be recognized as "writings."[12]

Fundamental problems with the existing international regimes—going well beyond their failure to anticipate electronic commerce—ensure that they cannot adequately address the problems that inevitably arise in implementing the new technologies that we are considering at this colloquium. All three of the existing regimes are too narrow in at least two different ways. It is perhaps better recognized that they are too narrow in their geographic scope of application. The Hague and Hague-Visby

---

8 27 Stat. 445 (1893). The Harter Act was recodified in 2006, and the current version is now found at 46 USC §§ 30701–07.

9 See generally, e.g., M. Sturley, "The History of COGSA and the Hague Rules", 22 *Journal of Maritime Law and Commerce*, 1, 15–17 (1991) (discussing, e.g., the Shipping & Seamen Act 1903 (N.Z.); Sea-Carriage of Goods Act 1904 (Austl.); Water Carriage of Goods Act 1910 (Can.)).

10 The Hague-Visby Rules are the Hague Rules as amended by the Protocol to Amend the International Convention for the Unification of Certain Rules of Law Relating to Bills of Lading (Hague Rules), Feb. 23, 1968, 1412 UNTS 128 [hereinafter Visby Protocol], and also (perhaps) the Protocol Amending the International Convention for the Unification of Certain Rules of Law Relating to Bills of Lading, Dec. 21, 1979, 1412 UNTS 146.

11 United Nations Convention on the Carriage of Goods by Sea, Mar. 31, 1978, 1695 UNTS 3 [hereinafter Hamburg Rules].

12 Hamburg Rules art. 1(8).

Rules apply only on a tackle-to-tackle basis,[13] while the Hamburg Rules apply only on a port-to-port basis.[14] As a result, none of the existing regimes by its terms governs the entire contract for a typical door-to-door multimodal transaction.[15] In addition, the existing regimes are too narrow to facilitate electronic commerce in the range of topics that they cover. The Hague, Hague-Visby, and Hamburg Rules are all primarily liability conventions; they provide answers when things go horribly wrong, and cargo is lost or damaged. As I will explain in more detail below,[16] a legal regime must provide answers for how transactions work when things go right if it is to address the needs of electronic commerce.

2.2 Domestic statutes, judicial doctrines, and customary trade practices

Because the international conventions governing the carriage of goods by sea focus almost exclusively on liability issues, other sources of law must address the other issues that arise in international shipping transactions. Indeed, those other sources are typically more important than the international conventions governing liability because liability issues rarely arise while principles regulating the transfer of rights, for example, arise every time a cargo is sold *en route* and a bill of lading is negotiated.

In the absence of relevant international conventions, domestic statutes often supply the necessary rules. The British Bills of Lading Act 1855[17] is a classic example of such a domestic statute.[18] Many other countries passed their own statutes to address the same issue. In the United States, the Pomerene Act of 1916 addresses the same subject but with some fundamental differences. It has been recodified, but it remains in force without substantial change over a century after its enactment.[19] Most Commonwealth jurisdictions passed statutes based directly on the British 1855 Act,[20] or incorporated the 1855 Act by reference,[21] with the result that the substance of the 1855 Act still applies in some countries long after it was repealed at home. The British statute that repealed and replaced the 1855 Act—the inaptly named Carriage of Goods by Sea Act 1992[22]—has also served as a model for other countries.[23]

---

13 *See* Hague Rules art. 1(e); Hague-Visby Rules, art.1(e). Because the Visby Protocol did not amend art.1(e) of the Hague Rules, the Hague and Hague-Visby Rules are identical on this point.
14 See Hamburg Rules, art. 1(6).
15 See below, notes 27–29 and accompanying text.
16 See below, notes 53–64 and accompanying text.
17 Eventually repealed by the Carriage of Goods by Sea Act1992.
18 Statutes addressing the rights that pass on the transfer of a bill of lading are not the only domestic statutes that affect the relationship between carriers and cargo interests, but because they are particularly relevant in the present context no further illustrations are required.
19 The Pomerene Act, also known as the Federal Bills of Lading Act, is currently codified at 49 USC §§ 80, 101–16.
20 See, e.g., Bills of Lading Act, RSC 1985, c. B-5 (Can.).
21 See, e.g., the Civil Law Act 1956, s 5(1) (Malaysia) ("with respect to mercantile law generally, the law to be administered shall be the same as would be administered in England in the like case at the date of the coming into force of this Act").
22 In force from September 1992.
23 See, e.g., Bills of Lading Act 1994 (Singapore).

As every common-law lawyer knows, even the best statutes inevitably leave some questions unanswered (or at least fail to answer a question satisfactorily) and the courts are required to step in to supply the necessary rules. Judicial decisions have established many of the fundamental principles regulating the carriage of goods. *Brandt v. Liverpool, Brazil and River Plate Steam Navigation Co.*[24] and *Lickbarrow v. Mason*[25] provide classic examples in English law, but countless other examples from England and many other jurisdictions could illustrate the point. The judicial doctrines that arise as a result are an essential part of the commercial law governing the transactions under consideration here.

Customary trade practices are closely related to judicial doctrines. Indeed, they often form the basis for judicial doctrines, or even for statutes. The preamble to the British Bills of Lading Act 1855 explicitly acknowledges its debt to "the Custom of Merchants." And the particular custom mentioned—when a bill of lading is transferred by indorsement, the property in the goods covered by that bill of lading may pass to the new holder as a result—remains an essential part of commercial law, even in countries in which the custom has not been explicitly codified by statute.

Domestic statutes in some countries provide formal recognition for electronic records to replace paper documents,[26] but no domestic statute provides a sufficient legal basis for electronic records to replace bills of lading in international trade. And it is hard to imagine how a judicial doctrine could provide a sufficient legal basis, even if judges were prepared to take that step. Customary trade practices could in theory fill the gap, much as they did for years before international conventions and domestic statutes appeared on the scene. But a trade practice regarding electronic records cannot develop, let alone become customary, until those in the trade start using electronic records on a regular basis. Because the industry is unwilling to risk the success of transactions with third parties unless a sufficient legal basis ensures that electronic records will serve their intended purpose, the resulting chicken-and-egg problem can be predicted to keep the new technologies on the drawing board.

2.3 International conventions, domestic statutes, and common-law doctrines governing other modes of carriage

In the container trade, which carries over 90% of the world's manufactured goods, door-to-door multimodal contracts are now routine.[27] A shipper can conclude a single contract with a single carrier to transport goods from an inland point of

---

24 [1924] 1 KB 575.
25 (1787) 2 TR 63.
26 *See, e.g.*, Sea-Carriage Documents Act 1997, s 6 (N.S.W.). The British COGSA 1992, ss 1(5)-(6), as amended by the Communications Act 2003 authorized regulations to accommodate "cases where an electronic communications network or any other information technology is used for effecting transactions corresponding to" transactions involving traditional paper documents. The government has not yet invoked that authority.
27 Of course not every contract of carriage is multimodal. Particularly in bulk trades, port-to-port shipments are still common. Even some containerized cargo is carried on a port-to-port basis.

origin (such as a manufacturer's plant) to an inland destination (such as a retailer's warehouse). During the performance of that contract, the goods will typically travel by different modes of transportation, including inland vehicles (trucks or trains) and ocean vessels. The multimodal carrier will generally sub-contract with other carriers to perform particular parts of the journey.[28] For example, an ocean carrier may undertake to move a container of cargo from Berlin to Chicago, but it will carry the container itself only on the sea voyage from Antwerp to New York; it will sub-contract with a European trucker to haul the container from Berlin to Antwerp and with a US railroad to move the container from New York to Chicago.[29]

Because the international conventions governing the carriage of goods by sea apply only to the port-to-port ocean carriage (in the case of the Hamburg Rules[30]) or even more narrowly to the tackle-to-tackle period (in the case of the Hague and Hague-Visby Rules[31]), some other legal regime necessarily applies to the inland portions of a multimodal contract. In other words, a single contract of carriage could easily be subject to three (or more) different legal regimes. In the hypothetical contract mentioned in the previous paragraph,[32] for example, the road journey from Berlin to Antwerp would be governed by one legal regime, the sea voyage from Antwerp to New York would be governed by a second legal regime, and the rail journey from New York to Chicago would be governed by a third legal regime.[33]

It is bad enough to have a single contract governed by multiple regimes,[34] but the problems are compounded by the existence of different regimes in different places and under different circumstances. Within Europe, regional regimes governing the carriage of goods by road (CMR)[35] or rail (CIM-COTIF)[36] apply to international road or rail movements. Otherwise national law generally governs an inland leg preceding or following the sea carriage. Elsewhere in the world, national law is generally the only option. In my Berlin-to-Chicago hypothetical,[37] therefore, CMR would presumably govern the European road leg (but Belgian national law would have governed if the

---

28 The multimodal carrier may even sub-contract for *every* leg of the journey. A non-vessel-operating carrier (NVOC) typically has no capacity to carry anything except by sub-contracting with other carriers. In the shipment at issue in *James N. Kirby Pty Ltd v Norfolk Southern Railway Co*, 543 US 14, 2004 AMC 2705 (2004), for example, an Australian NVOC contracted with an Australian trucker to carry the goods from an inland point to the Port of Sydney; with a German liner to carry the goods from Sydney to a US port; with a US railroad to carry the goods from that port to the railhead; and with a US trucker to carry the goods from the railhead to the buyer's plant.
29 I will use this Berlin-to-Chicago hypothetical further below.
30 *See* Hamburg Rules, art.1(6). See also above, note 14 and accompanying text.
31 *See* Hague Rules, art.1(e); Hague-Visby Rules, art.1(e). See also above, note 13 and accompanying text.
32 See above, note 29 and accompanying text.
33 See below, notes 37–42 and accompanying text.
34 In *James N. Kirby Pty Ltd v Norfolk Southern Railway Co*, 543 US 14, 29, 2004 AMC 2705, 2715 (2004), the US Supreme Court observed that "[c]onfusion and inefficiency will inevitably result if more than one body of law governs a given contract's meaning."
35 See Convention on the Contract for the International Carriage of Goods by Road, 19 May 1956, 399 UNTS 189 (CMR).
36 See Uniform Rules Concerning the Contract for International Carriage of Goods by Rail, Appendix B to the Convention Concerning International Carriage by Rail (COTIF) of 9 May 1980, as amended by the Protocol of 3 June 1999. An earlier version governed rail movements in 1965.
37 See above, note 29 and accompanying text.

shipment had originated in Brussels instead of Berlin, and German national law would have governed if the shipment had passed through the port of Hamburg instead of Antwerp). For the sea voyage, the Hague-Visby Rules would apply, at least in a court that was bound to apply the Hague-Visby Rules according to their terms.[38] But if a US consignee sued in New York or Chicago, the US court would instead be bound to apply the US Carriage of Goods by Sea Act (COGSA),[39] which is the US domestic enactment of the Hague Rules.[40] And the rail journey from New York to Chicago would be governed not by the Carmack Amendment,[41] the US statute that governs domestic road and rail shipments, but by the general maritime law of the United States.[42]

Not surprisingly, few of those various legal regimes gave any thought to the needs of electronic commerce. And even if some of them did, that would not be adequate to facilitate the new technologies that we are considering here. Without consistent rules that apply uniformly during every stage in the performance of a contract, commercial parties will not have the certainty and predictability that they need in order to develop efficient new technologies.

3 The Rotterdam rules

The Rotterdam Rules[43] are designed to supersede the Hague, Hague-Visby, and Hamburg Rules. The new convention continues to govern carriers' liability for cargo loss or damage, building on the experience of the prior regimes.[44] But—in

---

38 See Hague-Visby Rules, art.10(b).

39 Ch. 229, 49 Stat. 1207 (1936), *reprinted in* note following 46 U.S.C. § 30701.

40 By its terms, the US COGSA applies to inbound and outbound shipments. See COGSA enacting clause & § 13. A US court would be bound to follow that statutory directive and apply its own COGSA to the inbound shipment to New York—even though a German or Belgian court would be bound to follow the directive of the Hague-Visby Rules to apply that regime to the outbound shipment from Antwerp. See, e.g., *Ferrostaal, Inc v M/V Sea Phoenix*, 447 F.3d 212, 218–19, 2006 AMC 1217 (3d Cir. 2006) (holding COGSA applicable "by its own terms," and declaring that "[it] makes no difference that the Hamburg Rules purport to apply to every shipment from a contracting state," even if that would have been relevant in the court of a contracting state).

41 49 U.S.C. §§ 11706 (rail), 14706 (road). Remarkably, the inland leg of a multimodal *import* shipment is not governed by the Carmack Amendment. See *Kawasaki Kisen Kaisha Ltd v Regal-Beloit Corp*, 561 US 89, 100, 2010 AMC 1521 (2010). It is unclear whether the Carmack Amendment applies to the US road or rail leg of a multimodal *export* shipment. Compare, e.g., *Smallwood v Allied Van Lines, Inc*, 660 F.3d 1115, 1120 n.5, 2012 AMC 370, 374 n.5 (9th Cir. 2011) (holding that the Carmack Amendment applies to the inland leg of a multimodal shipment under a through bill of lading in an export shipment), with, e.g., *CNA Insurance Co v Hyundai Merchant Marine Co*, 747 F.3d 339, 366–70, 2014 AMC 609 (6th Cir. 2014) (holding that the Carmack Amendment does not apply to the inland leg in a similar export shipment).

42 See *Kirby*, above note 28 (holding that a multimodal contract of carriage is a maritime contract, and thus governed by the general maritime law, which permitted the parties to agree by contract to apply the US COGSA beyond the tackle-to-tackle period).

43 United Nations Convention on Contracts for the International Carriage of Goods Wholly or Partly by Sea, Dec. 11, 2008, General Assembly Resolution 63/122, U.N. Doc. A/RES/63/122 [hereinafter Rotterdam Rules]. Minor amendments were adopted in January 2013 to correct two editorial mistakes. *See* Correction to the Original Text of the Convention, U.N. Doc. C.N.105.2013.TREATIES-XI-D-8 (Depositary Notification) (Jan. 25, 2013). Those two amendments have no direct bearing on the issues discussed here.

44 See Rotterdam Rules, chs. 5, 6, 7 & 12.

an effort to modernize the law governing the carriage of goods by sea—it addresses a much broader range of issues than have previous maritime conventions.[45] Of particular relevance here, the Rotterdam Rules seek to facilitate electronic commerce in the shipping industry.[46] They also provide the first systematic response to the container revolution, which has completely changed international shipping over the last 50 years.[47] In other words, the Rotterdam Rules are much more than just a liability convention.

3.1 The genesis of the Rotterdam rules

Although much of the literature about the Rotterdam Rules has focused on the liability provisions, those provisions were not the primary focus in the evolution of the convention. The genesis of the new regime is instead found in UNCITRAL's desire to facilitate electronic commerce.

In March 1994, UNCITRAL's Working Group on Electronic Data Interchange (EDI) exchanged views about the "legal issues relevant to the increased use of EDI" and considered its future work in the area.[48] One suggestion was that the Working Group "could focus on the preparation of a functional equivalent to a negotiable bill of lading or ... explore the establishment of a new kind of document of title. Wide support was expressed in favor of that proposal."[49] After discussion, "[t]he prevailing view was that it would be appropriate for [UNCITRAL] to undertake the preparation of uniform law on the issue of negotiability in a computer-based environment."[50]

The following year, the EDI Working Group had a more detailed discussion of the subject.[51] It recognized that bills of lading serve three functions,[52] and that EDI could easily accomplish the receipt and contract functions.[53] But the Working Group recognized that the third function—"giving the holder a number of rights, including the right to claim and receive delivery of the goods at the port of discharge and the right to dispose of the goods in transit"[54]—"raised difficulties in an EDI environment."[55] The Rotterdam Rules' solution of that difficulty is the primary reason that the new convention facilitates electronic commerce in ways that existing law cannot. And the EDI Working Group's report of the 1995 session

---

45 See Rotterdam Rules, chs. 3, 9, 10 & 11.
46 See, e.g., Rotterdam Rule,s ch. 3 (arts. 8–10).
47 The Hague-Visby and Hamburg Rules each address containerization in a single provision that addresses only the calculation of the package limitation. See Hague-Visby Rules, art.4(5)(c); Hamburg Rules art.6(2)(a). Substantially the same provision is included in the Rotterdam Rules (see art.59(2)), but other provisions also address the problems of containerization.
48 Report of the Working Group on Electronic Data Interchange (EDI) on the Work of Its Twenty-Seventh Session, ¶ 154, U.N. Doc. A/CN.9/390 (1994).
49 Ibid. ¶ 155.
50 Ibid. ¶ 157.
51 See Report of the Working Group on Electronic Data Interchange (EDI) on the Work of Its Twenty-Ninth Session, ¶¶ 106–118, U.N. Doc. A/CN.9/407 (1995).
52 Ibid. ¶ 107. The Working Group noted the three classic functions of a bill of lading—serving as (1) a receipt for the goods, (2) evidence of the contract of carriage, and (3) a document of title.
53 Ibid. ¶ 108.
54 Ibid. ¶ 107.
55 Ibid. ¶ 108.

demonstrates that it was already focusing on those issues that would assume central importance in the Rotterdam Rules:

> The Working Group engaged in a general debate, with a view to identifying the scope of possible future work and issues that could be addressed. ... [One] suggestion was that, while work could include transport documents of title in general, particular emphasis should be paid to maritime bills of lading since the maritime transport area was the area in which EDI was predominantly practised and in which unification of law was urgently needed in order to remove existing impediments and to allow the practice to develop. In support, it was pointed out that EDI messaging was currently restricted to the exchange of information messages in the North Atlantic maritime routes and could not develop without the support of a legal regime that would validate, and provide certainty about, transport documents in electronic form. For example, it was stated that there was a need to facilitate delivery of the cargo at the port of discharge without production of a paper bill of lading ....[56]

After discussion, the Working Group "agreed that future work could focus on EDI transport documents, with particular emphasis on maritime electronic bills of lading,"[57] and that the issues to be addressed would include "the uniqueness of an electronic bill of lading that would allow its 'holder' to dispose of the cargo in transit by electronic means while protecting the carrier from the risk of misdelivery,"[58] "the definition of the holder in an EDI environment,"[59] "the rights and obligations of the holder and the issuer of EDI transport documents (e.g., right of the holder to give instructions in transit and obligation of the issuer to receive and execute those instructions),"[60] and "the effects of transfer of EDI transport documents on third parties."[61] All of those are important issues that the Rotterdam Rules address in order to facilitate electronic commerce.[62]

In May 1995, the Commission—acting on the EDI Working Group's recommendation—decided that the proposed project should proceed with the Secretariat's "preparation of a background study on negotiability and transferability of EDI transport documents, with particular emphasis on EDI maritime transport documents, taking into account the views expressed and the suggestions made at the 29th session of the Working Group with regard to the scope of future work and the issues that could be addressed."[63]

Finally, in June 1996, the Commission launched the new project that would ultimately culminate in the Rotterdam Rules. From the beginning, the focus was

---

56 Ibid. ¶¶ 111–112.
57 Ibid. ¶ 113.
58 Ibid. ¶ 114.
59 Ibid. ¶ 115.
60 Ibid. ¶ 115.
61 Ibid. ¶ 117.
62 See, e.g., Rotterdam Rules, art.47 (allowing the holder of an electronic transport record to dispose of the cargo in transit by electronic means while protecting the carrier from the risk of misdelivery); art.1(10)(b) (defining the holder of an electronic transport record); art.50–56 (addressing the right of the holder to give instructions in transit and obligation of the issuer to receive and execute those instructions); art.57 (addressing the effects of transfer of electronic transport records on third parties).
63 Report of the United Nations Commission on International Trade Law on the Work of Its Twenty-Eighth Session, U.N. GAOR, 50th Sess., Supp. No. 17, ¶ 309, U.N. Doc. A/50/17 (1995).

on the EDI aspects. For example, the Commission limited the scope of the project to establishing "uniform rules in the areas where no such rules existed and with a view to achieving greater uniformity of laws than has so far been achieved."[64] Because uniform liability rules already existed, that subject that was outside the scope of work for the new project. The Commission instead called attention to the problems with existing law that hindered efforts to introduce electronic commerce:

> [E]xisting national laws and international conventions left significant gaps regarding issues such as the functioning of the bills of lading and seaway bills, the relation of those transport documents to the rights and obligations between the seller and the buyer of the goods and to the legal position of the entities that provided financing to a party to the contract of carriage.[65]

In an effort to address those problems, the Commission authorized the Secretariat to start gathering information with a view to deciding "on the nature and scope of any future work that might usefully be undertaken by [UNCITRAL]."[66] The Secretariat then invited the Comité Maritime International (CMI) to begin the preparatory work for a new convention. It was not until over a year later that the CMI's International Sub-Committee was finally authorized to add liability issues to the agenda, but even then the focus was to be on "areas of transport law, not at present governed by international liability regimes."[67] Although the Rotterdam Rules ultimately modernized the liability aspects of the existing legal regimes, and that modernization is a valuable benefit of the new convention, it was never the primary goal of the process. Facilitating electronic commerce was the first goal.

UNCITRAL understood that a successful regime for electronic transport records would require "functional equivalence." The electronic substitutes for traditional paper documents must still be able to fulfil the functions of those traditional documents. As the EDI Working Group recognized when the project was first forming,[68] it is not particularly difficult for an electronic transport record to act as a receipt for the goods and as evidence of the contract of carriage. Both of those functions address the relationship between the shipper and the carrier—the two original parties to the contract.[69] The "document of title" function causes more difficulties. With a paper bill of lading, a holder can transfer rights in the goods to a third party outside of the original contractual relationship. Achieving functional equivalence in that context was a primary challenge for the drafters of the Rotterdam Rules.

---

64 Report of the United Nations Commission on International Trade Law on the Work of Its Twenty-Ninth Session, U.N. GAOR, 51st Sess., Supp. No. 17, ¶ 210, U.N. Doc. A/51/17 (1996) (hereinafter UNCITRAL Twenty-Ninth Session Report), reprinted in 1996 CMI YEARBOOK 354.

65 Ibid.

66 Ibid. ¶ 215, *reprinted in* 1996 CMI Yearbook 355.

67 *See* S.Beare, *Issues of Transport Law: Introductory Paper*, 1999 CMI Yearbook 117, 117. Mr Beare chaired the CMI's Working Group and its International Sub-Committee.

68 See above, notes 52–53 and accompanying text.

69 To the extent that the industry is successfully using electronic equivalents of traditional paper documents today, it is generally in situations in which the "document of title" function is irrelevant. For example, when a shipper sends goods to itself, no third parties are involved in the transaction and electronic transport records can more easily serve as receipts for the goods and evidence of the contracts of carriage.

3.2 The explicit provisions authorizing electronic commerce under the Rotterdam rules

Chapter 3 of the Rotterdam Rules, titled "electronic transport records," explicitly authorizes anything that can be done with a paper transport document to be done with an electronic transport record (if the parties agree);[70] specifies that various actions performed with an electronic transport record have the same effect as the corresponding actions with a paper transport document;[71] provides for procedures governing the use of electronic transport records;[72] and enables paper transport documents and electronic transport records to be substituted for each other.[73] Chapter 3 is thus the obvious starting point for any discussion of the role that the Rotterdam Rules play in facilitating electronic commerce.

Provisions that are substantially like those in Chapter 3 are without doubt a necessary condition for a legal system that seeks to facilitate electronic commerce, particularly in the context of a long history of international conventions that are limited in their application to transactions "covered by a bill of lading or any similar document of title."[74] In a world in which legal systems cannot agree whether well-established paper substitutes for the classic bill of lading are "similar document[s] of title,"[75] carriers cannot have any confidence that their electronic substitutes would be recognized in the absence of provisions substantially like those in Chapter 3, let alone that transactions involving those electronic substitutes would have the intended effects. Chapter 3 is accordingly a necessary first step to facilitate electronic commerce.

3.3 The Rotterdam rules' implicit provisions to facilitate electronic commerce

Although Chapter 3 (or something very like it) is a necessary first step to facilitate electronic commerce, Chapter 3 is not by itself sufficient. Article 8(b), for example, may specify that various actions performed with an electronic transport record have the same effect as the corresponding actions with a paper transport document, but unless the effect of using a paper transport document is itself clear there will be ambiguities in the use of electronic transport records.

---

70 Rotterdam Rules, art.8(a).
71 Rotterdam Rules, art.8(b).
72 Rotterdam Rules, art.9.
73 Rotterdam Rules, art.10.
74 Hague-Visby Rules, art.1(b).
75 Although US commercial law is largely derived from English law, US and English law do not fully agree on the meaning of the term "bill of lading." US law generally recognizes a non-negotiable document such as a "sea waybill" as a type of bill of lading that need not be surrendered to obtain delivery of the goods. English law, by contrast, treats a "sea waybill" as something distinct from a "bill of lading." Cf *The Rafaela S* [2005] UKHL 11, [2005] 2 AC 423 (distinguishing a "straight bill of lading" from a "sea waybill" and treating a "straight bill of lading" as a "bill of lading or ... similar document of title" for purposes of applying the Hague-Visby Rules). Even within England, not all lawyers would have predicted the conclusion in *The Rafaela S* that a "straight bill of lading" is a "bill of lading or ... similar document of title" under the Hague-Visby Rules.

The right to demand delivery of the goods provides a useful illustration of the problem. The Hague and Hague-Visby Rules do not specify who is entitled to demand delivery, or under what conditions.[76] They do not even impose an obligation on the carrier to deliver the goods. The Hamburg Rules hint at the issue only indirectly.[77] Indeed, delivery under most contracts of carriage generally occurs *after* the expiration of the period of the relevant convention's mandatory application.[78] Thus the carrier's obligation to deliver the goods, and the consignee's corresponding right to demand delivery, is typically governed by the patchwork of domestic statutes, judicial doctrines, and customary trade practices discussed above.[79] As UNCITRAL recognized over 20 years ago,[80] that patchwork is far from uniform, and the lack of uniformity hinders the introduction of electronic substitutes for paper documents.

More fundamentally, the nature of the patchwork makes its application to electronic transport records uncertain. Even if a common-law principle were to apply universally, it would not necessarily be clear how that principle would apply in an electronic context. Suppose, for example, that every legal system accepted the principle that a person properly in possession of a negotiable bill of lading (the "holder") is entitled to demand delivery of the covered goods by tendering the bill of lading to the carrier. Because that principle is tied to the holder's possession of a physical piece of paper, it is ambiguous how it translates to a context in which no physical piece of paper exists. How does someone become the holder of an electronic transport record? It cannot be by the physical indorsement and delivery of a piece of paper—as with traditional bills of lading—because there is no physical piece of paper to indorse or deliver. How should the holder tender the electronic transport record to the carrier? It cannot be by offering to surrender a physical piece of paper that does not exist.

It is not inordinately difficult to formulate answers to these questions, but the questions must be answered (and must be answered uniformly in the different jurisdictions that may be concerned about a particular transaction). Moreover, it is not enough to say "we will do it the same way as we do with paper documents." The rules for paper documents are not uniform, and even if they were it would still be necessary to translate them to the electronic context. The legal regime must actually

---

76 Article 3(6) of the Hague and Hague-Visby Rules recognizes that there will be a "person entitled to delivery" of the goods, but it offers no guidance in identifying that person.

77 Article 1(7) of the Hamburg Rules defines "bill of lading" as "a document ... by which the carrier undertakes to deliver the goods against surrender of the document," thus indirectly suggesting that a person who surrenders a bill of lading is entitled to demand delivery—but there is no mention of any conditions or limitations that might apply. And the definition presumably does not apply to traditional paper documents that need not be surrendered to obtain delivery.

78 Because the Hamburg Rules apply on a port-to-port basis, delivery under a port-to-port contract may be subject to the mandatory application of the Hamburg Rules (although only a small proportion of world trade is subject to the Hamburg Rules). For the Hague and Hague-Visby Rules, which apply on a tackle-to-tackle basis, the conventions would mandatorily apply only when cargo is delivered on discharge from the vessel (or before). None of the existing international conventions governing the carriage of goods by sea would mandatorily apply to delivery under a multimodal, door-to-door contract of carriage with an inland destination—a routine situation for containerized cargo.

79 See above, notes 17–42, and accompanying text.

80 See above, notes 48–50, and accompanying text.

decide on rules—applicable to both paper and electronic transactions—to determine whether a carrier is obligated to deliver the cargo to a particular person under specified circumstances. Unless those rules are clear, carriers will be justifiably hesitant to commit the resources necessary to develop and implement the new technologies that we are discussing here.

Delivery is a good example of an issue that must be addressed before widespread electronic commerce transactions will be feasible, but it is not the only example. Of course a carrier needs to know to whom it should deliver the goods, and a potential consignee needs to know if it will be entitled to demand delivery. But while the goods are still in transit, the parties also need to know who has control of the goods. Who has the right to give instructions to the carrier with respect to the goods, and to whom should the carrier look if it requires instructions for the safe handling of the goods? With whom should the carrier negotiate if it becomes necessary to change the contract of carriage (for example, to designate a new destination), and who has the right to enter into those negotiations with the carrier? Finally, when a particular person has rights under the contract of carriage, such as the right to demand delivery of the goods or the right of control while the goods are in transit, how may those rights be transferred to a third party?

Over the centuries, the commercial world has developed answers to these sorts of questions in the context of traditional paper documents. Different sources—ranging from international conventions and domestic statutes to judicial decisions and trade practices—have supplied the answers, and those answers have not always been consistent among different jurisdictions. For the most part, the answers have been tied to the physical piece of paper, and as a result the answers do not automatically translate to a new context in which the physical piece of paper has been replaced by an intangible electronic record. For electronic commerce to work—for the new technologies under discussion at this colloquium to be implemented in the present context—the commercial world needs answers that will work in the electronic context.

The Rotterdam Rules meet the need for answers to these questions with Chapters 9, 10, and 11, which were included in the convention primarily to facilitate electronic commerce (although that purpose was less obvious for those three chapters than it was for Chapter 3). Chapter 9 addresses delivery, Chapter 10 addresses the right of control, and Chapter 11 addresses the transfer of rights. None of the three is very extensive; all of them leave the parties with considerable freedom to work out their contractual obligations in their own contract.[81] But the three chapters together (along with Chapter 3) provide the necessary framework to enable the parties to agree to use electronic substitutes instead of the more expensive paper documents that have been the norm for centuries.

---

[81] See, e.g., Rotterdam Rules, art.43 (linking the obligation to accept delivery to the contractual terms); art.45(a) (linking the carrier's obligation to deliver the goods to the contractual terms); art. 46(a) (same); art.47(1)(a) (same); art.47(2) (limiting the right to deliver the goods without surrender of the negotiable transport document or electronic transport record to cases in which the parties agreed to that option); art.56 (permitting the parties by agreement to vary the effect of provisions relating to the right of control).

4 Conclusion

It is no secret that current maritime commercial law is inadequate to accommodate new technologies such as blockchain—at least in the context of regulating cargo-carrier relationships. It is also no secret that the Rotterdam Rules offer a ready solution to the problem. Legal scholars who specialize in the field have long recognized the convention's advantages for e-commerce,[82] but that recognition is not limited to legal specialists. In an April issue of *The Economist*, a three-page story titled "Thinking outside the box" focused on the changing nature of the transportation industry and its use of data.[83] The story considered why the industry has not been able to implement new technologies that would significantly reduce costs and improve performance. The story explained:

> One answer is regulation; there are a lot of institutional obstacles to reform. For instance, in 2008 a UN convention put electronic documents in international shipping on a firm legal footing. But for these "Rotterdam rules" to come into force, the agreement must be ratified by 20 countries. Owing to a lack of interest in the subject among politicians the tally so far is just four ...[84]

Even in the non-legal community, sophisticated journalists recognize that current commercial law is standing in the way of progress and that ratifying the Rotterdam Rules would provide a solution.

It is less obvious, even among legal experts, how the Rotterdam Rules are able to solve the well-recognized problem. Some have criticized the new convention for being too complex, often complaining about the decision to go beyond liability issues to address the problems of delivery, the rights of the controlling party, and the transfer of rights. Yet it is precisely the treatment of those non-liability issues that provides the firm legal basis that will permit the industry to rely on the new technologies and move past the slavish adherence to paper documents that has created so many problems.

If we are to see the new technologies that everyone in the industry seems to desire, and achieve the improved efficiencies that would benefit carriers, cargo owners, and ultimately consumers, we can only hope that politicians can be persuaded to show enough interest in the Rotterdam Rules that the new convention not only enters into force but also achieves widespread acceptance. In the meantime, we are all burdened with an antiquated commercial law system that is no longer facilitating commerce in the way that it should.

---

82 Shortly after the General Assembly adopted the Rotterdam Rules, months before the convention was even opened for signature, legal experts—both those who had been deeply involved in the drafting process and those who had not been involved in the negotiations but who had evaluated the finished product—recognized the potential benefits for electronic commerce. See, e.g., G.van der Ziel, "Delivery of the Goods, Rights of the Controlling Party and Transfer of Rights", 14 J. Int'l Mar. L. 597 (2008) (an article by one of the convention's principal drafters); M.Goldby, "Electronic Alternatives to Transport Documents and the New Convention: A Framework for Future Development", 14 J. Int'l Mar. L. 586 (2008) (article by an expert on electronic commerce who had not been directly involved in the negotiations).
83 "Thinking outside the box", *The Economist* (London, 28 April 2018), at 20–22.
84 Id. at 21, col. 2.

CHAPTER 4

Electronic signatures in shipping practice

Professor Erik Røsæg[*]

1 Introduction

When someone asks me to sign a letter, I usually add a picture (facsimile) of my signature and return the document by email. This is always accepted. I do not run any risk by doing this. If a third party uses a copy of a person's signature on a document without permission, that person is obviously not responsible or bound by any agreement. However, facsimiles of signatures pose a problem for the receiver, because it is difficult to determine whether they have been added by the right person or not.

A picture of a signature is a signature, and it may be electronic, but it is not considered a real electronic signature. A real electronic signature gives the receiver confidence that the signature represents a legally binding commitment. Furthermore, a real electronic signature is actually more trustworthy than a conventional pen-and-ink signature because it cannot be copied and is linked to a person's identity even if a previous signature sample is not available for comparison.[1]

There are some technicalities involved. It is necessary to understand the mechanisms in order to evaluate the signatures. The basis for this discussion on electronic signatures is European Community law.[2]

In this paper, the mechanisms and legal framework for electronic signatures will be discussed.

---

[*] Professor of the Scandinavian Institute of Maritime Law, University of Oslo.

[1] On signatures in general, see Erik Røsæg, IT: Avtaleslutning og behovet for lovreform, In: L. Gorton (ed.), Festskrift till Gunnar Karnell 657 (1999); C. Reed, 'What is a Signature?', (2000) 3 *Journal of Information Law & Technology* (2000) (https://warwick.ac.uk/fac/soc/law/elj/jilt/2000_3/reed, all URLS accessed 21 December, 2018); S. Mason, 'Documents Signed or Executed with Electronic Signatures in English Law', (2018) 34 *Computer Law & Security Review* 933; O. A. Orifowomo and J. O. Agbana, Manual Signature and Electronic Signature: Significance of Forging a Functional Equivalence in Electronic Transactions, (2013) 10 *International Company and Commercial Law Review* 357; S. Mason, *Electronic Signatures in Law* (3rd Ed., 2012), Ch. 1 and 7.

[2] Regulation (EU) No 910/2014 of the European Parliament and of the Council of 23 July 2014 on electronic identification and trust services for electronic transactions in the internal market and repealing Directive 1999/93/EC (eIDAS Regulation). Other states may also explicitly recognize electronic signatures. See for example 15 U.S. Code § 7001 et seq. for US interstate and foreign commerce (that is, contract matters regulated by federal law).

2 Asymmetric encryption

Asymmetric encryption refers to the use of keywords explaining how one can know that an electronic signature emanates from a specific person, and is not forged or copied. Asymmetric encryption means that you cannot use a simple reverse of the decryption key to encrypt a message. This will be explained in the text below.

An example of a message in cipher is Mfnaødjhøslgaæsdkdfæa. On the Internet, I have announced in a safe way a public key to the cipher. When a public key is applied, the message becomes readable: *eureka*. A reader naturally assumes the message is from the signature holder because the public key to the cipher works. Similarly, if a physical key opens a door, one would assume one has found the right door. By means of a public key, one receives an independent verification that the message is from the sender. Thus, the signature in the document is not the sole indication of credibility.

However, if one can use a key to decipher a code, one can usually also figure out how to encrypt a message. This reality weakens the assumption that the signature holder sent the message. Someone else could have intercepted the message, encrypted a different message, and sent it in the original sender's name. If the receiver applies the public key and sees a (false) confirmation that the message is from the original sender, the receiver may read a message unintended by the original sender (e.g., *alea iacta est*). This danger makes it necessary to use a form of encryption that prevents third parties from deriving the encryption key from the decryption key. This is called asymmetric encryption. With asymmetric encryption, a person can be sure that a message that can be decrypted using the sender's public key is truly from the sender, because the sender is the only one who can create a matching encrypted message by means of a private encryption key (secret code). The private key cannot be derived from the public key. Either the correct message is shown (in this case *eureka*), or the message remains garbled.

The principle of an electronic signature is that if a person, or the person's computer, receiving a message or document can decipher a message allegedly from the sender by means of the sender's public decryption key, then the receiver knows the sender's cipher, or signature, is valid. There are several reasons why this principle is counterintuitive.

- First, people are not used to a physical key that can unlock a physical door but not lock it. This thinking simply has to be changed in regard to electronic encryption keys.
- Second, people generally consider encryption to involve keeping something secret. This is not the case with electronic encryption. A message can be enclosed in readable text rather than a cipher. Encryption is used to verify the sender, not to ensure secrecy.
- Third, a lack of trust in messages on the Internet abound. This problem is resolved by an infrastructure service under public license that verifies the public keys.

One may wonder how it is possible to create a secure asymmetric encryption process. This is perhaps due to experience with very simple encryption algorithms, like substituting a letter with the number corresponding to its place in the alphabet with the addition of the number three. In such systems, if one understands the system for decryption, one can also encrypt messages, and the private key can be derived from the public key; if you can encode the message you understand how it is encrypted. However, there are functions used for encryption that are less transparent. As a very simple example, one can use algorithms based on modulo functions used as encryption/decryption algorithms that yield a remainder after the division of a fixed number by the encrypted letter's corresponding number in the alphabet. Their yield from input with a regular pattern (e.g., 1, 2, or 3) appear as an irregular pattern. Table 4.1 demonstrates the difficulty of reversing a calculation if a modulo function is used:

Table 4.1 Example of application of modulo function

Letter	q	r	s	t	u	v	w	x	y	z
Place in alphabet	15	16	17	18	19	20	21	22	23	24
Simple algorithm	18	19	20	21	22	23	24	1	2	3
Modulo algorithm[3]	3	3	5	9	15	3	12	1	13	3

It is easy to guess that the number added to row 2 in row 3 is 3; therefore, the value of each letter in row 1 can be calculated. Furthermore, the values in rows 2 and 4 have a defined relationship (defined by the modulo function). It is more difficult to guess or calculate an encryption algorithm, even if the values are known. (In fact, the formula is mod(243,n)). An encryption is more complicated in many ways so that inferring a private key from a public key is virtually impossible.

By such asymmetric encryption, it is possible to verify the sender of a specific message. A message that can be decrypted by the public key is encrypted by the holder of the private key and no one else. An electronic signature is one application of asymmetric encryption. The sender signs with a private key, and the signature is verified by the matching public key. The system requires a computer to handle the algorithms and trusted services to provide the public keys.

3 The user interface

One does not have to be a cryptology expert to deal with digital signatures. Indeed, knowledge of cryptology would not be as (un-)useful in dealing with digital signatures as graphology is in dealing with pen-and-ink signatures because digital signatures are scrutinized automatically by computers.

---

3 Some of the numbers in this row are identical. This problem can be resolved but will not be discussed here.

Figure 4.1 Screenshot of PDF Advanced Electronic Signatures

There are several formats for digitally signed documents. One example is the so-called PDF Advanced Electronic Signatures (PAdES) format. When a document is opened in Adobe Acrobat, a blue line at the top indicates that the document is digitally signed and identifies who signed. It is possible to verify the signatures, simply and safely, by pressing the button marked 'Signaturpanel' as shown in Figure 4.1.[4]

This is simple and safe.

Like other computer records, a PAdES document can be electronically copied, and the digital signature can be verified in all copies. None of the copies has a special status as an original. Therefore, it would not be meaningful to refer to an original electronic bill of lading, and the special properties of an original paper bill of lading must be taken care of by other techniques, which are discussed in the following section.

All parties can thus have a signed document to verify and prove an agreement. The possession of a computer document—whatever that would be—means nothing. Thus far, however, Norwegian practice of, for example, banks is not to give the other party a record of the agreement that can be verified electronically. This practice puts that party at a disadvantage if questions arise about what was actually agreed to and signed.

This mechanism can be utilized in many ways. An electronic signature can be associated with a particular document and used to mark an intent to be legally bound. It can also be used only to identify the issuer.[5] Furthermore, it can be used as a seal serving as proof that a physical connection has not been broken (e.g., the lid of a medicine bottle) or that the wording of a document has not been changed without the authorization of the signer. An electronic signature can also replace a company seal, which is used in common law countries to verify acts of the company as opposed to acts of its agents on its behalf.[6] The best way of doing this is to issue a digital signature for the company as opposed to a signature for a signing agent. While applications of asymmetric encryption are numerous, the basic asymmetric code techniques are the same.

Algorithms for encryption of digital signatures can be complicated and difficult to break, protecting the identity of the person who issued the signature. Mechanisms can be used to further secure electronic signatures, such as complicated

---

4 One can see how this works here: https://developer.signicat.com/wp-content/uploads/2017/09/sbid_authbased_signflow_pades.pdf. The document can be opened in Adobe Acrobat.

5 See further C. Sullivan, 'Digital Identity–From Emergent Legal Concept to New Reality', (2018) 34 *Computer Law & Security Review*, 723.

6 See, in the UK, the Companies Act 2006, ss 45 et seq.

passphrases or the use of an electronic device to generate one-time passwords in case communication is intercepted. The best standard in EU legislation is called a qualified signature. In general, digital signatures have a good user interface and can be used for a number of purposes.

4 Blockchains

Digital signatures form the basis for blockchains. The details of blockchains are explained elsewhere in this volume. Here the intention is to explain the relationship between digital signatures and blockchains.

In the shipping industry, an example of a possible use for blockchains is to transfer transport documents.[7] The starting point is a master of a ship digitally signing an electronic transport document, like a bill of lading. The assignment of that document, or the right to the cargo pursuant to the assignment, can then be carried out by adding an electronically signed statement of the assignment to the document. The signature of the assignor refers to the assignment and the signed transport document, which becomes a block. The next assignor includes all these elements, or a representation of them,[8] as well as her own assignment in the record she signs.

In this way, the blocks represent the transfer history of the document, or put another way a ledger. As each block includes and builds on the previous, no single assignor can change its tenor. The different electronic signatures involved make that virtually impossible.

Asymmetric encryption can be used to identify the assignor and the assignee. When person A assigns a document to person B, she signs, encrypts the message with B's public key, and sends it to B. Then B can prove that she is the assignee by decrypting the message with her private key. If B can read the message, she is the right person. This is an example of electronic signatures used in reverse.

This procedure does not prevent double-spending: person A first assigns the document to person B and then to person C. In the shipping industry, the simplest way to prevent double-spending is to notify the carrier or her computer of who is entitled to the cargo. This mechanism satisfies the criteria in the Rotterdam Rules.[9]

Cryptocurrencies like Bitcoin work in the same way as the blockchains explained in the text above.[10] However, the double-spending problem is partially resolved by giving preference to the blockchain that contains the greatest amount of computational work, which is a consolidation of a ledger, and there is a special way to provide proof of that work. This computational work requires much energy and is

---

7 For extremely early accounts of this possibility, see K. Reinskou, 'Konnossementer og EDB—Utkast til et Dokumentløst System for Varetransport til Sjøs' (1980) 59 *Marlus* 1; K. Reinskou, 'Bills of Lading and ADP. Description of a Computerized System for Carriage of Goods by Sea', (1981) 2 *Journal of Media Law and Practice* 160.

8 This connection between the signature and the signed statement is important, see N. Bohm, 'Watch What You Sign', (2006) 3 *Digital Evidence and Electronic Signature Law Review*, 45.

9 See the Rotterdam Rules, Ch. 3.

10 S. Nakamoto, 'Bitcoin: A Peer-to-Peer Electronic Cash System' available at <https://bitcoin.org/bitcoin.pdf> accessed December 2018.

perhaps unsuitable for shipping. This system has the advantage that it is distributed, meaning that it is not dependent on a central authority, like a central bank or a shipowner.

As a blockchain can serve as a ledger for the transfer of ownership of cargo, a blockchain can also record the full history of the logistics of a shipment: who handled the cargo, where it was located at a particular time, and what its condition is. The procedure is the same as described in this section, but there is no double-spending problem with transfer of ownership, so a mechanism to deal with that is unnecessary. The information in the ledger can be open to all involved, or it can be encrypted.

It is perhaps confusing that an option for an open ledger is available when encryption is often used for other purposes, like protecting electronic signatures. However, encryption with the absence of clear text is optional, as in all other contexts.

Blockchains extend the usefulness of electronic signatures. If one wishes, one can make a record of the movements or ownership of cargo that is difficult to manipulate, which increases the security of the record. However, the fact that the possibility of such protection exists does not mean it should necessarily be utilized. Sometimes commercial considerations warrant that extensive records should not be required, even in encrypted form.

5 Monopoly and interoperability

One of the advantages of pen-and-ink signatures is that paper and pens are available almost everywhere. While the mechanisms of electronic signatures work well, they are dependent on a digital infrastructure. First, as already explained, someone must vouch for the identity of the person signing and the integrity of her public key. There are a number of electronic identification service providers, with brand names like BankID and Commfides. Second, the receiver of the signature must have the necessary data equipment to read and verify the signed message.

The EU policy is apparent from the regulation of electronic signatures. The legal systems should accept and recognize all electronic signatures that satisfy the criteria.[11] This applies even to signatures vouched for by trust service providers in other EEA states. There is a free flow of digital signatures. However, individuals and businesses are under no such obligations, at least not expressly.

Digital signing is rarely used among small and medium-sized businesses (SMBs). It is typically offered by major institutions, such as banks, which have the necessary equipment and programming ability. User-points (as I will refer to them below) either offer their own services, such as bank services, or are facilitators for the use of electronic signatures between two SMBs.

---

11 See the eIDAS Regulation (fn. 2), articles 6 and 25. This is in line with the UNCITRAL Model Law on Electronic Signatures, article 6 (available at <www.uncitral.org/uncitral/en/uncitral_texts/electronic_commerce/2001Model_signatures.html> accessed December 2018). Less sophisticated signatures could be difficult to enforce. See W. Norton, 'Enforcing Simple Electronic Signatures in an International Context', (2012) 9 *Digital Evidence & Electronic Signature Law Review* 74. Security is relatively more emphasized for electronic signatures than for pen-and-ink signatures: see J. Gregory, 'Must E-Signatures Be Reliable', (2013) 10 *Digital Evidence & Electronic Signature Law Review* 67.

In any event, user-points will regularly choose to accept only a few brands of digital signatures and, depending on the market, not necessarily from foreign companies. For SMBs, this means that they would have to subscribe to the trust service of the brand recognized by the user-point they wish to deal with. They may purchase a number of electronic signatures of different brands with the associated, electronic devices and passphrases.

In this respect, pen-and-ink signatures are much simpler. A user-point may prefer to limit the number of brands of electronic signatures that can be used by SMBs. The marginal benefit of recognizing additional brands is likely small, while the cost and effort of setting them up may be significant. In addition, there may be a wish to promote one particular brand of electronic ID. One example is Norwegian banks, which only offer electronic signatures with their own brand, BankID. The user-points may even have a commercial interest in the brand of electronic signatures they favour.

Ideally, users of electronic signatures would choose a brand that is used worldwide. However, users of electronic signatures are also likely to want to avoid the problems of creating a monopoly, such as excessive pricing, in the entire market and at each user-point. At this stage, the market is developing. One can only hope that the fittest brands of electronic signatures will survive and that the remaining brands can communicate. In the PC market, a few standards have emerged, so perhaps this will happen in respect of electronic signatures as well. Intervention by authorities or legislation may be necessary to prevent monopolies from forming. The Norwegian Maritime Law Commission has proposed a new legal basis for secondary legislation to regulate the market of electronic signatures in connection with electronic transport documents.[12]

6 Liability

Because the use of electronic signatures is dependent on digital infrastructure, the issue arises of the potential liability of the infrastructure providers. One cannot assume that a trust service provider never commits an error, such as issuing an electronic signature to the wrong person.

There are no rules for strict liability and no insurance requirements in this field of law. The users of electronic signatures trust them and use them at their own risk, even if they have no control over the infrastructure. This trust is similar with pen-and-ink signatures. However, with pen-and-ink signatures, unlike electronic signatures, there is no one selling trust, and the situation may be more transparent.

The provider of an electronic signature service has negligence liability for failing to fulfill the obligations under EU Regulation.[13] With due diligence, the system may work well. However, service providers often limit their liability in relation to their customers (the persons who sign), many to only about GBP 500. That amount is not

---

12 Official Norwegian Reports NOU 2012: 10 Gjennomføring av Rotterdamreglene i sjøloven, Ch.15.51.

13 eIDAS Regulation (fn. 2), Arts.11 and 13.

much to compensate losses if the service provider has verified a signature by error in a contract for the selling of real estate or a vessel, as example.

The service provider has the option to limit the use of a signature and thereby limit its liability.[14] Even if use is limited, the signature can still be used for transactions above that liability amount, but the liability is limited as if the limitation on the use were complied with. This concept is similar to purchasing a Ferrari with a warranty against things going wrong, but only at speeds of up to 30 mph; no-one expects a Ferrari driver to maintain that low speed.

In addition, a third party may suffer loss as a result of errors by the service provider. A provider may trust and act in reliance on an agreement that later is declared unenforceable because it was signed by the wrong person, despite the appearance of a proper electronic signature. A third party does not have to respect limits of liability in the service contract between the service provider and the owner of an electronic certificate. However, the third party can accept the limits in a separate agreement with the service provider, for example a contract regarding her own electronic signature.

The limit can also appear in the signature itself.[15] Apparently, it is considered sufficiently communicated and accepted by the third party if she relies on the signature.[16] However it could be so difficult to dig out the limits from the certificate[17] and so difficult to reject a signature referring to the limitation of liability of the service provider that the limitation of liability communicated in this way would not be considered accepted by a third party. It is like a driver invoking a limitation of liability written under the bonnet of his car after running into a pedestrian.

Generally, there is no basis for governmental liability in respect of electronic signatures relied on despite being issued in error. There may be exceptions if signatures form part of a system that proves faulty.[18] A government that submits wrongful identity information across an EEA border will, however, be liable under a special rule, presumably to enhance trust in such information.[19]

7 Defences

An electronic signature is as valid as a handwritten signature. The additional security added by a trust provider and the possibility of incorporating electronic signatures into an automated decision system may suggest to some that there is more finality to an electronic signature than to a pen-and-ink signature. However, while the EU Regulation states that an electronic signature must have the effect of a handwritten signature, it does

---

14 eIDAS Regulation (fn. 2), Art.13(2).
15 Norwegian Parliamentary Report Ot.prp. nr. 82 (1999–2000) p 56.
16 Ibid.
17 See the explanation of what you do for one type of certificate to see its details at www.bankid.no/privat/los-mitt-bankid-problem/se-ditt-bankid-sertifikat/.
18 E. Røsæg et al., 'Elektronisk tinglysing. Forslag til endringer i tinglysingsloven mv. for å tilrettelegge for elektronisk tinglysing. Avgitt til Justis- og politidepartementet' 1.6.2010, 46 et seq. (<www.regjeringen.no/contentassets/3701927744d046a2bbcb22ae2bfb5c8d/rapporte-tinglysingsutvalget.pdf>).
19 eIDAS Regulation (fn. 2), article 11 and 7(f).

not require any more than that.[20] This means that an alleged signer may put up the defence that she did not sign (in other word, that the signature is a forgery). In addition, other defenses relating to the conclusion of contract are available, such as a mistake.

Similarly, the defence that the person signing with her own personal signature acted outside her authority is available, whether she signed on behalf of a company or of another person. If a third party knows that a signature was given by another person rather than the owner of the digital signature, she is likely to know that the use is a violation of its terms and should not be allowed to rely on it. If the third party does not know that another person is involved, the matter is better dealt with under the rules of forgery, as the third party cannot rely on any apparent authority. If an electronic signature is issued to a company, the defenses relating to lack of authority may not be available. The idea is to avoid agency issues, just like a conventional company seal under common law jurisdictions.[21] Other defenses are, however, still available.

Even if forgery and authority defences can be invoked, the person whose electronic signature has been abused and has had her identity stolen is not entirely safe. Other rules may also come into play. One example under Norwegian law pertains to a vessel being sold through the misuse of the owner's electronic signature.[22] If the purchaser registers his ownership and resells the vessel to another purchaser in good faith, the purchaser may acquire a good title to the vessel despite the defects if his seller's title.[23] The provision is interpreted as meaning that the real owner can only invoke circumstances she could not guard against. Lack of control of a passphrase and an electronic security device for the electronic signature is certainly not a circumstance of this kind, but perhaps the unlikely event of a systems failure at the trust provider is one such circumstance.[24]

The owner of an electronic signature certainly has a strong obligation to protect the passphrase and any electronic security devices.[25] This does not mean that giving away control of these implies unlimited authority to the person obtaining control, and there is no basis for establishing contractual ties by giving away control. In certain relationships, it is conceivable that the parties agree that they shall be contractually bound even if the electronic signatures are abused.[26] However, the starting point is that the person who has lost control over her electronic signature is liable in torts only. A difference

---

20 eIDAS Regulation (fn. 2), article. 25.

21 See fn. 6 above.

22 Digital registration if ships in Norway is coming soon. See <www.sdir.no/sjofart/regelverk/utgatte-horinger/horing—forslag-til-endringsforskrift-til-forskrift-av-30.-juli-1992-nr.-593-om-registrering-av-skip-i-nor-og-forskrift-av-30.-juli-1992-nr.-592-om-registrering-av-skip-i-nis/> accessed December 2018.

23 Norwegian Maritime Code 1994, Art. 26.

24 Some commentators on the corresponding provision for real estate in Norway submit that the list of defences is exhaustive. But they have probably not had this defence in mind, which is unknown in the classic law of contract.

25 This may follow, inter alia, from the user agreements.

26 Some one-sided agreements of this kind have been made for situations like family members drawing on a bank credit.

between being bound in contracts and being liable in torts is that the torts claim typically involves a monetary claim. If a vessel has been sold by abuse of the owner's electronic signature, it can be claimed back, but the owner may have to cover the losses thereby incurred by the purchaser.

There is no basis for strict liability, but there is negligence liability toward those who are likely to suffer loss because they wrongfully trust an electronic signature. Negligence liability by the owner of an electronic signature is unlimited, in stark contrast to the regularly limited liability of the professional service provider for its negligence.[27] In some states, for example Norway, torts liability can be mitigated by the courts if reasonableness requires.[28]

Despite the possibility of mitigation, the liability for not keeping control over the passphrase and electronic security device can be considerable. However, it is comparable with the risk of using agents. Unlike powers of attorney, the risk is not manageable by limiting the scope of the electronic signature to certain types of transactions or certain amounts, as this service is not offered by any trust service provider.[29]

8 Conclusion

Real electronic signatures are here to stay,[30] because the use of asymmetric encryption can resolve two problems elegantly. First, the identity of the issuer can be ascertained without resorting to an original, because only the private encryption key can be used to create a message that can be deciphered by the matching publically announced (public) key. Second, the identity of the receiver of a cargo or another holder of a right can be ascertained, because only the holder of a private key can decipher a promise encrypted by the matching publically announced (public) key. In this way, one can make sure that the right person signs electronically for the cargo or another value. These two functions can be combined. In this way, an electronic message can mimic the essential functions of a real negotiable paper document that represents a right.

The mechanism is based on encryption, involving pairs of encryption and decryption keys that cannot be derived from each other. It is this property of the pairs of encryption and decryption keys that makes them 'asymmetric'. Each pair consists of a publicly announced key and a private key. Both can be used both for encryption and decryption.

The use of encryption connects the properties described above to the message that should be electronically signed, etc. It is the message or a representation of it that is encrypted. However, secrecy is not a necessary part of this. One can chose to accompany the message signed by encryption with an unencrypted version of the message.

---

27 See above in Section 6.
28 See the Norwegian legislation contained in the Torts Law 1969, Art.5–2.
29 Compare this to Section 6 above on limiting the scope of electronic signatures for the purpose of managing the liability of the service provider.
30 For an essay of the perspectives, see E. Morse, 'From Rai Stones to Blockchains: The Transformation of Payments', (2018) 34 *Computer Law & Security Review* 946.

If the electronic infrastructure to publicize the public keys in a reliable way is in place, electronic signatures are more convenient to use and safer than pen-and-ink signatures. However, special attention is needed, as there is no original document, the liability rules are somewhat underdeveloped, and there is a possibility of creating monopolies. Electronic signatures are not more binding than other signatures, and the defences of forgery and lack of authority are available.

CHAPTER 5

Pinning down delivery

Glencore v MSC and the use of PIN codes to effect delivery

*Simon Rainey QC**

1 Introduction

The decisions in *Glencore International AG v MSC Mediterranean Shipping Co SA (The Eugenia)*,[1] both at first instance and in the Court of Appeal, have attracted sustained interest from academics and practitioners alike.[2] Whilst in many ways the decision turned on a handful of particular and relatively peculiar facts, the interest, no doubt, derives in large part from the decisions' wider implications. The judgments provide a microcosm for a wider conflict at the sharp end of English maritime law and practice; that between established legal doctrine and burgeoning technical development; the merits of certainty and the need for progress; tradition and modernity.

The validity of the eventual outcome in *Glencore v MSC* is beyond doubt and serious critique. As many have concluded,[3] the decision calls for parties to consider carefully whether their standard terms and conditions should be updated, in order to capture logistical developments in their commercial relationships. Nonetheless, that is not the only insight the case provides.

The decision leaves certain issues unresolved, as well as resolving certain issues unsatisfactorily. This chapter analyses both decisions in the case, with a view to suggesting the avenues that they leave open to interested parties, as well as the avenues that might be worthy of re-opening, if the issues are again the subject of litigation.

---

* Barrister at Quadrant Chambers. London; Honorary Professor of School of Law at the University of Swansea, Visiting Fellow at the Institute of International Shipping & Trade, University of Swansea. The author was greatly assisted in the preparation of this chapter by Jamie Hamblen, barrister, Quadrant Chambers.

1 [2015] EWHC 1989 (Comm); [2015] 2 Lloyd's Rep 508 and [2017] EWCA Civ 365; [2017] 2 Lloyd's Rep 186.

2 See A. Tettenborn, "Bills of Lading and Electronic Misdelivery", [2017] *LMCLQ* 2017, pp. 479–481; M. Goldby, "What is Needed to Get Rid of Paper? A New look at Delivery Orders" [2015] *JIML*, 21, pp. 339–347. M. Bridge et al., *Benjamin on the Sale of Goods*, 10th ed. (Sweet & Maxwell, 2017), para. 18–253 to 257, (hereinafter referred to as "Benjamin").

3 A. Tettenborn in "Bills of Lading and Electronic Misdelivery" at p. 481, and *Benjamin* at para 18–257.

2 The facts of *Glencore v MSC*

The case concerned the misappropriation of two containers of cobalt briquettes whilst stored at the Port of Antwerp in June 2012. Pursuant to a negotiable bill of lading dated 21 May 2012 ("the Bill of Lading"), three containers were shipped aboard the *MSC Eugenia* from Fremantle to Antwerp.[4] Glencore International AG ("Glencore") were the named shipper, C Steinweg NV ("Steinweg"), Glencore's agents at Antwerp, were named as "Notify Parties", and MSC Mediterranean Shipping Co SA ("MSC") were carriers.

The Bill of Lading included an express "Delivery Term" which provided:

> [if] this is a negotiable (To order/of) Bill of Lading, one original Bill of Lading, duly endorsed must be surrendered by the Merchant to the Carrier ... In exchange for the Goods or a Delivery Order.

Prior to 2012, MSC and Glencore had contracted for carriage to Antwerp on materially identical terms for a number of years. Usually, on presentation of the bill of lading, MSC would provide Steinweg with a paper release note, whilst the cargo would be held in a dedicated area of the terminal operated by MSC Home Terminal NV ("MSC Home"). Steinweg would then present the release note to the terminal, in exchange for release of the cargo.

On 1 January 2011, the Port of Antwerp introduced a new electronic release system ("the ERS"). Pursuant to the ERS, on presentation of the bill of lading, the carrier would issue a PIN code which would be emailed to an address specified by the cargo receiver, as well as to the terminal. The receiver would then present the codes at the terminal, in order to obtain delivery of the cargo. MSC's local agent in Belgium, MSC Shipping Co Belgium NV ("MSC Belgium") decided to adopt the ERS from January 2011.

Between January 2011 and June 2012, MSC carried 69 shipments of cobalt briquettes on behalf of Glencore to the Port of Antwerp. Each time, the ERS was used without complaint or complications. On the 70th occasion, as on other occasions, in exchange for the Bill of Lading at Antwerp, MSC provided Steinweg with a release note and three PIN codes ("the release note and PIN codes"). The release note provided (*inter alia*):

> [d]ischarge of the cargo will constitute due delivery of the cargo. After discharge the cargo will remain on the quay at the risk and at the expense of the cargo, without any responsibility on the shipping agent or the shipping company/carrier.

Having received the release note and PIN codes, on 26 June 2012 Steinweg sent the PIN codes to its hauliers, Cargo Trans. On 27 June, Cargo Trans went to collect the containers from MSC Home. On arrival, it was discovered that two of the three containers had already been collected. It appeared that an unknown party had obtained the PIN codes and used them to take possession of the containers.

---

4 En route the containers were transhipped to the *MSC Katrina*, although this caused no issue in the proceedings.

As a consequence of the foregoing, Glencore brought a claim against MSC for misdelivery in breach of its duties in contract, bailment, and for having converted the containers. At first instance, a number of important factual and legal findings were made by Andrew Smith J including that Glencore had no knowledge of the ERS at Antwerp and that the PIN codes, once provided to Steinweg, remained revocable by MSC Belgium.

Following the theft of the containers at Antwerp, along with at least one other occasion of theft, MSC and Steinweg altered their arrangements. As a consequence, containers would only be released to a driver who was from a specific transport company, who provided identification and who was using a vehicle with a specified registration number.

3 MSC'S defences to the misdelivery claim

At first instance, MSC put forward four defences: (a) that a release note and PIN codes constituted a "Delivery Order" per the Delivery Term[5] (b) alternatively, the Bill of Lading was varied such that provision of the release note and PIN codes constituted delivery[6] (c) alternatively, that the previous course of dealing/unexpressed intentions of the parties/of requirement for business efficacy dictated that the Bill of Lading contained an implied term to the same effect[7] (d) alternatively, that Glencore were estopped from contending that provision of the electronic PIN amounted to a breach of the Delivery Term.[8] In addition to these arguments, Andrew Smith J considered the reasons why provision of the release note and PIN codes would not constitute actual delivery of the goods.

In the Court of Appeal, MSC did not contend that the Bill of Lading had been varied or included an implied term. In addition to the arguments on the correct construction of the phrase "Delivery Order" and estoppel, MSC, in light of Andrew Smith J's consideration of whether actual delivery could have occurred, contended that provision of the release note and PIN codes constituted symbolic or constructive delivery of the Containers.[9]

Across both hearings, each of the arguments was dismissed. Commentators have universally concluded that the decision should provoke carriers to consider including express terms that deal with ERS in their bills of lading. For example, Professor Andrew Tettenborn has concluded:

> in the long term the Glencore case may simply lead to carriers and P&I interests trying subtly to redraft their terms of carriage, so as to say that supply of a PIN to the consignee is to amount to delivery of the goods. This would not be quite as revolutionary as it looks; it would merely transfer the risk of theft or fraud during the brief period of

---

5 [2015] EWHC 1989 (Comm); [2015] 2 Lloyd's Rep 508 at [19].
6 Ibid., at [30].
7 Ibid., at [26].
8 Ibid., at [33].
9 [2017] EWCA Civ 365; [2017] 2 Lloyd's Rep 186, at [25].

the handover process after discharge from carrier to consignee, as indeed is sometimes done already.[10]

He is entirely correct in reaching this conclusion. First and foremost, the decision clearly affirms the Court's restrictive approach to construing bills of lading as negotiable instruments. The obvious and sensible conclusion is that carriers must include explicit terms in their bills of lading, if an ERS or similar system is to be used in the way MSC hoped the system at Antwerp was being used. There are, however, aspects of the decisions which leave open arguments as to the effectiveness of a release note and PIN code, absent express contractual provision.

Hence, as to whether or not a release note and PIN code can effect delivery, it may be argued that the decision does not exclude the possibility, even without amendments to standard contractual terms. As to the meaning of "ship's delivery order", it may also be contended that the Court of Appeal went too far and a PIN code, accompanied by appropriate undertakings, could and should qualify as a "ship's delivery order". Finally, it may be argued that the decision leaves open the possibility of carriers avoiding liability for damage sustained to the cargo, in the period after discharge but before delivery.

4 The implications for interpreting bills of lading

At first instance, MSC's arguments as to the correct construction of the Delivery Term were supported by two primary contentions: (a) prior to implementation of the ERS, Steinweg had accepted a release note as opposed to a formal ship's delivery order and (b) irrespective of Glencore's actual knowledge, Glencore were to be imputed with Steinweg's knowledge, including their familiarity with the ERS and MSC's use of that system.

Andrew Smith J rejected both contentions. Glencore were found to have no knowledge of the ERS. Steinweg's knowledge could not be imputed for the purpose of construing the bill of lading, as Steinweg were not Glencore's agent for the purpose of entering into bills of lading or making contracts.[11] In any event, the course of conduct between the parties or their agents could only play a limited role when construing a negotiable bill of lading, as made clear by Lord Hoffman in *Homburg Houtimport BV v Agrosin Private Ltd (The Starsin)*.[12]

The conclusion on imputation is significant. No authority was cited in support of the proposition that knowledge imputed to the principal for one purpose would not be imputed for another. Imputation has, however, always been viewed as contingent on an antecedent purpose.

Hence, as stated in *Bowstead & Reynolds on Agency*,[13] as quoted by Lords Toulson and Hodge in *Bilta (UK) Ltd v Nazir (No.2)*:[14]

---

10 A. Tettenborn in *Bills of Lading and Electronic Misdelivery* at p. 481.
11 [2015] 2 Lloyd's Rep. 508, p. 514 at [23].
12 [2003] UKHL 12; [2004] 1 A.C. 715; [2003] 1 Lloyd's Rep. 571.
13 PG Watts (ed.), 21st ed., (Sweet & Maxwell, 2017), at para 8–214.
14 [2015] UKSC 23; [2016] A.C. 1; [2015] 2 Lloyd's Rep. 61; at [191].

[b]efore imputation occurs, there needs to be some purpose for deeming the principal to know what the agent knows.

Andrew Smith J's decision, therefore, is defensible, albeit the consequence is that shippers and consignees will rarely be saddled with the knowledge of their agents at any given port. This, in turn, will make it hard for carriers to demonstrate that a particular practice at any given port has a bearing on the meaning of the contract of carriage. Obtaining evidence of the shipper's actual knowledge, therefore, will become all the more important.

Andrew Smith J's conclusion on the role of a general course of conduct when construing a bill of lading is clearly in accordance with high authority. Beyond the dicta of Lord Hoffman in the *The Starsin*, Lord Bingham in *Dairy Containers Ltd v Tasman Orient CV* stated that:[15]

> [t]he contract should be given the meaning it would convey to a reasonable person having all the background knowledge which is reasonably available to the person or class of persons to whom the document is addressed.

In the context of a bill of lading, as noted by Lord Hoffman in *The Starsin*, the class of persons to whom a bill of lading is addressed include merchants and bankers who may have no experience of the particular technology in place at certain ports. Consequently, *Lewison on the Interpretation of Contracts*[16] now cites *Glencore v MSC*[17] as support for the proposition that: "in the case of a negotiable bill of lading the role of background is very restricted."

Taken together, these principles place a high bar in front of parties seeking to rely on traditional bill of lading terms to govern innovative technical practices. The immediate handling of the goods will usually be carried out by agents, whose knowledge is unlikely to be imputed to the principal (absent authority to enter into and alter contractual relations on behalf of the principal). Even if the principal can be shown to have the requisite knowledge, imputed or otherwise, it will be necessary to show that the meaning would be acceptable to parties who are unlikely to have any knowledge of recent developments in the industry. Even if ERS proliferated widely, parties may struggle to convince a tribunal that bankers are sufficiently aware, so at to permit a purposive construction of the bill.

Ultimately, however, it must be remembered that the particular facts in *MSC v Glencore* created a strong incentive for the Court to avoid lending the bill of lading a progressive construction. In particular, Glencore were found not to know of the ERS,[18] MSC were found to have provided no undertaking to deliver to Glencore or anybody else[19] and MSC were found to have retained the ability to revoke Glencore's right to collect the containers from the terminal.[20] If MSC had been able to show that Glencore were in no way prejudiced by use of release notes

---

15 [2004] UKPC 22; [2005] 1 W.L.R. 215; [2004] 2 Lloyd's Rep. 647, at [12].
16 6th ed., (Sweet & Maxwell, 2017) at para 3.18.
17 [2015] EWHC 1989 (Comm); [2015] 2 Lloyd's Rep 508.
18 [2015] EWHC 1989 (Comm); [2015] 2 Lloyd's Rep 508 at [23].
19 Ibid., at [25].
20 Ibid., at [8].

and PIN codes, it is suggested the Court might have been prepared to lend the Bill of Lading a sensible and contemporary interpretation. The fact that a banker may be unaware of the underlying technology should not prevent this. The Court is not concerned with the intention of third party merchants or bankers when interpreting a bill of lading; it is concerned with the parties' objective intention, in light of the fact that the bill may pass into the hands of such third parties. Emphasis, therefore, should be on the value and quality of the rights provided by the bill, as that is what such third parties will be primarily concerned with. Consequently, it is submitted that, provided MSC could have demonstrated that Glencore were in no worse a position by virtue of being provided a release note and PIN codes, as compared to having obtained delivery or a delivery order, a different conclusion could have been reached, on a number of the issues in the proceedings. The sections that follow seek to substantiate that submission.

5 Provision of the release note and pin codes as "actual" delivery

5.1 The decisions

As set out above, the Delivery Term required MSC to either deliver the goods or a delivery order, in exchange for the original bill of lading. At first instance, MSC did not contend that, on the original terms of the Bill of Lading, delivery of the goods could be achieved by provision of the codes. Nonetheless, Andrew Smith J "set the scene"[21] by dealing with why, in his view, provision of the codes would not constitute delivery of the goods. Relying on Diplock LJ in *Barclays Bank Ltd v Commissioners of Customs and Excise*,[22] the judge held that the carrier under a bill of lading must surrender possession by divesting himself of all powers to control any physical dealing in the goods, to the person entitled under the contract to obtain possession.[23] Whilst his lordship accepted in "some circumstances, delivery might be effected by putting goods into a port authority's custody",[24] in general, delivery could not be effected merely by putting the goods into the custody of a person who is not the agent of the consignee.[25] Delivery had not occurred at Antwerp, because the containers were put into an MSC Terminal and MSC had a power (albeit not a contractual right as against Glencore) to invalidate the PIN codes.[26] This meant that MSC had not divested itself of its powers of control and delivery had not taken place.

On appeal, MSC questioned Andrew Smith J's finding that MSC had control. Revocation, it was argued, was irrelevant, provided that MSC did not have the right, as against Glencore, to revoke the PIN codes and Steinweg's right to collection. In giving judgment on behalf of the Court of Appeal, Christopher Clarke LJ

---

21 Ibid., at [17].
22 [1963] 1 Lloyd's Rep 81 at p. 89.
23 [2015] EWHC 1989 (Comm); [2015] 2 Lloyd's Rep 508 at [17].
24 Ibid., at [18].
25 Ibid., at [17].
26 Ibid., at [8].

divided his analysis between actual delivery and symbolic delivery. As to the first, he accepted that the judge had found that the codes could be revoked by MSC and that MSC Home would act at the behest of MSC Belgium[27] He went on to hold that Diplock LJ in *Barclays Bank Ltd v Commissioners of Customs and Excise* was concerned with a question of physical control, irrespective of whether the exercise of such control by the donor would put them in breach of obligations owed to the done.[28] Consequently, in the ordinary case, where a shipowner discharges goods into a storage facility, the goods remain undelivered so long as any order given by the shipowner to the facility remains revocable, citing the judgment of Tomlinson LJ in *Great Eastern Shipping Co Ltd v Far East Chartering Ltd (The Jag Ravi)*.[29] In agreement with Andrew Smith J, therefore, the Court of Appeal held there was no actual delivery, as MSC retained power to control physical dealing in the goods. Christopher Clarke LJ went on to question whether provision of the PIN codes could ever effect delivery, holding:[30]

> I do not think that delivery of the code can, itself, constitute delivery. Delivery usually means actual delivery, not delivery of a means of access, and nothing is spelt out in the contract to the contrary.

Whilst it must be correct that provision of a code by "itself" will almost certainly be insufficient, it is worth considering what, if anything, could accompany the codes, so as to effect delivery.

5.2 Analysis

Diplock LJ's definition of delivery has a positive and negative aspect; the donor must divest itself of all powers to control the goods, whilst the person entitled to possession must obtain the power to control the goods. This question is not a pure question of fact, as the degree of control required must be determined by the particular legal and contractual context in which delivery is being considered; a point made by Christopher Clarke LJ in *Glencore v MSC*.[31] Nonetheless, the correct question is whether sufficient control has been divested by the donor and vested in the donee, in light of the amount of control required by the contract. If the requirements are met, then delivery will have taken place in the eyes of the law. This will constitute "actual" delivery, as opposed to symbolic or constructive delivery.

In *Glencore v MSC*, the provision of the release note and PIN codes was insufficient to achieve delivery, as MSC were held to have retained control over the containers. It is not hard to conceive, however, of circumstances where the carrier could be found to have not retained any control over the cargo, either by virtue of a lack of a contractual arrangement to that effect or express terms within a contractual relationship. If that could be shown, it would then be necessary to show that

---

27 [2017] EWCA Civ 365; [2017] 2 Lloyd's Rep 186 at [37].
28 Ibid., at [40].
29 [2012] EWCA Civ 180; [2012] 1 Lloyd's Rep. 637, at [45].
30 Ibid., at [41].
31 [2017] EWCA Civ 365; [2017] 2 Lloyd's Rep 186 at [31].

provision of the PIN codes would be sufficient to perfect the positive aspect of delivery i.e. that it would vest sufficient control in the consignee.

In agreement with Christopher Clarke LJ, it is submitted that the codes alone would be insufficient. The point, however, would be arguable, if the codes were coupled with an attornment by the Terminal or sub-bailee of the goods, to the consignee, provided the terms of the attornment granted sufficient control to the consignee. Andrew Smith J[32] and Christopher Clarke LJ[33] in *Glencore v MSC*, as well as Tomlinson LJ in *The Jag Ravi*, all noted that an attornment will be of relevance when considering delivery. As it was put by Tomlinson LJ in *The Jag Ravi*[34] (albeit construing delivery in the context of an LOI):

> [d]elivery does not necessarily involve that the shipowners must themselves physically hand over the cargo to the receivers in the sense of physically shovelling the coal onto the consignees' lorries.

As the citation from Diplock LJ makes clear, what is involved in this context is the divesting or relinquishing of the power to compel any dealing in or with the cargo which can prevent the consignee from obtaining possession. Such divesting must of course be effective. The judge held that as a matter of construction of the letter of indemnity the issue of the delivery order and the discharge of the cargo were sufficient to amount to delivery. I do not agree that this alone was sufficient, for as the facts here show a shipowner may attempt to revoke the authority given by a delivery order and may succeed in doing so. Whether in any given case a shipowner will in fact succeed in revoking an authority given in that way will no doubt depend upon the law governing the relationship between the shipowners and the person to whom the delivery order is addressed, *and may be affected by the question whether the addressee of the delivery order has subsequently attorned to the consignees named in the bill of lading.* (emphasis added)

Matters would undoubtedly turn on the particular terms of the attornment. If, however, the terms provided a high degree of control to the consignee, then it is submitted that delivery could be found to have occurred. This is consistent with the case law, where it has been held that provision of a physical key is sufficient to transfer possession and effect "actual" delivery.

Hence, the point was explored in detail by Rowlatt J in *Wrightson v Mcarthur & Hutchisons Ltd.*[35] In that case, the defendant set aside specified goods in two rooms within its premises. The parties purported to enter into a transaction by which the goods would be transferred to the plaintiff, as security. The rooms were locked and the keys provided to the plaintiff, along with an undertaking that the plaintiff had the right to remove the goods as desired. The defendant went into liquidation and the liquidator contended the transaction was invalid under s. 93 of the Companies (Consolidation) Act 1908. The validity of the transaction turned on

---

32 Ibid., at [31].
33 Ibid.
34 [2012] EWCA Civ 180; [2012] 1 Lloyd's Rep. 637, at [45].
35 [1921] 2 K.B. 807.

whether possession of the goods had passed to the plaintiff. Rowlatt J held that possession had passed, finding that:[36]

> [t]he point to which this case is now reduced is whether the circumstance that the rooms, the keys of which were delivered, were within the defendants' premises, prevents the delivery of the keys conferring possession of the contents of the rooms. If the keys delivered had been the outside key of the whole warehouse containing these goods I should have felt no difficulty, nor should I have felt any difficulty had the key been of an apartment or receptacle in the premises of a third party as was the case in *Hilton v. Tucker* (1888) 39 Ch. D. 669. On the other hand if, the rooms being in the defendants' premises, the keys had been given without the licence to go and remove the goods at any time I should have thought it clear that possession of the goods did not pass. It would be merely a case of the goods remaining in the defendants' possession with the security that they should not be interfered with, but without any power of affirmative control at the free will of the plaintiff. It would be like the case of furniture left in a locked room in a house that is let furnished, where the lessor has no right to enter except upon reasonable notice and at reasonable times. The actual question has to be considered in the light of the principle that delivery of a key has effect not as symbolic delivery, but as giving the actual control. This was the view expressed by Lord Hardwicke in Ward v. Turner (1752) 28 E.R. 275, where he says the key is the means of coming at the possession. The matter was fully discussed in the light of all the cases in Pollock and Wright on Possession in the Common Law, p. 61 and following pages. In *Hilton v. Tucker*, already referred to, in a judgment delivered since the date of that work, Kekewich J. observes "that the delivery of the key in order to make constructive possession must be under such circumstances that it really does pass the full control of the place to which admission is to be gained by means of the key." If I might criticise that statement my criticism would only be as to the propriety of the use of the word "constructive" in the connection in question.

In light of the above, there are clearly circumstances in which a key or, in theory, PIN code would provide sufficient control so as to effect delivery of goods. It is, of course, highly relevant that *Wrightson v Mcarthur & Hutchisons Ltd.*[37] concerned a pledge and not delivery pursuant to a bill of lading. Nonetheless, the underlying question of control remains pertinent. If an attornment alone would not suffice, then it may be open to contend that the attornment gives rise to a relationship of agency between the consignee and terminal or sub-bailee in possession of the goods. If the terminal or sub-bailee could be construed as acting as the consignee's agents, it is trite law that delivery would be effected.[38] Furthermore, there is nothing inconsistent with the terminal or sub-bailee acting as the carrier's agent during the initial stages of discharge and then the consignee's agent at the point in time at which the carrier divests itself of any control and the terminal/sub-bailee attorns to the consignee.[39] It will be possible for the carrier to defend against arguments to the effect that this form of delivery is beyond the expectation of third party merchants or bankers. This approach to delivery is premised on

---

36 Ibid., at 816–817.
37 [1921] 2 K.B. 807.
38 *British Shipowners v Grimond* (1876) 3 R. 968.
39 See *The Jaederen* [1892] P. 351 and *Cooke on Voyage Charters 4th ed.* (Informa Law, 2014) (hereinafter referred to as "Voyage Charters") at para 10.2

conventional, traditional and well-established mechanisms of conferring possession and completing delivery. As a result, provided the carrier can establish (a) that it divested itself of control and (b) that the consignee has obtained a sufficient degree of control, delivery may still be found to have taken place, even if the bill of lading is silent on the use of an ERS or like system.

6 Symbolic delivery

Having rejected the possibility of actual delivery on the facts of the case, Christopher Clarke LJ considered whether symbolic delivery could have occurred. His lordship accepted that:

> where the parties have agreed that symbolic delivery suffices, then such delivery takes place when the symbol is delivered, notwithstanding that the deliverer of the symbol may in practice be able to deprive the recipient of the actual goods after the symbol has been handed over.[40]

This finding was of no help to MSC. Equally, it will not be of help to parties saddled with a bill of lading that makes no express reference to the method of delivery being relied upon. The passage, however, does clarify that parties are free to agree a method of effecting delivery, even if that method does not meet the standard legal definition of delivery. As a consequence, it should lend parties confidence that a properly drafted clause would succeed in ensuring delivery occurred at the time the clause dictates e.g. on provision of PIN codes.

7 The correct construction of the term "delivery order"

7.1 The decisions

Given that MSC could not establish that actual delivery took place, the only other avenue open to them was to rely on the substitute option of providing a delivery order in exchange for the bill of lading, as per the Delivery Term. At first instance, over and above the fact that Glencore were found to have no knowledge of the ERS, Andrew Smith J held it was inherently improbable that a shipper would agree to "surrender its rights" against the carrier without receiving in return either the goods themselves or the benefit of a substitute undertaking.[41] The phrase "delivery order" should be construed as meaning ship's delivery order, the essential characteristic of which is that it provides a substitute undertaking from the carrier to the person entitled to the goods. For similar reasons, MSC's argument that there was an implied term that provision of the release note and PIN codes would constitute delivery was rejected, albeit Andrew Smith J also found such a term conflicted with, if it did not contradict, the Delivery Term itself.[42]

---

40 [2017] EWCA Civ 365; [2017] 2 Lloyd's Rep 186 at [41].
41 [2015] EWHC 1989 (Comm); [2015] 2 Lloyd's Rep 508 at [19].
42 Ibid., at [27].

In the Court of Appeal, MSC refined and developed its arguments, contending that, by the time a release note and PIN codes were issued, its contractual uses were exhausted. Consequently, it functioned as an administrative key. Whoever surrendered the bill to the carrier would have contractual rights, by virtue of the Carriage of Goods by Sea Act 1992 ("COGSA 1992"). Such rights would not be extinguished by passing the bill to the carrier. In the alternative, it was contended that the release note and PIN codes amounted to a ship's delivery order because it was an undertaking to deliver to the bearer of the order i.e. the party that typed in the PIN codes at Antwerp.

Whilst the Court of Appeal accepted that the delivery order need not be a physical piece of paper and could be transmitted by email;[43] Christopher Clarke LJ agreed with Andrew Smith J that the delivery order should provide a substitute undertaking.[44] In the case itself, such an undertaking could not be found, as the release note contained the phrase "discharge of the cargo will constitute due delivery of the cargo."[45] When that fact was coupled with the findings that (a) Glencore did not know of the system and (b) a course of conduct is of limited relevance when construing negotiable bills of lading, the conclusion is easily explicable and justifiable. Merchants and bankers are unlikely to care about the particular mechanics of delivery of the delivery order, provided they are afforded the same standards of protection. The Court's conclusion, therefore, that the release note and PIN codes needed to provide equivalent protection can readily be defended. The Court's reasoning as to what would qualify as equivalent protection is, however, questionable.

7.2 Analysis

Christopher Clarke LJ, like Andrew Smith J, concluded that the phrase "delivery order" must refer to a "ship's delivery order" as defined in s. 1(4)(b) of the Carriage of Goods by Sea Act 1992.[46] He went on to find that it was:

> implicit in those circumstances that the parties intended that the delivery order should have the key attribute of a bill of lading, namely an undertaking by the carrier to deliver the goods to the person identified in it, which would, here, have to be Glencore or Steinweg, Glencore's agent.

This view was held to be supported by the decisions in *Waren Import Gesellschaft Krohn & Co v Internationale Graanhandel Thegra NV*,[47] *Colin & Shields v W Weddel & Co*[48] and *Cremer v General Carriers SA*.[49]

As a consequence of this analysis, if a release note and PIN code were provided, along with an undertaking to deliver to the first party to utilise the PIN code:

---

43 [2017] EWCA Civ 365; [2017] 2 Lloyd's Rep 186 at [61].
44 Ibid., at [46].
45 Ibid., at [57].
46 Ibid., at [46].
47 [1975] 1 Lloyd's Rep 146.
48 [1952] 2 All ER 337.
49 [1974] 1 WLR 341.

it is not the delivery order called for by the B/L, namely to deliver to Glencore/Steinweg. A promise to deliver to whoever first enters the right code, whether or not that is Glencore/Steinweg, is not the same.[50]

This conclusion is open to criticism, as it implies that it is a requirement of a ship's delivery order that the undertaking it provides must be to a named party. This is not and has never been a requirement of a ship's delivery order. Hence, prior to COGSA 1992, the position at common law was that a ship's delivery order could be made out to the holder of the order, as opposed to a particular named party. *The Rights of Suit: Carriage of Goods by Sea Report*, produced by the Law Commission in 1991 ("the 1991 Report") provides at 5.26 that:

> Ship's delivery orders are [...] (a) documents issued by or on behalf of shipowners while the goods are in their possession or under their control and which contain some form of undertaking that they will be delivered to the holder or to the order of a named person ...[51]

With regard to the cases cited by the Court of Appeal in *Glencore v MSC*, two of the cases provide support for this proposition and, indeed, were cited at paragraph 5.26 of the 1991 Report. Hence, Kerr J in *Waren Import Gesellschaft Krohn v Internationale Graanhandel Thegra N. V.*, citing the GAFTA Board of Appeal stated as follows:[52]

> The term "Ship's Delivery Order" in the context of G.A.F.T.A. contract form No. 100 does have a special trade meaning, in relation to any goods of the kinds normally sold on the terms of this contract form, and means a document issued by the Owner or Master of the carrying vessel or their agents at a time when the goods are on board ship by the terms of which the Owner or Master expressly undertake to deliver the goods to the holder or his order.

It is not without irony, in light of the Court of Appeal's reliance on *Waren Import Gesellschaft Krohn v Internationale Graanhandel Thegra N. V.* in *Glencore v MSC*, that Kerr J went on to question the validity of restricting the phrase "ship's delivery order" to a "special trading meaning", holding that:[53]

> [t]he special trade meaning found by the Board of Appeal would, however, have the effect that only a document as there set out, and no other, would satisfy the description of "ship's delivery order" in cl. 13 (2), although other similar documents may have the same effect in practice and in law. I need only give two examples. The finding requires the document in question to be "issued by" the owner or master of the carrying vessel or their agents. This would apparently exclude a document which had originally emanated from the sellers, being addressed to one of these persons, and which had thereupon been endorsed by them with an undertaking as specified in the finding, but which was not issued direct to the buyers because as a matter of convenience it may have been handed back to the sellers or their agents and then transmitted to the buyers by them. Such a document might not qualify as having been issued by the persons referred to in the finding. Secondly, the finding would require an express undertaking

---

50 [2017] EWCA Civ 365; [2017] 2 Lloyd's Rep 186 at [56].
51 See further N. Teare, Ship's Delivery Orders [1976] *LMCLQ* 29.
52 [1975] 1 Lloyd's Rep. 146 at 152.
53 Ibid., at 153.

to deliver the goods "to the holder or his order". This would apparently exclude a document, albeit issued direct to the buyers, containing an undertaking to deliver the goods to them nominatim or to their order. In the light of the authorities referred to hereafter, which show the general uncertainty as to what is or is not comprised in the term "ship's delivery order", it seems highly improbable that because parties happen to use this particular form of contract, they also intended that only a document complying precisely with this finding would suffice, and no other, however irrelevant the differences in form and content might be. This is a further reason against treating the finding as one which binds the Court to the exclusion of other forms of documents.

The decision in *Waren Import Gesellschaft Krohn v Internationale Graanhandel Thegra N. V*, therefore, does not sit easily with the Court of Appeal's assumption in *Glencore v MSC* that the phrase "delivery order" can only mean an order that meets the statutory definition. Furthermore, it supports the view that a delivery order could traditionally be made out to the holder, as opposed to a named party.

A similar view can be found in *Peter Cremer GmbH v General Carriers SA (The Dona Mari)* (equally relied upon by the Court of Appeal in *Glencore v MSC*) where Kerr J held:[54]

> In other cases, they may be what are sometimes referred to as "ship's delivery orders," that is documents which are usually issued by shipowners' agents addressed to the master or chief officer or other persons authorising delivery to the holder or to the order of a named person.

At common law, therefore, there was no requirement for an undertaken to be given to a named party, as opposed to the holder of the order. To the extent that the Court of Appeal viewed s.1 COGSA 1992 as requiring a more restrictive interpretation, a practical approach similar to that of Kerr J in *Waren Import Gesellschaft Krohn v Internationale Graanhandel Thegra N. V.* should be preferred. In any event, it is equally questionable whether COGSA 1992 in fact requires the beneficiary of the undertaking to be named. If that is the effect of COGSA 1992, it would certainly be surprising, given that the 1991 Report recommended that:

> the holder of a ship's delivery order to whom a sea carrier has undertaken to deliver the goods be given statutory rights of suit against the carrier.

Section (4)(b) of COGSA 1992 provides that a "ship's delivery order" must contain:

> an undertaking which—(a) is given under or for the purposes of a contract for the carriage by sea of the goods to which the document relates, or of goods which include those goods; and (b) is an undertaking by the carrier to a person identified in the document to deliver the goods to which the document relates to that person.

Section 1(4)(b), however, has to be read alongside s 5(3) which provides:

> References in this Act to a person's being identified in a document include references to his being identified by a description which allows for the identity of the person in question to be varied, in accordance with the terms of the document, after its issue.

---

54 [1973] 2 Lloyd's Rep. 366, at 372.

It is submitted that the wording of both sections is consistent with a delivery order that provides an undertaking to the holder. Indeed, that view best explains the somewhat obscure wording of s. 5(3). Hence, an undertaking made out to the holder of a delivery order is an example of the identification by description envisaged by s. 5(3).

It follows that the Court of Appeal's analysis in *Glencore v MSC* created a false dichotomy by finding that a ship's delivery order would necessarily contain an undertaking made out to either Glencore or Steinweg. A ship's delivery order could have provided an undertaking to the holder of the order itself, whoever that might be.

Seen in its proper context, the difference between an undertaking to a holder of a paper document and the recipient of an email containing an encrypted PIN code are relatively fine. Christopher Clarke LJ contended that an email containing a PIN code may be subject to hacking, such that the Court cannot assume it would have been assented to. But that reasoning alone, seems strained. There are plenty of risks inherent in there being a single paper copy of a delivery order that can be avoided by using an encrypted PIN code, not to mention the time and expense that can be saved. Indeed, the very types of precautions now undertaken at the port of Antwerp by MSC and Steinweg are probably more secure than any past procedures, including the use of a physical delivery order. It is submitted, therefore, that this aspect of the Court of Appeal's judgment goes too far. A PIN code, coupled with an undertaking to deliver to the first person to apply that code at the Terminal, can properly be construed as a ship's delivery order.

8 Estoppel, variation, and waiver

8.1 The decisions

As to estoppel, at first instance it was contended by MSC that by accepting delivery through the ERS without complaint for 69 shipments, Glencore represented it was content with this mode of delivery. Andrew Smith J held that this argument faced many of the same difficulties as the other submissions.[55] In particular, the representation needed to go further than allow for use of the ERS, delivery needed to take place at the time the codes were provided.[56] Furthermore, the arguments were answered by the finding that Glencore had no knowledge of the ERS.[57]

In the Court of Appeal, MSC contended that an estoppel preventing Glencore from contending that MSC could not use the delivery system would alleviate them from responsibility. Furthermore, Glencore's knowledge was irrelevant for the purposes of a representation by their agents. Whilst the judge had found that Steinweg did not have authority to enter contractual relationships, they clearly had authority to accept delivery and, consequently, make representations as to what form of

---

55 [2015] EWHC 1989 (Comm); [2015] 2 Lloyd's Rep 508 at [33].
56 Ibid., at [33].
57 Ibid., at [33].

delivery was acceptable. As a result, Steinweg's knowledge could be imputed to Glencore in this context, if not in the context of varying or implying terms.

The Court of Appeal rejected the estoppel argument, emphasising that throughout the 69 shipments no issue had arisen as to when delivery was in fact made.[58] The complaint was not that delivery was made against the codes but that it had not been made at all. The Court also rejected the contention that Steinweg had any authority to make such a representation as:

> [a]uthority to make arrangements to ensure delivery to Glencore pursuant to the B/L or Delivery Oder did not impliedly extend to accepting that delivery pursuant to the B/L would validly be made by delivery to the first presenter of the codes whether that was Glencore or a thief, especially when Glencore was not even aware of the ERS system.[59]

Whilst both judgments dismissed the particular estoppel arguments run by MSC, they do not rule out the possibility that Steinweg's dealings with MSC could have estopped Glencore from contending that the use of a release note and PIN codes was, itself, a breach of contract.

In a similar vein, with regard to variation, MSC contended that Glencore had actual authority to vary the Delivery Term as they were authorised to do what was necessary to obtain release of the containers. In the alternative, it contended that Steinweg had apparent/ostensible authority.

Andrew Smith J could not identify a specific point at which Glencore could be said to have accepted an offer to vary the contract.[60] Equally, he rejected that Steinweg had actual or apparent authority to vary the Delivery Term in the way contended for by MSC.[61] In particular, he found that Steinweg could not have accepted any offer provided by the release note, as this expressly set out that delivery was to occur on discharge, which was clearly beyond any authority they might have. He noted, however, that he did not need to decide whether Steinweg could reach a contractual agreement, binding on Glencore, about how delivery might be affected in accordance with the B/L.[62]

8.2 Analysis

The Court's findings suggest that variation or estoppel arguments are unlikely to avail carriers charged with misdelivery. To do so, it would be necessary to establish that the agent had authority to alter when delivery should be deemed to occur, which is unlikely to be the case. They leave open, however, the question of whether an agent's use of an ERS or similar system would preclude a consignee claiming the carrier was in breach at the time they did not provide a delivery order or the goods, in exchange for the bill of lading. It is possible, therefore, that MSC would

---

58 [2017] EWCA Civ 365; [2017] 2 Lloyd's Rep 186 at [67].
59 Ibid., at [68].
60 [2015] EWHC 1989 (Comm); [2015] 2 Lloyd's Rep 508 at [30].
61 Ibid., at [31].
62 Ibid., at [31].

not have been found to have breached the contract of carriage, merely by warehousing the goods without provision of a delivery order.

In any event, as Dr Miriam Goldby has argued,[63] it was open for MSC to contend that Steinweg waived compliance with the Delivery Term on behalf of Glencore. Such an argument would not run into the same issues regarding actual or ostensible authority, in light of the decision in *The Happy Day*.[64] Whilst the preceding arguments may not avail a party faced with a misdelivery claim, they would be pertinent to any claim for damage sustained to the cargo, during the period after discharge but before delivery. In particular, they could preclude a claim that the carriers were in breach, merely for providing a release note and PIN code in lieu of a delivery order.

It is an open question whether the Hague/Hague-Visby Rules, if incorporated into the bill of lading, would continue to apply during this period, in the absence of an express term that decided the question.[65] The weight of judicial and academic opinion suggests, in the absence of clear words to the contrary, the rules will continue to apply.[66] Hence, Longmore LJ noted in *Trafigura Beheer BV and another v Mediterranean Shipping Company SA (The MSC Amsterdam)* held:[67]

> It must follow from this that the parties are free to agree on terms other than the Hague Rules (or the HVR) for periods outside the actual period of the carriage. No doubt if no agreement is made for the period after discharge, it might be easy to say that the parties have impliedly agreed that the obligations and immunities contained in the Hague Rules continue after actual discharge until the goods are taken into the custody of the receiver.

Nonetheless, it is suggested that the point is clearly arguable. Carriers and cargo interests alike may wish to rely on the Hague/Hague Visby Rules, depending on the particular facts of the case.[68]

If, however, the Bill of Lading expressly excluded application of the Rules after discharge, such a clause is likely to be upheld and no issue as to Article III r 8 should arise, per Brandon J in *The Arawa*.[69] Consequently, whilst the outcome in *Glencore v MSC* will disappoint some carriers, it provides the potential for protection, by variation, estoppel, or waiver, with regard to claims arising out of damage to the cargo, after discharge from the Vessel.

---

63 M. Goldby, "What Is Needed to Get Rid of Paper? A New Look at Delivery Orders", [2015] *JIML* 339–347.
64 [2002] 2 Lloyd's Rep. 487.
65 On the point in general, see *Carver on Bills of Lading 4th Ed.* (2017) ("Carver") at para 9–130, *Voyage Charters* at para 85.79–82.
66 See *Carver* at para 9–130 and *Seafood Imports Pty. Ltd v ANL Singapore Ltd* (2010) 272 A.L.R. 149. For the contrary view, see *Aikens, Lord and Bools on Bills of Lading 2nd Ed.* (2015) at para 10.94.
67 [2007] EWCA Civ 794; [2007] 2 Lloyd's Rep 622 at [23].
68 For example, a carrier may wish to rely on the Article III r 6 time bar whilst a cargo interest may wish to contend that the carrier should not be permitted to rely on the Article IV r 2 exceptions. Conversely, a cargo interest may wish to rely on Article III r 8 whilst a carrier may wish to rely on express exclusions of liability in the bill of lading.
69 [1977] 2 Lloyd's Rep. 416 at pp. 425–426.

9 Conclusions

Carriers who use ERS or, indeed, any system which materially alters how they physically deliver the cargo, are now well advised to ensure the bills of lading they use have explicit terms dealing with such systems. The judgements in *Glencore v MSC* reveal the limits of how flexible the Court can (or will) be when construing a bill of lading that has no express terms dealing with novel systems and procedures. It is, for the most part, a victory for legal conservatism over commercial innovation.

Nonetheless, this chapter has attempted to show that the decision should not necessarily be viewed as closing all potential avenues, to a carrier that finds itself in a similar position to MSC. In particular, the concept of delivery and delivery orders should not be considered as ossified. To the extent that the decisions in *Glencore v MSC* suggest otherwise, it is submitted that their example should not be followed, if English law is to maintain its reputation as a commercially pragmatic and dynamic legal system, attuned to the contemporary concerns and expectations of modern commercial parties.

PART 2

ARTIFICIAL INTELLIGENCE AND SHIPPING

CHAPTER 6

Autonomous shipping and maritime law

Paul Dean* and Henry Clack†

1 Introduction

Once mere science fiction, autonomous ships (known as Maritime Autonomous Surface Ships or "MASS") will soon become a part of commercial reality. Whilst the international law of the sea has, in its current format, historically been flexible enough to cope with the rise of steam power and the use of containers, some reform will be required in order to allow MASS to operate beyond the limits of territorial waters. This chapter examines the legal standing of MASS in relation to international conventions which govern the use of commercial vessels and discusses their potential contractual and non-contractual realities.

2 What is a MASS?

Generally, MASS routinely operate with little or no human involvement and have some or all of the following characteristics. They are man-made and unmanned assets which operate in the marine environment; they are also capable of being operated un-tethered (i.e. without the use of a fibre optic or a wired communications link) or by any other form of direct control, (e.g. radio, acoustic) although it is accepted that a MASS may also be capable of receiving and acting on further instructions sent to it (e.g. a MASS controlled by a shore operator); they are capable of moving through the surrounding water mass using an onboard power source; and finally, once deployed, they can be controlled by onboard computers using "artificial intelligence" ("AI") and/or remotely operated via a wireless link to a shore based controller.

In our view, the following would not be considered MASS: deployed over side equipment; Remote Operated Vehicles ("ROVs"); remotely controlled mine disposal vehicles; "MASS" attached to a mother platform (e.g. by crane); unpropelled water sensors (such as bathythermographs); diving bells; submarines; drift nets or moorings.

---

* Senior Partner at HFW; London Head of Shipping and Global Head of Offshore; Head of HFW's Autonomous Vessel Group.
† Associate at HFW; Member of HFW's Autonomous Vessel and Cyber Groups.

The level of autonomy of a MASS depends on its function. Existing MASS display a number of varying degrees of autonomy and can be subdivided into different classes. The different classes are as follows:[1]

2.1 Autonomy assisted bridge ("AAB")

A MASS with an AAB will have a bridge which is continuously manned and the crew will be able to intervene in the ship's operations. These ships will display the lowest level of autonomy. Examples include otherwise normal vessels fitted with a collision avoidance system which will work in tandem with an officer of the watch.

2.2 Periodically unmanned bridge ("PUB")

These MASS could operate without members of the crew on the bridge for limited periods of time (e.g. in good weather conditions whilst the vessel is in open sea). However the crew would remain on board the ship and would call to the bridge as and when issues arise.

2.3 Periodically unmanned ship ("PUS")

MASS falling into the category of PUS would be able to operate without a crew on board for extended periods of time (e.g. during deep-sea voyages). However, a boarding team and/or pilot would board the ship and take control at certain key points. These situations could include when the ship was coming into port, entering areas where navigation was difficult such as the Suez or Panama canals or the English Channel or where local laws do not permit a ship to operate autonomously. These ships are likely to be treated the same as CUS.

2.4 Continuously unmanned ships ("CUS")

These ships will operate without physical human intervention at all times, except, perhaps, in emergency situations. No members of the crew, if there are any onboard, would be authorised to take control of the bridge. Any members of the crew remaining onboard would be tasked with care of the cargo (such as stockmen), passengers (onboard cruise ships) or maintenance.

The above definitions are for guidance only and there are certain vessels which may fall into a number of categories at certain stages. MASS have an enormous number of potential uses and are currently used in a variety of sectors. These include commercial, scientific and defence/security. This chapter considers maritime law as it applies to the commercial and scientific research sectors; it does not cover MASS engaged in

---

1 Norwegian Forum for Autonomous Ships (NFAS) "Definitions for Autonomous Merchant Ships", Rev 1.0. 2017–10-10 http://nfas.autonomous-ship.org/resources/automon-defs.pdf (last tested on 31 March 2019).

military activities although much of the same regulatory framework will still apply save that, in the UK at least, MASS may be entitled to Crown immunity.

3 The current state of MASS

The use of MASS is still in its infancy and today's MASS are modest in size, with the largest MASS seldom more than 25 metres in length. However, the latest generation of MASS are growing in size and we set out below a number of examples of MASS which are in use and/or development.

The UK Ship Register has registered its first unmanned vessel, "C-WORKER 7" (owned by ASV Global), to the UK flag. The vessel has been described as operating under the direct control of an operator as well as having semi-manned and completely unmanned modes. "C-WORKER 7" will be used for subsea positioning, surveying and environmental monitoring work. Whilst the "C-WORKER 7" is not on the same scale as the projects that are being developed by Yara and Rolls Royce (see below), the significance that the UK Ship Register has permitted the first unmanned vessel to be registered is a welcome development and one which will no doubt assist with the adoption of MASS technology in the marine industry.

In late June 2018, Italian shipbuilder Rosetti Marino teamed up with Purple Water to demonstrate the remote control of the Lloyd's Register-certified 26 metre long, double-ended tugboat, "GIANO". During the demonstration, a number of tug operators from France, Denmark, the Netherlands and Italy trialled remote monitoring and control of this tug. Prior to this demonstration, Rosetti Marino tested the remote control of the "GIANO" over more than 1,000 nautical miles of offshore sailing, manoeuvring it remotely from a shore console.

Robert Allan Ltd and Konsberg Maritime are collaborating to develop a new remotely-operated fireboat. The new design will allow coast guard and salvors to attack fires with minimum risk to the lives of first responders by offering in-close firefighting and "eye in the fire" fire fighting capabilities. Specifically, fires involving hydrocarbons or toxic chemicals can be attacked faster where toxic smoke or risk of explosion would otherwise delay or prevent fire fighting operations.

KOTUG, based in the Netherlands, have also demonstrated the use of a remotely controlled tug. The Tug "RT BORKUM", located in Rotterdam, was controlled from the floor of the International Tug, Salvage and OSV Convention in Marseille (a distance of some 700 miles).[2]

Developed by Kongsberg, the "YARA BIRKELAND" is designed to be the world's first fully electric and autonomous container ship. The vessel is a 120 TEU open top container ship. The concept is to reduce the number of diesel powered truck journeys between 3 ports in southern Norway (Herøya, Brevik and Larvik) by 40,000 journeys per year. A detachable bridge will be fitted and when the vessel is ready to move from manned to fully autonomous operations in 2022 this module is intended to be removed.

---

2 See, https://gcaptain.com/watch-captain-demos-remote-controlled-tugboat-from-700-miles-away/ (last tested on 31 March 2019).

DNV GL has developed an unmanned 60-metre-long, zero emission vessel. According to the company's website,[3] the vessel is designed to help reduce increasing levels of traffic congestion on inland waterways and offers "a solution to the growing need for transport capacity". DNV GL estimate that vessel's increased load capacity and low operating and maintenance costs could result in a saving of USD 34 million over the vessel's 30 year lifetime.

4 Do MASS fall into the legal definition of ships?

The key UK statute governing the maritime sphere is the Merchant Shipping Act 1995 (the "MSA"). The MSA 1995 defines a ship as "every description of vessel used in navigation".[4] While there is a significant body of case law considering whether or not a particular asset is a "ship" or is "used in navigation", no authorities have sought to define "ship" and, to date, there has been no specific case law with respect to MASS.

There is however guidance available from case law where, for example, the courts have taken into consideration what the particular asset looks like and what it does. In the case of *Polpen Shipping Co Ltd* v *Commercial Union Insurance Co Ltd*[5] the Court found that a flying boat was not a ship. However, the Court helpfully stated that a ship "was any hollow structure intended to be used in navigation i.e. intended to do its real work on the seas or other waters, and capable of free and ordered movement thereon from one place to another".

In *Perks* v *Clark and Others* (which decided that a jack-up rig was a ship for the purposes of the Income and Corporation Taxes Act 1988) the Court of Appeal considered all the relevant case law and held that:[6]

> [so] long as "navigation" was a significant part of the function of the structure in question, the mere fact that it was incidental to some more specialised function such as dredging or the provision of accommodation did not take it outside the definition; and "navigation" did not necessarily connote anything more than "movement across water"; the function of conveying persons and cargo from place to place was not an essential characteristic.

Therefore, it is our considered view that (at least in terms of English law) there is no single feature or characteristic which makes a "ship" and each type of MASS must be looked at on its own merits.

There are, however, a number of other potentially relevant sections of the MSA 1995 with respect to MASS. Section 88 of the MSA 1995 was specifically drafted to regulate manned submersibles, inferring that submersibles (both manned and unmanned) were not included in the definition of a ship, although the issue of whether the MSA 1995 applies to MASS is not specifically addressed.

Previously, section 311 of the MSA 1995 recognised potential issues with defining what was meant by "ship" and gave the Secretary of State power to provide that

---

3 Available at: www.dnvgl.com/technology-innovation/revolt/index.html (last tested 31 March 2019).
4 Section 313(1) of the MSA 1995.
5 [1943] KB 161.
6 [2001] EWCA Civ 1228; [2001] 2 Lloyd's Rep 431, at [42], per Carnwath, J.

certain assets designed or adapted for use at sea should be treated as ships; however this has since been repealed and amended by section 112 of the Railways and Transport Safety Act 2003. There is no doubt, however, that these powers could be exercised to apply to merchant shipping legislation if it was deemed necessary to legislate for MASS while a more formal framework was drawn up. However, no such regulations have been made.[7]

Notwithstanding that there is no statutory definition of a "ship" under the MSA, it is our view that a MASS would be considered a "ship" under English law. It should be noted that each State signatory to the various international conventions will incorporate these conventions' articles and their amendments into national law in different ways.

The Dutch Civil Code understands "ships" to be all things "that are not an aircraft, which pursuant to their construction are intended for flotation and which float or have floated".[8] The People's Republic of China defines "ship" as "seagoing ships and other mobile units, but does not include ships or craft to be used for military or public service purposes, nor small ships of less than 20 tons gross tonnage".[9] Whilst German law does not provide a codified definition of the term, the Bundesgerichtshof in 1951 provided a widely cited definition which defines a "ship" as "every ship of more than insignificant size, capable of floating and provided with a hull, the purpose of which is to be moved on water".[10] Norwegian law also uses a vessel's size to determine whether a vessel is a "ship". For a vessel to be recognised as a ship under Norwegian law, it must be at lea*st 15 metres long. We understand that military and research vessels* often fall outside the definition of "ship" as well.[11] *Given that m*any existing MASS are relatively small, these vessels will fall outside the definition of "ship" for the purposes of Norwegian law, as will those MASS which are built for military and/or research purposes.

The US legal system also applies a broad definition of the word "vessel". As per Section 3 of the Rules of Construction Act, the word "vessel" includes every description of watercraft or other artificial contrivance used, or capable of being used, as a means of transportation on water.[12] Applying this definition in the case of *Stewart v. Dutra Construction Co*,[13] the court found that the dredge used in the construction of the Ted Williams Tunnel under Boston Harbor was a vessel.[14] In doing so, the court concluded that the definition was satisfied only when a watercraft was "practically capable of being used" as a means of transportation on water. It therefore seems

---

7 It should be noted that SI. 2005/74, made under section 112 of the Railways and Transport Safety Act 2003, concerns oil rigs and other platforms and not MASS.

8 Article 8.1 Dutch Civil Code.

9 E. Van Hooydonk, "*The Law of Unmanned Merchant Shipping – An Exploration*" (2014) 20 Journal of International Maritime Law at 403–423.

10 1 ZR84/51 (1951) [1952] Neue Juristische Wochenschrift 1135.

11 Definitions of autonomous merchant ships. FOR-1992-07-30-593 "Forskrift om registering av skip i norsk ordinært skipsregister" – §2 "Hva som forstås med skip mv".

12 1 U.S.C. § 3.

13 543 U.S. 481; [2005] AMC 609.

14 D. Robertson and M. Sturley, "Vessel Status in Maritime Law: Does Lozman Set A New Course" (2013) *JMLC* 393.

that, if applied to MASS, this definition would include MASS involved in the carriage of goods. However, the situation remains unclear in relation to other types of MASS, such as firefighting or survey vessels. Interestingly, in *Lozman* v *City of Riviera Beach*,[15] the US Supreme Court had to decide whether a floating home was a "vessel" for the purposes of the Rules of Construction Act. The home was a plywood construction above an empty bilge space, measuring 60ft by 12ft and lacked any means of propulsion. The Supreme Court held that the home would only be a ship if a reasonable observer, looking objectively at the physical characteristics and activities of the structure, would consider it to have been designed for the transportation of things and people on water. This definition would also exclude several of the existing MASS set out above, such as those MASS designed as tugs or firefighting vessels.

The French Code des Transports 2017 (as amended) defines the term "ship" as:

> Except as indicated to the contrary, for the purposes of the present Code ships are any floating craft, built and *manned* for maritime merchant navigation, or for fishing, or for yachting and dedicated to it" (emphasis added).[16]

Articles L.5000–4 and 5522–2 of the French Code des transports, respectively provide as follows:

> A ship is said to be equipped when she is fitted out with the technical, administrative and *human means* necessary for the considered maritime activity.
>
> *Each ship has to be equipped with a sufficient number of seamen* with the professional qualifications necessary to guarantee the safety and security of the ship and of the people on board, and that the obligations of look-out, working hours and rest are respected.

It therefore appears that, in *order* for a craft to be a "ship" for the purposes of French law, the craft must be manned inorder to qualify, although the crew may not necessarily need to be on board. If this is the case, then MASS with a sufficient degree of autonomy would fall outside the existing French regulatory framework. This is important because under French law the owners of ships in France are strictly liable for any damage caused by them.[17] However we understand that the French legislature is discussing a bill which would allow the relevant authorities to authorise drones and/or MASS to navigate in French waters under defined circumstances on the condition that the appropriate risk assessments are submitted to the authority in advance.

5 The interaction between MASS and maritime law

Given that MASS will be treated as "ships" by the English legal system and by the majority of national legal systems as set out above, we must now examine how maritime law, as it currently exists, will interact with the use of MASS. This usage will likely be, at least initially, limited to vessels which are primarily developed for MASS research. However there are already vessels, such as the "YARA

---

15 (2013) 133 S Ct 735; [2013] AMC 1.
16 Art.L.5000–2
17 French Civil Code Art. 1384.

BIRKELAND", which will be used for commercial trading. However this trading will be limited to voyages in national waters and, until the issues we highlight below are rectified, will not be able to take to the high seas.

So, what is maritime law? For the purposes of this chapter, maritime law refers to a range of laws which govern the legal framework surrounding ships and their operation. The definition covers a wide range of legal systems, from international law to local and national rules. It includes both civil law issues (such as compensation and liability for salvage, damage and insurance) and matters relating to public law (for example environmental regulations, health and safety and national security).

Whilst none of the conventions and laws touched on below were written with MASS in mind, some will require little to no modification. Others will require modification to varying degrees. We set out our review of these issues below.

5.1 International conventions

5.1.1 The UN convention of the law of the sea ("UNCLOS")
UNCLOS deals with a broad range of jurisdictional issues and sets out individual states' rights and obligations in respect of the sea. The key issues that UNCLOS deals with are as follows: the right to navigate different areas of the sea, a state's obligations regarding ships flying their flag and the rights that other states have to interfere with the navigation and operation of ships flying other states' flags. UNCLOS also sets out the rules for establishing and delimiting maritime zones and provides detailed rules for each zone with respect of states' rights and obligations.

The terms "ships" and "vessels" are used interchangeably in UNCLOS however neither term is explicitly defined. However, UNCLOS provides that each state shall fix the conditions for the grant of its nationality to ships (Article 91). The implication therefore is that the national laws of each flag state will be critical for the definitions used. As set out above, we consider that, at least with regards to English law, MASS would be considered to be ships. If MASS are to be considered to fall within the definition of ship for the purposes of UNCLOS, then a number of issues arise. We consider them to be as follows.

Broadly, whilst a flag state's jurisdiction applies regardless of a vessel's location, other coastal states' parallel jurisdiction over a vessel increases as the vessel approaches that coastal state. For example, if a foreign-flagged ship is present in a coastal state's ports or internal waters, then that state has broad jurisdiction over that ship. Under Article 2, internal waters form part of the sovereignty of the state. Further, there is no general right for a foreign-flagged vessel to enter a port and UNCLOS provides a wide discretion as to the conditions of entry for foreign ships (Articles 25(2), 211(3) and 255). Therefore a coastal state may refuse a foreign-flagged MASS entry to its ports or internal waters, subject to a general test of reasonableness (based on non-discrimination, proportionality and that the prohibition does not amount to the abuse of a right). This may have significant consequences for the freedom of movement of MASS. For example, currently it is common in certain jurisdictions, such as India, for vessels performing cabotage voyages to be Indian flagged and crewed by Indian nationals. It is possible that these restrictions will remain following the use of MASS in international trade in order to ensure that there is a sustainable source of jobs.

At Article 94(4)(b), UNCLOS requires that flag states ensure

> that each ship is in the charge of a master and officers who possess appropriate qualifications, in particular in seamanship, navigation, communications and marine engineering, and that the crew is appropriate in qualification and numbers for the type, size, machinery and equipment of the ship.

Whether or not a MASS will be able to comply with this provision is dependent on the MASS' degree of autonomy. Whilst it may be met if the MASS is remotely operated or has a PUB, it may be more difficult for a fully automated MASS which fall into the PUS and CUS categories to meet this obligation. This situation is further complicated by the fact that the degree of automation of a MASS may vary depending on locations, the amount of sea-traffic and local regulations.

Further, flag states are under a duty to require that the master of a ship flying its flag "render assistance to any person found at sea in danger of being lost" (Article 98(1)). As set out above, it is arguable that, in certain circumstances and depending on the degree of autonomy exhibited by the MASS, that the MASS has no master. Whilst a MASS may be able to assist by relaying radio communications, it is unclear how a MASS would be able to render physical assistance to a person in danger without a crew onboard. However, the duty to provide assistance is a qualified one. A master is only required to render assistance "in so far as he can do so without serious danger to the ship, the crew or the passengers" (Article 98(1)) and *"in so far as such action may reasonably be expected of him"* (Article 98(1)(b)). Some commentators have argued that, there is no "quid pro quo with other *sea-users* in this respect"[18] as, since there will be no obligation on coastal states or other vessels to render assistance to MASS due to the fact that there will be no lives onboard, then there would be no obligation on a MASS to provide assistance beyond alerting other manned vessels or the relevant search and rescue authorities.

5.1.2 The limitation of liability for maritime claims ("LLMC")

This is a critical area for those owning and operating ships and is a cornerstone of maritime law. By extension, this ought to include MASS. However, in the unlikely event that the definition of a "ship" does not extend to MASS, then the owners and operators of MASS will have to look to other ways of limiting their liability.

Limited liability, or "one ship" owning, companies have traditionally been used to ensure that any liability accrued by a company is limited to the value of its assets or capital. However, this traditional model will not fit all situations. For example, companies entering into a contract with another company that has limited resources (e.g. companies established by universities for scientific development) will want to ensure that the company of limited resources has sufficient security to cover potential

---

18 R. Veal and M. Tsimplis, "The Integration of Unmanned Ships into the Lex Maritima' (2017) *LMCLQ* 303 at 330.

liabilities, such as some form of external guarantee or liability insurance. In addition, there are some circumstances where officers of a limited liability company can be held liable in their own right for acts or omissions of the company, which makes limiting liability against the world desirable for MASS operators, where possible.

There are a number of conventions on the limitation of liability for Maritime Claims. These include the 1957 Brussels International Convention relating to the Limitation of the Liability of Owners of Sea-going Ships (the "1957 Brussels Convention") and the Convention on Limitation of Liability for Maritime Claims 1976 ("LLMC"). The UK has enacted the LLMC 1976, the 1996 Protocol and the Amendments to the 1996 Protcol (which increased the limits of liability under the LLMC), which are incorporated into English law by section 185(1) of the MSA 1995. However, some states still apply the 1957 Brussels Convention which has lower limits, and a number of other states that have enacted the LLMC 1976 have not yet implemented the higher limits of the 1996 Protocol or the Amendments thereto.

The LLMC grants owners, charterers, managers or operators of "ships" the right to limit their liability by reference to the registered tonnage of the vessel, for loss or damage following a collision or other casualty. The LLMC does not contain a separate definition of "ship" (although it refers to the requirement for the vessel to be "used in navigation"). It would therefore be a matter of interpretation of English law as to whether a MASS would be considered a "ship" under the LLMC. However, as a MASS is likely to be considered as a "ship" for the purposes of the MSA 1995, it seems that they would also be treated as "ships" for the purposes of the LLMC.

The limits of liability pursuant to the Amendments to the 1996 Protocol applicable under English law are as follows:

(a) in respect of claims for loss of life or personal injury,
  (i) 3.02 million Units of Account for a ship with a tonnage not exceeding 2,000 tons
...
(b) in respect of any other claims,
  (i) 1.51 million Units of Account for a ship with a tonnage not exceeding 2,000 tons

"Units of Account" refer to Special Drawing Rights ("SDRs") which are published daily on the International Monetary Fund's website.[19]

The right to limit enables the shipowner (or other party with a right to limit) to obtain a limitation decree or constitute a limitation fund (which may or may not have to be paid into court) against which claimants may enforce their claims, if liability is so established. The amount of the fund/limitation decree is determined by the above calculation. A claimant cannot recover more than the amount in the limitation fund and will receive a pro-rata share of their proven claim if the total amount of claims exceeds the fund. A ship owners' right to limit can only be "broken" in exceptional circumstances.[20]

---

19 International Monetary Fund (online) available at: www.imf.org/external/np/fin/data/rms_sdrv.aspx (last tested on 31 March 2019).

20 The Article 4 of the LLMC, as amended, provides as follows: "A person liable shall not be entitled to limit his liability if it is proved that the loss resulted from his personal act or omission, committed with the intent to cause such loss, or recklessly and with knowledge that such loss would probably result".

By enabling ships (and by extension MASS) to limit their liability, the effect of the LLMC is to allow insurers to offer lower rates of premium to shipowners than would otherwise be available, as the insurer is effectively able to take the benefit of the limits on behalf of the assured.

5.1.3 The international regulations for averting collisions at sea 1972 ("COLREGS")

For non-contractual liabilities, the most common basis for bringing a claim under English law is under the tort of negligence. However, even this is not clear cut. Although it is likely that the English courts will measure the standard of care required of MASS operators and owners to the same standards as set out in the COLREGS – particularly if they are being used "as a means of transportation on water" – these rules were written with conventional ships in mind. Thus, while AI technology currently exists to allow MASS to comply with the manoeuvring rules, there are still a number of rules which MASS may be unable to strictly comply with.

For example, Rule 2 governs the responsibility of vessels, owners, masters and crew. Part (a) of the rule sets out that nothing shall exonerate the former for the consequences of neglecting to comply with the rules that "may be required by the ordinary practice of seamen", which indicates the requirement for real-time human judgement. Rule 2(b) goes on to say that "due regard shall be had to all dangers of navigation and collision and to any special circumstances, including the limitations of the vessels involved, which may make a departure from these rules necessary to avoid immediate danger". It is questionable whether a MASS operating on AI alone would be able to comply with this Rule, although arguably a shore-based controller with suitable bridge experience may be able to fulfil this role. However, this raises questions as to whether a MASS in these circumstances could be considered to be truly autonomous.

Rule 5 of the COLREGS requires every vessel at all times to "maintain a proper look-out by *sight and hearing* as well as by all available means appropriate in the prevailing circumstances and conditions so as to make a full appraisal of the situation and of the risk of collision" (emphasis added). This rule suggests that look-out must be maintained by seamen. It is questionable how a MASS, especially one controlled by AI, would be able to strictly comply with the requirements regarding sight and hearing, and other rules such as safe speed (Rule 6). Consideration will have to be given as to whether the use of cameras and microphones onboard the MASS can be considered a proper means of maintaining a look out for the purposes of this Rule.

In *The Atlantik Confidence* [2016] EWHC 2412 (Admlty); [2016] 2 Lloyd's Rep 525 cargo insurers sought to "break limits" by defending an application by the owners of the vessel to constitute a limitation fund pursuant to the LLMC and obtain a declaration that they were entitled to limit their liability. They successfully argued that the loss of the vessel along with her cargo was caused by the "personal act or omission" of the owners. In his judgement, Teare J concluded that the vessel's sinking was a deliberate scuttling.

Rules 7 and 8 of the COLREGS deal with risk of collision and action to avoid a collision. While trials have demonstrated that MASS can successfully avoid collisions, strict compliance with Rule 8 is likely to be more difficult. Rule 8 requires that any action to avoid collision shall "be positive, made in ample time and with due regard to the observance of good seamanship". Again, as with the other rules analysed above, elements of this rule are subjective and it is questionable whether a MASS operating in autonomous mode would be able to strictly comply with the "observance of good seamanship" part of this Rule, particularly in areas of high traffic density where action to avoid collision with one vessel may lead to risk of collision with another.

MASS are still a relatively new concept, and as yet there is no case law testing the ability of a MASS to comply with the COLREGS. Undoubtedly the issues will eventually be overcome from a technological perspective and research in developing collision avoidance algorithms is already well underway.[21] However, perhaps the greatest obstacle that developers face is enabling AI machines to learn "seamanship" behavioural characteristics that will enable a MASS to interact in a way that is predictable to both manned and un-manned ships, as well as programming "any special circumstances" to enable the MASS to meet its responsibilities under Rule 2 and "make a departure from these rules necessary to avoid immediate danger".[22]

Should there be a requirement for intervention from a shore based controller; another issue which arises is how the streaming of real-time data from a MASS to the shore base is going to be achieved. The data link between the MASS and the shore based control facility would need to be fast enough to allow an operator to make a full appraisal of a situation so he may take appropriate action under the COLREGS. Putting aside the issues of cyber security, the lack of satellite coverage in some areas of the world raises questions as to whether a ship can be fully autonomous for a trans-ocean voyage.

For MASS to operate effectively they will require collision avoidance systems that are compliant with the COLREGS. Whilst a number of companies have developed effective collision avoidance systems, as pointed out above, full compliance with the COLREGS is difficult because this requires real time human judgement to consider making a departure from the Rules necessary to avoid immediate danger.

Nevertheless, some companies, such as ASV Global have demonstrated collision avoidance systems that can operate on autonomous test beds in complex waters in compliance with the manoeuvring rules of the COLREGS.[23] These collision avoidance systems generally use a combination of sensors such as fused AIS, LIDAR (Light Detection and Ranging), Infrared Cameras and radar to support the detection of

---

21 See, for example, the MAchine eXecutable Collision regulations for Marine Autonomous Systems research project (**MAXCMAS**).

22 For example, taking appropriate action when another (manned) ship is not complying with the COLREGS.

23 See for example ASV Global's video titled Autonomous Collision Avoidance and Situational Awareness (www.youtube.com/watch?v=J9YNGyhYszU).

objects. While the detection of vessels is straightforward, automatically classifying vessels to act in accordance with the COLREGS can be challenging, particularly in respect of small vessels not using AIS. One of the benefits of these collision avoidance systems is their potential to be integrated with existing systems on conventional ships to assist bridge awareness. Shipowners will be keen to investigate the possibility of having both a human watch keeper and an autonomous collision avoidance system if it means potentially reducing the number of accidents and therefore insurance premiums.

5.1.4 The convention on standards of certification, training and watch keeping ("STCW convention")

The STCW Convention sets out the qualification standards for masters, officers and watch keeping personnel onboard ships. Article III of the STCW Convention expressly applies to "seafarers serving on board seagoing ships entitled to fly the flag of a Party". Difficulties could arise with respect to the STCW Conventions' watch keeping requirements as set out in Chapter 8 (Standards Regarding Watchkeeping). At part 4, paragraph 10 this chapter states "when deciding the composition of the watch on the bridge ... the following factors, inter alia, shall be taken into account: ... at no time shall the bridge be left unattended". This clearly presents issues for MASS. Further, at paragraph 24 the officer of the watch is required to "keep the watch on the bridge" and "in no circumstances leave the bridge until properly relieved".

Prima facie, the STCW Convention will not apply to MASS. The rise of MASS will result in a completely different set of roles relating to the navigation of a MASS at sea. These will include shore-based controllers and programmers who currently lack a formal qualification regime. If MASS are to receive wide-spread acceptance, it is likely that these individuals will require a similar qualification regime to that set out in the STCW Convention. As set above, Rule 2 of the COLREGS governs the responsibility of vessels, owners, masters and crew and requires that a ship must be able to conform to the requirement for good seamanship. In order to be able to discharge this duty, shore-based operators will, therefore, have to be suitably qualified in maritime navigation and be suitably technically trained to be able to work with the IT and operational technologies which increasingly form part of modern vessels' navigation systems.

5.1.5 Safety of life at sea convention 1974/1978/1988 ("SOLAS")

SOLAS sets out a specific list of categories of ships to which it applies as follows: passenger ships, cargo ships (defined as ships which are not passenger ships), tankers, fishing vessels and nuclear ships. Where a MASS falls within these categories of ship, SOLAS will apply. SOLAS is incorporated into English law by sections 85 and 86 of the MSA 1995. There are a number of regulations under these sections.

According to the IMO, the main objective of SOLAS is to specify minimum standards for the construction, equipment and operation of ships, compatible with their safety and applies to "ships entitled to fly the flag of State of Governments of which are contracting Governments". The objectives and minimum standards are codified into main articles specifying general obligations of contracting states and twelve chapters setting out different safety and technical requirements.

Under SOLAS, contracting flag States, which account for approximately 98% of all merchant ships, are responsible for ensuring that ships under their flag comply with the aforementioned requirements. This is achieved through a number of certifications, further enforced by port state authorities of other contracting states which, under SOLAS, retain the right to conduct inspections where there are clear grounds for believing that a ship and its equipment do not comply with the technical and safety provisions set out in the convention. A limited number of exceptions apply to SOLAS, for example, cargo ships of less than 500 gross tonnes and ships not propelled by mechanical means. Therefore, whilst the current generation of MASS may be exempt from SOLAS, it is likely that MASS built for commercial purposes will have to comply with the convention.

5.1.6 ISM code

The ISM Code is incorporated into English law by way of the Merchant Shipping (International Safety Management (ISM) Code) Regulations 2014/1512 made under section 85 of the MSA 1995. Regulations 2014/1512 apply to:

(a) "United Kingdom ships wherever they may be; and
(b) Other ships while they are within United Kingdom waters".

The Regulations state that a "ship" includes "a hovercraft, a mobile offshore drilling unit, a passenger submersible craft and a high speed craft". MASS are not specifically mentioned in the types of ships listed. However, where a MASS has been signed to the UK Ship Register, such as "C-WORKER 7" then arguably the ISM Code will apply to it. The IMO has stated that the purpose of the ISM Code "is to provide an international standard for the safe management and operation of ships and for pollution prevention". To this effect, the person assuming responsibility for operating the ship is required to establish a safety management system. One of the key parts of operating a safety management system is provision of shore based support with direct access to the highest level of management.

5.1.7 ISPS code

The International Ship and Port Facility Security (ISPS) Code was created in response to the terror attacks in New York on 11 September 2001. This new security regime for the maritime sector was added to SOLAS at chapter XI-2 and came into force in December 2002. The ISPS Code requires all ships to be equipped with a ship security alert system, to provide information to the IMO and to be in full control in port. This includes dealing with circumstances such as delay, detention and restrictions on operations, such as moving within, or expulsion from, a port. In order to be able to comply with these requirements, shipping companies "are required, under the ISPS Code, to designate appropriate officers and personnel, on each ship". These individuals are known as Company Security Officers ("CSO"). The CSO's role is to assess, prepare and implement effective security plans that are able to manage any potential security risk. This obligation presents an obstacle with a sufficiently high level of autonomy and it is unlikely that a shore based controller will be able to satisfy the requirements of the ISPS Code. However, Regulation XI-2/12 permits a flag state administration to allow equivalent security measures for particular ships or types of ships, provided that these measures are at least as effective as those prescribed in the ISPS Code. Provided that a MASS owner could implement these equivalent security measures, there is no reason why the ISPS Code should prevent the widespread adoption of MASS.

5.1.8 Load lines convention 1966 ("LLC") as amended 1971, 1975, 1979, 1983, 1988, 1995 and 2003

The LLC is incorporated into English law by the Merchant Shipping (Load Line) Regulations 1998/2241 made under sections 85 and 86 of the MSA 1995. The LLC places limitations on the draft to which a ship may be loaded with the purpose of ensuring her safety. These limits are given in the form of freeboards which, aside from external weathertight and watertight integrity, constitute the main objective of the LLC. The LLC applies to ships engaged on international voyages but specifically excludes ships of less than 150 gross tonnes and less than 24 metres in length. Therefore the LLC will apply to MASS of a sufficient size and engaged on international voyages.

5.1.9 Tonnage measurement convention 1969 ("TMC")

The TMC is incorporated into English law by the Merchant Shipping (Tonnage) Regulations 1997/1510 under section 19 of the MSA 1995. The TMC standardised and introduced a universal tonnage measurement system and applies to "ships engaged in international voyages". Article 4 provides that it does not apply to ships of less than 24 metres in length. Potentially, MASS could be subject to the TMC when employed on international voyages and if over 24 metres in length.

5.1.10 International convention for the prevention of pollution from ships 1973/1978 ("MARPOL")

MARPOL is incorporated into English law by section 128 of the MSA 1995, Merchant Shipping (Prevention and Control of Pollution) Order 1987/470 and the Merchant Shipping (Prevention of Pollution by Sewage and Garbage) Order 2006/2950. Following a series of tanker accidents, MARPOL was developed to offer a standardised framework for prevention and minimisation of pollution, whether arising in the course of routine operations or due to an accident. The convention addresses a range of specific and general pollution risks such as pollution by oil, sewage from ships or more broadly "harmful substances". MARPOL is stated to apply to "ships entitled to fly the flag" of a state party and, in our view, as a matter of English law some MASS will need to be flagged. MARPOL is therefore likely to apply to MASS.

5.1.11 The convention on the prevention of marine pollution by dumping of wastes and other matter 1972/1996 ("LDC")

The LDC is incorporated into English law by section 12 of the Food and Environmental Protection Act 1985 ("FEPA 1985"). FEPA 1985 sets out a requirement to obtain a licence from the Foods Standards Agency before dumping at sea. The LDC deals with the dumping of certain hazardous materials. Dumping is defined as "the deliberate disposal at sea of wastes or other matters from vessels, aircraft, platforms or other man-made structures". Vessels include "waterborne craft of any type whatsoever ... whether self propelled or not". Unless a MASS is going to be engaged in dumping material, the LDC and FEPA 1985 are unlikely to have an impact on a MASS. However, those MASS engaged in dumping material will be required to comply with FEPA 1985.

5.1.12 The convention for the protection of the marine environment of the north east Atlantic 1992 ("OSPAR")

OSPAR applies to the disposal of waste from vessels within the internal waters and territorial sea of the contracting states (including Belgium, Denmark, Finland, France, Germany, Iceland, Ireland, the Netherlands, Norway, Portugal, Spain, Sweden, the United Kingdom, Luxembourg and Switzerland, together with the European Union). The definition of vessels to which this convention applies includes waterborne craft of any type including "other man-made structures in the maritime area" which would extend to MASS.

5.1.13 Memorandum of understanding on port state control 1982 ("Paris MOU")

On the assumption that instruments to which the Paris MOU is related (SOLAS, MARPOL, STCW, COLREGS and the TMC 1969) are found to apply to MASS then the Paris MOU will apply to their enforcement.

5.1.14 Suppressions of unlawful acts convention 1988 ("SUAC")

SUAC provides a framework for prosecution of individuals using ships and as a means for unlawful acts. It is largely based on previous conventions tackling terrorism and applies to ships engaged on international voyages. Any unlawful acts committed within a state's territory are subject to national law only. Article 1 of the 2005 Protocol to this convention defines a "ship" as a "vessel of any type whatsoever not permanently attached to the sea-bed, including dynamically supported craft, submersibles, or any other floating craft". In our view this definition is wide enough to apply to MASS and covers acts said to jeopardise the safety of persons and property.

5.1.15 Intervention convention 1969/1973

The Intervention Convention 1969/1973 is incorporated into English law by section 108A of the MSA 1995. It provides for the intervention by states in oil spills resulting from marine casualties (e.g. collisions and/or grounding). The convention applies to "any seagoing vessel of any type whatsoever" (except warships) and is wide enough to cover MASS.

5.1.16 International convention on civil liability for oil pollution damage 1992 ("CLC") and fund convention

The CLC is incorporated into English law by sections 171 and 182 of the MSA 1995. Subject to limited exceptions, the CLC makes the ship owner strictly liable for any damage caused by oil pollution within the territory and the exclusive economic zone of the contracting state. The CLC defines a "ship" as "any sea-going vessels and sea-borne craft of any kind whatsoever constructed or adapted for the carriage of oil in bulk as cargo". The CLC requires a ship owner to maintain insurance or some other form of financial guarantee in respect of its potential liability, albeit this requirement is made with reference to ships registered in any other contracting state. The CLC has been signed by 134 states, covering 86% of the world's tonnage. These conventions would only apply to MASS that are constructed or adapted for the carriage of oil in bulk as cargo.

5.1.17 International convention on liability and compensation for damage in connection with the carriage of hazardous and noxious substances by sea 1996 ("HNS convention")

The definition of "ship" to which the HNS Convention applies includes "seaborne craft, of any type whatsoever", which would cover MASS. However, the convention only applies to pollution from "hazardous and noxious substances" which are "any substances, materials and articles on board a ship as cargo". Therefore unless a MASS is constructed or adapted to carry such hazardous substances as cargo, the HNS Convention is unlikely to apply.

5.1.18 International convention on civil liability for bunker oil pollution damage 2001 ("bunker convention")

The Bunker Convention entered into force on 21 November 2008 in the Merchant Shipping (Oil Pollution) (Bunkers Convention) Regulations 2006/1244 and is largely based on the CLC. It creates a compensation mechanism for persons who suffer damage as a result of pollution caused by the escape or discharge of bunker oil. The Bunker Convention defines a "ship" as "any seagoing vessel or seaborne craft, of any type whatsoever". The Bunker Convention will therefore apply to all MASS unless they use an electromechanical power source as a means of propulsion and do not carry bunker oil.

5.1.19 The Nairobi wreck removal convention 2007

The Nairobi Convention is incorporated into English law under Part IXA of the MSA 1995. It provides a legal framework regulating liability, compensation and compulsory insurance for removal of shipwrecks within exclusive economic zones. It places liability for removal on the registered owner of a ship and enables states to undertake the operation and recover any associated costs (including direct action against insurers) should the registered owners fail to engage. The Nairobi Convention defines a "ship" as "a seagoing vessel of any type whatsoever operating in the marine environment and includes ... submersibles". "Wreck" is defined as "a sunken or stranded ship, or any part thereof, including anything that is or has been on board such a ship". The Nairobi Convention will apply to MASS. However, for smaller MASS it is more likely practically that salvage would be relevant to a "wrecked" MASS.

5.1.20 Collision convention 1910
The Collision Convention applies to collisions between "sea-going vessels or between sea-going vessels and vessels capable of inland navigation", and assumes that there will be a master onboard the vessel. The convention sets out a two year time bar for claims resulting from collisions. It seems unlikely that the convention will apply to MASS which fall into the categories of PUS and CUS if they were involved in, for example, a collision with a ship. Practically, this means that national rules on the apportionment of liability and limitation would apply; under English law limitation this would be six years from the date of the tort causing the collision. However to avoid time bar arguments it would be prudent to observe the two year limit.

5.1.21 Salvage convention 1989
This convention is incorporated into English law by section 224(1) of the MSA 1995. So far, 69 states have signed up to the convention. The convention applies to any salvage operations subject to judicial or arbitral proceedings in a signatory state. A salvage operation means any act or activity undertaken to assist "a vessel or any other property in danger". The convention lays out a clear mechanism for the assessment of a salvage award. Under this convention, "vessel" is defined as "any ship or craft, or any structure capable of navigation". This would be broad enough to cover MASS so long as they are found to be "capable of navigation", i.e. the conveyance by water of people or property.[24]

5.1.22 Ship registration convention 1986 and UK ship register
Article 2 of the convention defines "ship" to mean "any self propelled sea-going vessel used in international seaborne trade for the transport of goods, passengers, or both with the exception of vessels of less than 500 gross registered tonnes". While MASS are likely to be considered vessels, the convention appears to only apply to MASS of 500 gross tonnes or more that carry passengers or goods (i.e. from one port to another). The carriage of scientific equipment for research or fire fighting equipment would not be considered as trade. However a MASS has already been registered in the

---

24 *Merchants' Marine Ins. Co.* V *North of England P&I Ass* (1926) 26 LlL Rep 201.

UK, although this might have been limited and dependent upon the individual characteristics of the "C-WORKER 7". The UK Ship Register will also register small commercial vessels under 100 gross tonnes and less than 24 metres long.

5.1.22 The international convention relating to the arrest of seagoing ships 1952 (the "arrest convention")

While the Arrest Convention does not define "ship", it is clear from the title and preamble that it applies to seagoing ships, and is likely to apply to those MASS which call from port to port in the same manner as a conventional ship. Those MASS which do not call from port to port may however be subject to some other civil seizure under national law for creditors seeking to enforce their claims.

5.1.23 Maritime liens and mortgages conventions 1926/1967/1993

At the present time, these conventions are unlikely to apply to MASS. This is because their aim is to give certain rights to financiers and other maritime creditors in the event of insolvency, and to give a certain priority to mortgages registered in the state of a ship's registry (i.e. flagged vessels). The conventions may become applicable in the future when the construction of larger MASS is financed by providing security over the MASS through a mortgage.

5.2 Other legal issues

5.2.1 Civil law – non-contractual liabilities

There are various legal bases of non-contractual liability for damage to property and/or persons involving MASS: the tort of negligence, strict liability regimes (such as that under the Harbours Docks and Piers Clauses Act 1847) and salvage claims.

The most common tort is the tort of negligence. In order for a claim to succeed under English law, it must satisfy: (a) that a duty of care was owed to a party to avoid physical damage; (b) that the duty of care was breached causing recoverable loss; (c) that the defendant's careless conduct was causative of the loss; and (d) the loss was not unforeseeable as to be too remote. On this basis, under common law a MASS operator would owe a duty of care to shipowners and crews of their ships that could reasonably be foreseen as suffering physical damage by its negligence, e.g. by causing a MASS to collide with another ship. In this example the standard of care required would be that of a reasonable prudent MASS owner or operator. In the absence of applicable national or international standards, the English courts would likely give weight to industry codes of practice such as the MASRWG Voluntary Code of Practice.[25]

---

[25] Originally launched in November 2017, an updated version of the Code of Practice was released on 2 November 2918. Maritime UK, (2018) (online). Available online at: www.maritimeuk.org/documents/305/MUK_COP_2018_V2_B8rlgDb.pdf (last tested on 31 March 2019).

5.2.2 Civil law – non-contractual liabilities

MASS operators could enter into a vast range of contracts, such as contracts for the carriage of goods. It is not possible to examine all contracts here, and each type of contract will have its own express clauses dealing with the allocation of risk. For example, MASS operators may have entered into a service contract with another party in which the usual rules of contract would apply for the law applicable to that contract. As with a number of oil and gas contracts, for example, a service contract for a MASS may have indemnity clauses whereby each contracting party will agree to assume responsibility for its own property. These are commonly known as "hold harmless" or "knock for knock" provisions.

Operators of merchant MASS may, in the future, charter their MASS; for example by entering into a time charter with another company for that MASS. There are numerous types of standard charter party forms available depending on the needs of the MASS operations. Where a contract has been breached the usual remedy is damages, which are generally calculated so as to place the innocent party in the position it would have been in if the contract had been properly performed. Key to any contract is the choice of law and jurisdiction clause. Some contracts, such as charter parties, have arbitration clauses. Generally the parties are free to choose the law applicable to their contract, and English law and jurisdiction are commonplace in maritime contracts.

5.2.3 MASS and salvage

Incidents leading to insurance claims in which a MASS has caused damage to third party property or injury to persons would hopefully be rare. Usual salvage case law is likely to apply to MASS and the MASRWG Voluntary Code of Practice provides that "[e]xisting maritime salvage case law as it applies to manned ships is deemed to apply to MASS. MASS owners will also make use of the existing standard salvage contracts such as Lloyd's Open Form (LOF)".

5.2.4 MASS and insurance coverage

Under English law, section 192A of the MSA 1995 gives the Secretary of State power to make regulations requiring that there must be a contract of insurance in place for a ship while that ship is in UK waters. There are no regulations or international conventions which require a MASS to carry insurance cover. However, Lloyd's Emerging Risks and Research division has looked into the risks for autonomous vehicles and recognises the issues in determining liability in the event of an incident, which will have an effect on the pricing and structure of risk transfer.

Any insurance should cover property damage (damage to the MASS) and liability cover. The International Group of P&I Clubs (the "IG") has formed a working group on MASS. The IG working group is expected to consider the extent that MASS present new risks to the shipping industry, and whether those risks are poolable. The IG's support for MASS will add substantial confidence to the industry.

The use of MASS in commercial trade will affect the risk profile faced by shipowners. The Shipowners' Club, who are the first IG Club to have published a policy, have reported that roughly 47% of claims involve human error to some degree.[26] In addition Allianz Global Corporate & Specialty, in their Safety and Shipping Review 2018 estimate that human error has cost $1.6 billion in losses in five years.[27] Removing a number of the key factors which contribute to human error (such as shift work, difficult sea conditions, fatigue and so on) should result in a reduction in navigational and other operational claims for MASS. As of December 2017, Shipowners' Club handles over 850 claims per year relating to crew (including injury, death and repatriation). These claims represent 34% of the claims expenditure paid out by the club. Further, in parallel to the development of MASS, there is a move to more environmentally friendly methods of propulsion, including the use of electric motors. These changes result in lower risks of environmental damage as there will be no bunker fuel onboard. However, the use of MASS in maritime trade comes with its own risks. For example, the risk of piracy may be greater, as a cyber attack may result in MASS owners being unable to manually override an attacker's actions.

As the uptake of MASS grows, there will inevitably be significantly more data transferred to facilitate their operation. This in turn will, potentially, increase the risk of a cyber event which could put at risk the safety of the vessel, its cargo and the environment. One of the most heavily relied upon navigational aids is GPS. However, GPS signals are vulnerable to "spoofing", a process whereby GPS information is falsified. In 2017, several spoofing attacks took place in the Black Sea, which resulted in a number of vessels reporting that their navigational equipment displayed their position to be a significant distance away from their actual positions – often in implausible locations, such as airports. While these attacks are unlikely to adversely impact manned vessels which can use secondary navigational methods such as plotting visual bearings and radar ranges on ECDIS or paper charts, MASS might be more vulnerable to these sorts of attacks.

In order to counter the increased risk of cyber events, cyber resilience must therefore go hand-in-hand with autonomy. In particular, BIMCO's Guidelines on Cyber Security Onboard Ships identifies ship to shore interfaces, such as engine performance monitoring, cargo, crane and pump management and voyage performance monitoring, as a source of potential vulnerabilities for all ships. Remote access to MASS must therefore be taken into consideration as an important part of assessing the risks of a cyber event.

6 Potential reform of maritime law in light of the issues presented by MASS

As set out above, MASS are considered differently, in certain respects, to conventional surface vessels and as such, the regulatory framework covering the use of

---

26 Shipowners' Club (2017) [online] Available at: www.shipownersclub.com/pi-cover-autonomous-vessels/ (last tested on 31 March 2019).

27 Allianz (2018) [online] Available at: www.agcs.allianz.com/insights/white-papers-and-case-studies/safety-and-shipping-review-2018/ (last tested on 31 March 2019).

MASS will require development. Currently, there are no specific regulations or international conventions relating to MASS. In June 2017 the Maritime Safety Committee ("MSC") of the IMO, agreed to undertake a regulatory scoping exercise to identify the extent to which MASS can fit within the existing regulatory framework. Initially, the scoping exercise identified current provisions in an agreed list of IMO instruments and assessed how they may or may not be applicable to ships with varying degrees of autonomy and/or whether they may preclude MASS operations. The agreed list of IMO instruments included those covering safety (SOLAS); collision regulations (COLREGS); loading and stability (Load Lines); training of seafarers and fishermen (STCW, STCW-F); search and rescue (SAR); tonnage measurement (Tonnage Convention); and special trade passenger ship instruments (SPACE STP, STP).

Once this preliminary stage is complete, an analysis will be conducted to determine the most appropriate way of addressing MASS operations, taking into account, *inter alia*, the human element, technology and operational factors.[28] The scoping paper was submitted at the 98th session of the MSC by Denmark, Estonia, Finland, Japan, the Netherlands, Norway, South Korea, the UK and the USA. The MSC met for its 99th session in May 2018 and established a correspondence group on MASS to test the framework of the regulatory scoping exercise and, in particular, its methodology. This group reported back on its preliminary findings at the 100th session held in December 2018.

The scoping exercise is likely to require two sessions of the MSC and is expected to run until June 2020. Once it is complete, and subject to the agreement of the IMO countries, work is likely to begin on revising regulations. The organisations behind the scoping paper are hopeful that a regulatory framework incorporating MASS will be in place by 2028. Conventional shipping will not disappear within the foreseeable future and it is understood that the IMO's intention is for the existing international framework to remain intact. If conventional vessels and MASS are to successfully co-exist and share the same waters then a number of hurdles will have to be overcome. These issues include liability issues, cyber security, maintenance and operation.

In 2015, the Comité Maritime International also set up the International Working Group for Maritime Law and Unmanned Craft ("IWG"). The purpose of the IWG was to identify the legal issues surrounding the use of MASS at sea and to provide an international legal perspective to the issues involved.[29] The CMI reported to the 98th session of the MSC, referred to above.

In March 2017, the IWG published a position paper identifying the particular sections of UNCLOS and other IMO regulations which may require amendment if MASS are to be able to comply with the wider law of the sea. The IWG also circulated a questionnaire to the National Associations of the CMI. The questionnaire

---

28 International Maritime Organisation (2018) [online]. Available at: www.imo.org/en/MediaCentre/PressBriefings/Pages/08-MSC-99-MASS-scoping.aspx (last tested on 31 March 2019).

29 Comite Maritime International (2017) [online]. Available at: http://comitemaritime.org/work/unmanned-ships/(last tested on 31 March 2019).

posed a number of questions regarding national laws and UNCLOS. These included whether MASS would constitute a ship under national law and whether MASS could be registered with the relevant flag state as well as questions regarding civil liability, the STCW Convention and the COLREGS.[30]

By 23 April 2018, the IWG had received 20 responses to the questionnaire and a summary of the various answers were submitted to the 99th session of the MSC. Separately, the IWG has also performed an analysis of the various IMO legal instruments and identified those sections which might need clarification in order to accommodate MASS in international waters. Whilst there are more than 50 IMO instruments which will need to be reviewed, the IWG has selected the most relevant instruments (i.e. those which directly relate to MASS) and will, initially, focus on these. Specifically, the IWG will focus on those instruments which govern the conduct of a master and crew whilst others, such as the liability conventions, will be reviewed later. The instruments that will be analysed by the IWG during the initial stage are as follows:

- International Convention for the Safety of Life at Sea;
- The International Convention for the Prevention of Pollution from Ships;
- The COLREGS;
- The STCW;
- The Facilitation of Maritime Traffic Convention;
- The International Convention on Maritime Search and Rescue;
- The Convention for the Suppression of Unlawful Acts against the Safety of Maritime Navigation; and
- The International Convention on Salvage.

In advance of the 99th session of MSC, the IWG also conducted an initial review of the LLMC, CLC, Bunker Pollution, Nairobi and Athens Conventions. In their current form, these conventions require little, if any, modification. *Prima facie*, the strict liability prescribed to the relevant shipowner, supplemented with limitation of liability and compulsory insurance requirements can function in the context of MASS. However, there may be issues for completely autonomous operations in respect of the standards of recklessness and intent and the liable person. The issue of whether a separate liability regime is required is a political one.

MASRWG was formed in August 2014 under the auspices of the UK Marine Industries Alliance to, amongst other things, formulate a regulatory framework for MASS that could be adopted by the UK and other states as well as the international bodies charged with the responsibility to regulate the marine and maritime world. During its third annual conference in November 2017 MASRWG launched a Voluntary Code of Practice (the "Code"). The aim of the Code, which has been reviewed by the UK Maritime and Coastguard Agency (MCA), is to "set initial standards and best practice for those who design, build, manufacture, own, operate

---

30 CMI International Working Group Position Paper on Unmanned Ships and the International Regulatory Framework (2017) [online]. Available at: http://comitemaritime.org/wp-content/uploads/2018/05/CMI-Position-Paper-on-Unmanned-Ships.pdf (last tested on 31 March 2019).

and control MASS of less than 24 metres in length". The second version of the code was released in November 2018, adding new guidance on the operation of autonomous vessels, with a particular focus on skills, training and vessel registration.

Significantly, the Code also deals with the subject of remote manning and the training and qualifications required of those who operate MASS. The Code's intent is to demonstrate equivalence with existing legislation and to provide a goal-based framework for the MASS industry to develop. The Code sets out objectives and practical guidance and seeks to address the requirements of key international instruments, such as COLREGS, SOLAS and MARPOL. By way of example, the Code defines a "Master" as "a specific person officially designated by the owning company ... as discharging the responsibilities of the Master of the vessel". This broad definition is hoped to provide a functional interpretation of IMO instruments and emphasises the need to co-exist within existing (or amended) legislative frameworks, as opposed to relying on a new legislative regime.

The Code also introduces original concepts, setting out new classes of MASS: ultra light (less than 7m); light (7–12m); small (12–24m); large (24m +); and high speed. This reflects the current use of small MASS units for scientific and offshore surveys, whilst providing scope for larger MASS in future. It is anticipated that the Code will act as a starting point in developing sound industry practice. The Code will continue to be updated as and when required when guidance from the IMO Regulatory Scoping Exercise is published. In the meantime, MASS technology continues to develop rapidly and the MASRWG hopes that the Code will be adopted by Maritime Administrations to facilitate due regulatory compliance.

7 Conclusions

As set out above, it is our view that MASS would be considered ships for the purposes of the MSA 1995, notwithstanding there is no statutory definition of MASS or decided case law on this point. None of the conventions listed in this chapter were drafted with MASS in mind. There is no uniform definition of "ship" or "vessel", although the majority of conventions would appear to apply to MASS. There is an argument that the STCW Convention and the COLREGS are intrinsic to maritime law. However, as currently drafted it is difficult to see how these conventions would apply to MASS. Whilst a MASS could be considered to be a sea-going ship for the purposes of the STCW convention, it is hard to see how the convention would apply to MASS, particularly where there would be no seafarers serving onboard. Second the COLREGS were written with conventional ships in mind, and while MASS may have the technology to comply with the manoeuvring rules, they will be unable to strictly comply with rules pertaining to lookout for example.

Maritime law, as an extension of general commercial law, exists, broadly, to facilitate commerce. The nature of commerce changes with time. New opportunities and cost saving measures are exploited and commercial law must continue to evolve if it is to keep up with these developments. Until there are statutory definitions of MASS that can be adopted or existing conventions have been extended so that the status of MASS can be regulated, there will always be ambiguity.

CHAPTER 7

Botport law – the regulatory agenda for the transition to smart ports

*Professor Dr Eric Van Hooydonk**

1 Our objective: an exploration of Botport law

The objective of this paper is to explore briefly what regulatory changes may be needed as ports become 'smarter'. The 'perfect' smart port is characterised by calls by unmanned ships, automation of port operations and digitisation of port-related processes and handling of data.

The rapid technological revolution we are witnessing today will most likely bring about fundamental changes in ports and port areas. Many ports have historically been developed as the land-water interface of a trading place. They developed together with and were integrated into the port city. The breakthrough of steam shipping and the increase in size of ships during the Second Industrial Revolution led to the expansion of ever larger port zones outside the cities. In addition to cargo-handling facilities, large ports also became large-scale industrial complexes. In the case of world ports such as Rotterdam and Antwerp, the port area is now many times larger than the city from which it grew. Yet these port areas still essentially remain workplaces for human beings. In the ultimate or maximum scenario, the 'smart port' becomes a fully robotised port, which I will refer to as 'Botport'. In Botport, unmanned ships will load and unload goods in a fully computer-controlled manner, without human intervention. Moreover, the same could apply to the supply and delivery of those goods from inland: they would be carried by unmanned land or railway vehicles, or by unmanned inland waterway vessels. In other words, the port will be a mere machine functioning exclusively on the basis of artificial intelligence. This contribution to the ongoing discussion explores current technological developments and the regulatory implications of the transition to Botport.

In recent years I have tried to make an inventory of port-related innovation ideas, projects, studies, start-ups, etc., which are indeed legion. Even though the final scenario of unmanned ports visited by unmanned shipping and vehicles may sound like science fiction, many practical tools are, in fact, already operational today; furthermore, as will become apparent, in many cases no legal issues arise at all.

This paper was deliberately conceived as a very general overview of smart port developments and prospects and as a high-level assessment of any need for regulatory

---

* Professor, University of Ghent; Advocate, Eric Van Hooydonk Lawyers, Antwerp.

intervention. As far as unmanned shipping is concerned, only a number of specific implications for ports will be under discussion. For a discussion of the legal aspects of unmanned shipping, I refer to my previous overview paper on this subject from 2014, which covered a few port aspects,[1] to numerous studies published since then by other authors,[2] and to the work undertaken by the International Maritime Organization (IMO) and the Comité Maritime International (CMI).

2 Ports and unmanned ships

2.1 Port access

Let us start with the impact on ports of the introduction of unmanned ships. The very first question that arises is, of course, whether such ships have any legal right to enter the port at all. At the international level, access to ports is largely left to international custom (which does not really recognise a general access right) and to bilateral trade, shipping, port, river or canal conventions (which may grant such access). But otherwise, coastal states and port authorities still decide in a sovereign manner whether to grant access to ships. Whether or not an unmanned ship will be granted access may require a policy decision in which consideration of safety and environmental risks, not to mention public acceptability, will probably play a major role. In this respect, it is worth recalling that in the 1960s many coastal states reacted rather defensively to the appearance of nuclear-powered ships and refused them access or at least imposed very strict conditions on a case-by-case basis. Possibly special traffic-routing measures for unmanned ships will be adopted, through the marking out of reserved traffic lanes at sea. Incidentally, the possible impact of the widespread deployment of unmanned shipping on the competitive position of ports has not yet received much attention. It seems obvious that ports along the coast will enjoy a comparative advantage because the entry and exit of unmanned ships to and from ports deep inland may be difficult, especially when twisty rivers or narrow canals have to be used. Whatever the case, once the unmanned vessel has arrived in port, it will in many cases be protected by the principle of non-discrimination, which is upheld both in international law – more specifically, under the 1923 International Convention and Statute on Maritime Ports[3] – and in EU law.[4]

---

1 See E. Van Hooydonk, 'The law of unmanned merchant shipping – An exploration' (2014) 20 *JIML* 403.

2 In addition to the other papers in the present book, see, for example, O. Daum & T. Stellpflug, 'The implications of international law on unmanned merchant vessels' (2017) 23 *JIML* 363; R. Veal, M. Tsimplis, A. Serdy, A. Ntovas & S. Quinn, *Liability for operations in Unmanned Maritime Vehicles with Different Levels of Autonomy* (published by the European Defence Agency, Brussels, 2016); R. Veal & H. Ringbom, 'Unmanned ships and the international regulatory framework' (2017) 23 *JIML* 100. On the specific insurance aspects, see K. Bernauw, 'The insurance of driverless vehicles, pilotless aircraft and unmanned vessels' (2017) 52 *ETL* 359.

3 Convention and Statute on the International Régime of Maritime Ports, done at Geneva, 9 December 1923.

4 More specifically, under the free movement rules and, where relevant, the competition rules as enshrined in the Treaty on the Functioning of the European Union (TFEU), as interpreted by the Court of Justice in numerous port-related cases.

2.2 The shore-based ship controller

Unmanned cargo ships have quickly become a realistic possibility. Not only have numerous technical studies been published; there are also pilot projects and, at the time of going to press, a special unmanned seagoing freighter was actually under construction.[5] In all hypotheses, however, there remains a human actor, usually referred to as the 'shore-based (vessel) controller'. He or she will be responsible for the remote control of one or more autonomously sailing ships, and will be able to intervene in cases of emergency or to prevent incidents. In such a scenario, the ship would not be steered remotely, but neither would it be completely without outside control.

Because he or she is not on board the ship, the shore-based controller is not a seafarer (under either the Maritime Labour Convention,[6] or the STCW Convention[7]). In order to determine his or her status, seafarer law is not really relevant. Nevertheless, the shore-based controller will assume huge responsibilities. In any case, the Collision Regulations[8] and the local port regulations, which usually complement them, will have to be complied with. The shore-based controller will also have to observe reporting duties, e.g., in the event of casualties. Importantly for the purposes of this paper, the shore-based controller should be able to interact with port authorities and port service providers such as pilots, towage providers, mooring men or cargo-handlers. At the moment, such interaction is mainly a matter for local port regulations.

The new function of shore-based controller still has to be defined in law. What shape his or her status will take will depend on technological, operational and economic factors. A variety of existing maritime rules concerning the ship's crew at different levels may need changes (SOLAS[9] and national laws on the status of the master, are two instances). With regard to ports specifically, port procedures, communication mechanisms and formalities will have to be redefined. How this will happen is at present an open question. Unless the usual VHF radio communication instruments (or similar devices) were to be considered adequate and sufficient, linking the communication tools and the other technology used by the shore-based controller with those of each individual port called at might be a challenge. If new equipment for ship-port interaction comes to be developed, technical standardisation at international level would seem unavoidable, for both efficiency and safety reasons. That such potential harmonisation of port procedures is not self-evident is clear from the difficulties experienced in recent years in the pursuit of a European alignment of reporting formalities in ports. The systems and practices in EU ports still

---

5 The *Yara Birkeland*: see www.yara.com.
6 Maritime Labour Convention 2006, done at Geneva, 23 February 2006.
7 International Convention on Standards of Training, Certification and Watchkeeping for Seafarers (STCW Convention), done at London, 7 July 1978.
8 International Regulations for Preventing Collisions at Sea 1972 as annexed to the Convention on the International Regulations for Preventing Collisions at Sea (Collision Regulations), done at London, 20 October 1972.
9 International Convention for the Safety of Life at Sea 1974, done at London, 1 November 1974.

differ considerably.[10] Local regulations concerning the human interactions among captains, pilots, VTS personnel and port officials also differ. It therefore seems likely that in the future the port sector will have to be subject to some global rules in this field. But before this can happen the technology will need to develop further.

A specific but important secondary aspect is that of strike action by shore-based controllers. While such a strike is already problematical when the unmanned ship is at sea, it can give rise to critical situations when the ship is near or in port. A form of government regulation seems to be imposing itself, but of course the localisation of the shore-based controller must be taken into account. Measures in the area of the right of access to the port and Port State Control could in all likelihood provide an appropriate solution.

2.3 Manned and unmanned tugs

A specific question is how the shore-based controller will interact with a port tug that offers assistance to the vessel when it approaches and enters the port, during mooring manoeuvres and upon departure. This is not only a technological, but also a legal question. For example, an answer will have to be given to the question which party in law has the command of the tow when the towed ship is unmanned. At present it is assumed in many maritime jurisdictions that in port towage it is the towed ship that gives the orders. The question arises whether this is responsible or even possible when the ship is under the control of the shore-based controller. An even more difficult question arises in the hypothesis that the tug becomes unmanned itself.

Port towage is today mostly regulated through local port regulations and/or contractual Terms and Conditions. There are no international treaties and most countries do not seem to have national legislation either. Therefore, a review of regulations and contracts will probably suffice. This, however, is again without prejudice to the possible need for international technical standardisation. In this respect, too, it must in any case be said that it is premature to draw up new rules and regulations as long as the technological and operational questions have not been answered.

2.4 Other unmanned port craft

To conclude the discussion of unmanned shipping, reference should be made to the use in ports of numerous miscellaneous craft, including floating cranes and derricks, mooring boats, bunkering barges, clean-up barges, fire-fighting boats, sounding boats, underwater inspection devices, port ferries and water taxis. In principle, nothing prevents such vessels from becoming unmanned as well. Actually, various

---

10 See PwC and Panteia, *Ex-post evaluation of Reporting Formalities Directive (RFD) and Directive on Vessel Traffic Monitoring and Information Systems (VTMIS)*, Final report, Brussels, European Commission, October 2017, 128 p.

projects in this sense are already in progress. For example, the port of Rotterdam uses an automated 'water drone' equipped with a camera system to inspect the port as well as an unmanned clean-up vessel.

The rules that apply to the operation of local port craft are in most cases defined at national or local level. Obviously, existing manning and also safety standards are the main issue. Traffic regulations and regulations on safe operations and environmental protection may have to be reviewed as well. Clearly, measures are already being taken at various levels to remove regulatory barriers. For example, the government of Flanders in Belgium has developed a package of rules to facilitate smart shipping. This is intended, of course under the appropriate technical conditions, to enable both unmanned freight transportation on inland waterways and the operation of other unmanned vessels. Local port regulations will also need to be amended where necessary. In Europe, some port craft may fall under the scope of technical rules developed at the level of the Central Commission for Navigation of the Rhine and the European Union.[11] Preparatory work to remove bottlenecks is already underway in this area as well.

3 Automated ports

3.1 The port manager

Port management and operations may be controlled by the public and/or the private sector. Main port management tasks include construction and management of port land and infrastructure, ensuring public order (through the introduction of port regulations and supervision and enforcement actions by a Harbour Master), collecting port dues and providing ancillary services (which may vary from port to port). Port management systems vary widely. In Europe, most ports are run under the landlord model, with the port authority managing the infrastructure, and private companies taking care of handling services. But in the UK, where private commercial operators act as infrastructure managers and as service providers, the integrated or comprehensive model prevails.

Many port authorities are actively engaged in innovation. These initiatives often concern operational applications for internal use, with little or no regulatory issues arising. With regard to the core task of managing the port infrastructure, the port of Antwerp has, for example, developed projects to monitor the condition – and maintenance of quays automatically, fenders and port bridges using IT-controlled cameras, and also to calculate the optimum use of the available berth space. The port is also working on a European project that will allow supervision activities to be developed over the gigantic port area using air drones, e.g., as a means of detecting water or air pollution. Another application is the remote operation of bridges and locks on inland waterways and/or at ports.[12] In the future these

---

11 See, *inter alia*, Directive (EU) 2016/1629 of the European Parliament and of the Council of 14 September 2016 laying down technical requirements for inland waterway vessels, amending Directive 2009/100/EC and repealing Directive 2006/87/EC, *OJ* 16 September 2016, L 252/118.

12 For an overview, see The World Association for Waterborne Transport Infrastructure (PIANC), *Developments in the automation and remote operation of locks and bridges* (s.l., 2017).

infrastructures will definitely also be able to function autonomously (for safety reasons possibly again under the supervision of a human actor).

The management of ports is mainly regulated at national and/or local level. Of course, where port management processes become automated this in itself has no regulatory impact.[13] Obviously, innovation also allows port managers increasingly to digitise their own administrative processes, and this may in turn help in implementing any new laws and regulations. If, for example, port charges are paid digitally, this can help in the fight against corruption and 'facilitation payments' that still exist in many ports and often seriously impede trade.

The introduction of novel technology may entail new liability risks. It is conceivable, for example, that a shipping accident is caused by a failing automatic system for the operation of a bridge or lock. In many countries, the liability rules for port management are those of general national liability law. That law (and insurance) will in many cases provide appropriate solutions, so that no specific regulatory agenda appears to arise in this area.

As of 29 March 2019, in the European Union access to the port services market and port charging are governed by the EU Seaports Regulation.[14] The Regulation is clearly based on the assumption that ports are manned. For example, it allows the imposition on port service providers of minimum professional qualifications and compliance with social and labour law. It also imposes an obligation to provide training to workers. Nevertheless, the transition to the Botport scenario seems to have little or no impact on the applicability or functioning of the Regulation. After all, the instrument has been conceived as a 'regulatory toolbox' which leaves the EU Member States great freedom to organise their port operations.[15]

The EU Seaports Regulation would allow port managing bodies to introduce differentiated charges for unmanned ships, on condition that the criteria for such a variation are transparent, objective and non-discriminatory, and consistent with competition law, including rules on State aid.[16]

A more fundamental question is whether the legal status of the port manager will have to be changed. In many countries there is special port legislation that regulates the status, tasks and internal organisation of port authorities. The automation of port operations as such does not seem to have an impact on the port management regime. Public sector ports are supervised by politicians and these are likely to remain in place, in order to ensure the proper functioning and performance of the port in the general interest of the city, the region and/

---

13 The impact on enforcement and supervision, traffic management, and handling of goods will be discussed separately later.

14 Regulation (EU) 2017/352 of the European Parliament and of the Council of 15 February 2017 establishing a framework for the provision of port services and common rules on the financial transparency of ports, *OJ* 3 March 2017, L 57/1.

15 For a thorough discussion of the Regulation, see E. Van Hooydonk, *The EU Seaports Regulation. A Commentary on Regulation (EU) 2017/352 of the European Parliament and of the Council of 15 February 2017 Establishing a Framework for the Provision of Port Services and Common Rules on the Financial Transparency of Ports* (Portius Publishing, Antwerp, 2019).

16 See Art. 13(4) of the Regulation.

or the nation. Therefore, the last remaining human being in Botport is likely to be *homo politicus*.

3.2 The harbourmaster

The daily activities of the harbourmaster, who is in fact a specialised police officer for the port area, can be considerably facilitated by innovative technology. As already mentioned, applications exist to improve the management and allocation of berth capacity and to detect oil pollution using drones. Smart surveillance cameras have long been used at numerous port terminals and railway stations. Traffic management can be further automated as well.

The powers of harbourmasters are in most cases defined in national law and/or local port regulations. Their enforcement actions are often governed by provisions in special port laws and regulations and/or by general criminal and administrative law. The relevant rules may have to undergo modifications. More generally, it seems obvious that as the work of the harbourmaster is automated and digitised, the provisions of the port regulations of an operational nature are adapted where necessary.

An important legal issue is that of the evidential value of reports of violations made using automated detection systems. This is a national matter, and it is possible that particular national laws already provide a general framework that does not require adaptation.

The introduction of unmanned merchant shipping will raise the question whether the local harbourmaster will be authorised to issue orders and possibly impose fines on the shore-based vessel controller, who is by definition located elsewhere, and possibly not even in the national territory where the criminal law applicable to the port applies. International agreements of some kind may prove necessary in this area. In this context, we also refer to the discussion of the Vessel Traffic Service later on.

Further, it will have to be examined whether the owner or operator of the unmanned ship and/or the service provider who remotely controls the ship and/or the IT service provider or manufacturer can be held criminally liable for violations of port regulations. This issue is linked to the regulation of the civil liability of these actors in the event of damage, which has already been the subject of considerable legal research.

3.3 The port state control officer

Port State Control (PSC) supervises compliance with (mainly) the technical safety and employment rules for shipping. Although in most countries PSC is not part of the port authority, it is nevertheless a very important actor in the port. Modern technology can undoubtedly facilitate inspection activities.

Obviously, unmanned merchant ships will also have to be checked. Inspections will have to cover not only the security of the ship's hull and equipment, but probably also the proper functioning of the hardware and software used to control the vessel, which will be vital to ensure maritime safety. In so far as there are international technological standards in force, compliance with them will of course have to be monitored.

The inspection of physical ship's documents on board becomes meaningless when the ship is unmanned. In other words, the ship documentation will have to be fully digitised, even more so than is already the case.

By analogy with the rights that the ship's crew have today, the shore-based controller should have the right to demand an inspection. More generally, the shore-based controller should be enabled to interact with PSC (as the master can under current law).

In a distant future, it is conceivable that PSC itself will be fully automated, i.e. that no human inspectors are needed anymore, but that problems will be automatically detected using cameras, sensors, alarm systems and software systems.

With a view to the introduction of unmanned shipping, the rules of the aforementioned SOLAS Convention will undoubtedly have to be reviewed. The regional PSC cooperation structures will undoubtedly have to reach specific agreements on how to treat unmanned ships.

3.4 The port security officer

In the era of unmanned ships and unmanned ports, there will still be illegal migrants, stowaways and possibly terrorists. The handling of the infringements in question is often in the hands of the general police services and/or the maritime police. To prevent intentional crimes, a Port Security Officer must be appointed in every port. The applicable provisions regulate that Officer's interaction with the ship and the security officer of the shipping company. It will have to be examined how this will be reorganised when the ship becomes unmanned.

Ship and port security are governed by IMO and EU rules.[17] These rules will have to be reviewed if unmanned ships are introduced. The same applies in relation to existing port security assessments and the role of the Port Security Officer. In theory, it is of course possible that this function will also disappear in Botport. But on the other hand, it is clear that the advent of unmanned ships will entail new security risks because they could be used as a terrorist weapon and target ports and port cities in particular.

3.5 The vessel traffic service

A Vessel Traffic Service (VTS) provides general nautical information, including weather reports, and also provides specific information, advice and/or orders to individual vessels that are on their way to or from the port. VTS is usually in contact with the master and

---

17 See the Chapter XI-2 of the SOLAS Convention; the ISPS Code; Regulation (EC) No 725/2004 of the European Parliament and of the Council of 31 March 2004 on enhancing ship and port facility security, *OJ* 29 April 2004, L 129/6; Directive 2005/65/EC of the European Parliament and of the Council of 26 October 2005 on enhancing port security, *OJ* 25 November 2005, L 310/28; and Commission Regulation (EC) No 324/2008 of 9 April 2008 laying down revised procedures for conducting Commission inspections in the field of maritime security, *OJ* 10 April 2008, L 98/5.

the pilot by radio. VTS stations are often equipped with shore radar. The work of a VTS also includes the management of ship data.

It is not surprising that VTS authorities are particularly attentive to technological developments in shipping. The International Association of Marine Aids to Navigation and Lighthouse Authorities (IALA) currently focuses on the development of 'e-navigation' which it defines in a very general manner as 'the harmonised collection, integration, exchange, presentation and analysis of marine information on board and ashore by electronic means to enhance berth to berth navigation and related services for safety and security at sea and protection of the marine environment'. Its Secretary-General stated recently that the increased dependence of ships' officers on automated systems, combined with a decline in traditional nautical skills, gives rise to concern.[18] Indeed, it should not be forgotten that many ships already use auto-pilot systems which can be synchronised with other bridge equipment such as the gyro compass and the Electronic Chart Display Information System (ECDIS).

From both a technological and a legal perspective, the interaction between the shore-based controller of an unmanned ship and the VTS still needs to be defined. Related questions are of course how autonomously navigating ships will communicate with each other, with harbour craft and with the VTS, and whether the VTS (a human VTS operator or an autonomously acting VTS system) should be able to intervene in and overrule the autonomous decisions of unmanned ships (or their shore-based controllers). More fundamentally, the question arises whether the decisions of collision avoidance systems of unmanned ships can ever become so sophisticated that local VTS guidance in and around ports becomes superfluous, or whether the role of VTS can be reduced to intervention in risk or incident situations. In other words, the issue is whether the shore control centre that monitors the navigation of the autonomous vessel and intervenes in the event of an emergency, can replace the local VTS and, if not, what their respective roles are, and whether these should be understood differently from those in the current relationship between master and VTS. An even more fundamental issue is that the Shore Control Centre, which supposedly depends on a commercial operator (ship owner or operator) may therefore have other priorities than the VTS, which aims to ensure the fluidity and safety of general shipping traffic and thus serves the public interest.

It appears to be the case that, in this area too, everything will depend, first of all, on technological developments but also on important policy considerations in relation to safety of shipping in and close to ports. At any rate, there can be no doubt whatsoever that the advent of unmanned merchant shipping means that the roles and responsibilities of VTS will have to be reviewed and rearranged.

Today VTS has a concise basis in SOLAS[19] and is regulated by IALA/IMO and EU standards, recommendations and guidelines.[20] The liability of VTSs is

---

18 F. Zachariae, 'E-Navigation: Opening the door to the future', presentation at the E-Navigation Underway North America Conference, November 2018, http://e-navnorthamerica.org, slide 30.
19 Chapter V, Regulation 12.
20 See, for example, Directive 2002/59/EC of the European Parliament and of the Council of 27 June 2002 establishing a Community vessel traffic monitoring and information system and repealing Council Directive 93/75/EEC, *OJ* 5 August 2002, L 208/10.

regulated at national level. Depending on the answers to the above questions, these instruments may have to be readjusted. To the extent that VTS will continue to make use of people, new rules will become necessary for the training and certification of VTS personnel,[21] the interaction, communications and hierarchy between the traffic management and the shore-based vessel controllers, reporting duties in connection with hazards, defects and pollution, and the capture, secure storage, retrieval and presentation of VTS-related information.

3.6 The pilot

The pilot is a local guide who advises the master on board when entering and leaving a port and carrying out other manoeuvres in it. The task of the pilot is already greatly facilitated today by the use of Portable Pilot Units (PPUs) which are composed of a laptop with pilot software and sensors. To avoid confusion, the PPU can never substitute for the pilot, but is nevertheless a vital information support.

When ships become unmanned and there is no master on board, the question arises whether there will still be a need for pilotage assistance and whether the pilot's profession will disappear together with the function of the master.

What seems to be certain is that local nautical expertise will still be needed. However, it is obvious that the role of the pilot will change. In theory, it is conceivable that – possibly only in the experimental phase – unmanned vessels will switch to the manned mode when calling at ports and that a pilot will still join an on-bridge team. If the pilot acts as a local guide but no longer comes on board, he may be able to act as a shore-based vessel controller himself, possibly by remotely steering the vessel. An alternative arrangement is that the pilot advises the vessel controller (either remotely or in the control station). Yet another possibility is that the pilot will function as a key person in a 'new style' VTS. The final outcome will once again depend on technological progress.

Together with the job content, the organisational model of pilot services may also undergo changes. The pilotage provider may of course remain an independent pilotage agency, but could also be integrated or absorbed into a shipowning or operating company, the port authority, the harbourmaster's office, the VTS, or a 'new style' manning agency. The pilotage provider may also become a public-private joint venture between (1) a shipowner or operator or manning agency, and (2) a port, a VTS and/or a pilotage agency.

Pilotage is mainly regulated at national and local level, although there are IMO Recommendations on training and certification.[22] Existing pilotage laws and regulations may have to be reviewed (if not repealed). The same applies to the aforementioned IMO Recommendations. Here too, changes are currently completely premature.

---

21 See the IALA Standards for Training and Certification of VTS Personnel (revised version of 16 June 2017), www.iala-aism.org.

22 See IMO Resolution A.960(23) of 5 December 2003 which adopted the Recommendations on training and certification and on operational procedures for maritime pilots other than deep-sea pilots (A 23/Res.960, 5 March 2004).

3.7 The mooring man

A mooring man or linesman secures the ship at its berth or in a lock. Automated self-mooring systems using vacuum mooring pads already exist, so the job of mooring man may also disappear in the future. But even in the case of automated mooring, safety standards will be needed and of course liability issues may still arise.

There is no international framework on mooring services in ports and hardly any national regulation is available either. Mooring is mainly regulated[23] at local level. So, it is likely that adjustments will have to be made to legislation, or that they will simply have to be repealed.

3.8 The shipping agent

The shipping agency sector is also making more and more use of innovation techniques. In Singapore, for example, drones are used for shore-to-ship delivery of documents.

If unmanned shipping ever comes about, the question arises whether an unmanned ship in a port should still be represented by a shipping agent and, if so, how this service provider will interact with the shipowner or operator and/or the shore-based controller.

In the shipping agency sector, freedom of contract applies. There are no international treaties and hardly any national statutes. If adjustments are necessary, it will probably suffice to update standard Terms and Conditions and individual contracts.

3.9 The freight forwarder

For the forwarding sector, the existential question arises whether freight forwarders are still needed where carriage and formalities can be arranged via digital tools. More and more websites appear that offer e-freight forwarding services.[24] The distribution giant Amazon has obtained an ocean-freight-forwarding licence from China.

As regards the regulatory agenda, reference may be made *mutatis mutandis* to what was mentioned above in relation to shipping agency. After all, freedom of contract also applies in freight forwarding. In addition, it may be advisable to review the existing liability rules on online intermediaries (but this goes beyond shipping law).

3.10 The terminal operator

There are already numerous high-tech applications in the cargo-handling sector, and the evolution continues. In the port of Rotterdam an automated container terminal opened back in 1993, and by the end of 2017 38 ports were reported to be operating 60 automated terminals, including 14 fully automated terminals.[25] Loading and unloading and

---

23 See, however, the IMO Guidelines on minimum training and education for mooring personnel (FAL.6/Circ.11/Rev.1, 20 April 2016).
24 See, for example, www.flexport.com.
25 See the data in UNCTAD, *Review of Maritime Transport 2018* (United Nations, New York, 2018), 78–79; World Maritime University, *Transport 2040: Automation, Technology, Employment – The Future of Work*, 2019, 85. On innovation in container transport, see also C. Fenton, P. Storrs-Fox, M. Joerss,

yard operations indeed become more and more automated (using remotely controlled or autonomous cranes, straddle carriers and terminal trucks). Better stowage planning ('smart stowage') and warehousing robotics (including stock-taking drones) also contribute to efficiency improvement in ports. Gate control procedures can be automated as well. Some believe that blockchain technology may replace pincode-based release of containers to truck drivers.[26] In the maximum Botport scenario, autonomous ships deliver to autonomous trucks or trains. Several ports such as Hamburg are investigating the possibility of transporting containers or goods to hinterland stations by means of a hyperloop, a kind of high-speed tube transportation system. Meanwhile, digitisation is also leading to new problems, such as cybercriminality in the international drugs trade.

The existing Terminal Operators Convention,[27] which regulates liability issues, will probably never enter into force. The liability towards the cargo interests of the goods handler as a 'maritime performing party' is regulated in the Rotterdam Rules,[28] which, however, have also not yet come into effect. For the rest, terminal operations are mainly governed by port usages and contractual Terms and Conditions. Probably the impact of further automation and digitisation will mainly be on operational procedures rather than on the legal fundamentals, including the liability principles. The development of unmanned ports can, of course, also be the subject of clauses included in port lease or concession agreements concluded with the port authority. Maybe hyperloop carriage to and from the hinterland in addition to the sea carriage will one day be covered by the Rotterdam Rules.

3.11 The docker

As automation of terminal operations progresses further, the hard and often dangerous manual job of the classic dock worker is losing its essential character and the whole profession may eventually be completely eliminated. This is also the case with specialised jobs, such as that of crane operator or driver. In several ports, container cranes no longer have a crane driver's cabin, but are operated remotely by crane men sitting behind consoles equipped with screens and joysticks. Ultimately, nothing will be able to prevent the cranes that load and unload unit loads from operating fully automatically. The tallyman disappears as well, because containers can be identified by means of Optical Character Recognition (OCR) technology, and the external condition and contents can be checked using scanners. Automated lashing and twist-locking systems are currently being researched. But since the transition to Botport will obviously not take place overnight, dock workers will continue to be needed for some time, if only because not all goods can be transported in unit loads and therefore

---

S. Saxon & M. Stone, *Brave New World? Container Transport in 2043*, TT Club/McKinsey&Company (s.l., s.d.), 78 p.

26 On the potential for blockchain technology in ports, see UNCTAD, *Review of Maritime Transport 2018* (United Nations, New York, 2018), 88–89.

27 United Nations Convention on the Liability of Operators of Transport Terminals in International Trade, done at Vienna, 19 April 1991.

28 United Nations Convention on Contracts for the International Carriage of Goods Wholly or Partly by Sea, done at Rotterdam, 23 September 2009.

non-routine handling will continue to be necessary. However, their job description will definitely change, and the workforce in ports will need training and reskilling.[29]

Dock work unions traditionally oppose the introduction of new technologies in ports. In many ports, this has a long history, going back for example to the time when steam-driven grain elevators were introduced, or to the very beginning of the container trade. Moreover, port labour pool monopolies and other restrictive rules and practices (e.g. mandatory gang composition rules, which must be observed regardless of the real needs of the work) are still issues in many ports. However, there is a clear trend to re-regulate port labour according to the general principles of labour law and to abolish special laws and regulations for dock work. Restrictive rules and practices in Europe encounter objections from the European institutions, for that matter, and are often an incentive for terminal operators to look at possibilities for further automation.[30] In any case, it is likely that social issues will occasionally arise with the further automation of port operations.[31] But in the ultimate Botport, port labour can, in any case, no longer be a bottleneck.

Although the International labour Organization (ILO) has elaborated a number of international conventions and recommendations on dock labour,[32] their impact is rather limited. Dock labour is mainly governed by national laws and regulations and collective labour agreements, which may have to undergo adjustment (if not abolition) as further automation measures are implemented. Artificial obstacles to the introduction of automation should be removed, where needed, with the help of courts and/or competition authorities.

4 Digitisation and data

Partly due to the increasingly complex regulation of maritime shipping and trade, masses of data are transmitted, collected and processed in ports.

---

29 See also World Maritime University, *Transport 2040: Automation, Technology, Employment – The Future of Work*, 2019, 85–88.

30 For a recent state of play, see E.Van Hooydonk, 'The Spanish Dock Labour Ruling (C-576/13): Mortal Blow for the Dockers' Pools' (2015) 50 *ETL* 551 (also at *Transportrecht* 2016, Vol. 39, Iss. 7–8, 275–289).

31 See, for example, X., 'Valencia. Union rejects automation bid', www.portstrategy.com, 15 November 2018, mentioning:

> *The Valencia branch of the Coordinadora port union has rejected the idea of the fourth container terminal being automated. It claims that this will not only put hundreds of jobs at risk, but will also decrease productivity and competitiveness.*
>
> *The local convenor, Óscar Martínez, told the port's daily newspaper that the union had been troubled by this prospect for several months.*
>
> *'We are not going to allow Valencia to fall into the nonsense of robotisation,' he said, arguing that automation should be regarded as holding the stevedoring profession in contempt as well as attacking many thousands of families that rely on the port for a living.*
>
> *The Coordinadora union has held several meetings not only with the port authority president, Aurelio Martínez, but also with prospective bidders for the concession. All were told that the union completely rejected automation and that 'in no way are we willing to allow this option'.*

32 See, for example, the ILO Convention No. 137 concerning the Social Repercussions of New Methods of Cargo Handling in Docks, done at Geneva, 25 June 1973; ILO Recommendation No. 145 on dock work which accompanies the aforementioned convention.

As far as purely nautical data are concerned, we can point, for example, to the international and European regulation of the installation and use of Voyage Data Recorders (VDRs), the purpose of which is to assist in casualty investigations. VDRs record, among many other things, VHF communications. In a similar way, the local VTS may record radio and shore radar data and make it available for investigation purposes. Of course, such tools have been in existence for quite some time now and can hardly be considered revolutionary today. But new applications keep popping up. An example is a website that offers techniques for satellite-based maritime tracking that help compute the position of ships.[33] A recent technology aims at the real-time text conversion of VHF communications, which could detect, for example, delayed arrivals at an early stage and contribute to, among other things, traffic planning to and from the port.[34]

Data play an essential role in the organisation of port formalities. At international level, special measures to facilitate international maritime traffic may become necessary as unmanned ships arrive on the scene, and to that end changes may have to be made to the FAL Convention.[35] The Annex to this Convention certainly supports the electronic exchange of information. At the European level, coordination and simplification is pursued through the introduction of rules on reporting formalities and the electronic transmission of data via a European Maritime Single Window environment. The existing Directive 2010/65/EU[36] will probably soon be replaced by a more ambitious and hopefully more effective instrument. However, the exact formalities for unmanned ships still need to be determined, so that specific regulatory changes seem premature at the moment.

Finally, local data collection and sharing initiatives have been developed in many ports. To give just one example, NxtPort is a data-sharing platform in the Port of Antwerp which collects and shares data from shippers, forwarders, shipping agents, carriers, terminals and insurance brokers and helps improve Customs processes. The regulatory agenda seems rather limited in these matters. Many issues can be dealt with under appropriate contractual arrangements. But that should in any case be checked on a project-by-project basis. That new legal problems can arise at any time is evident from the recent complaint that a new, publicly funded port community portal in Los Angeles would create a 'data monopoly' in which the port authority, it is claimed, would have no control or stewardship to prevent misallocation or unintended use of the data.[37]

---

33 See www.spire.com.
34 The tool is developed by Antwerp-based Port+: see www.portplus.be.
35 Convention on Facilitation of International Maritime Traffic 1965, done at London, 9 April 1965.
36 See Regulation of the European Parliament and of the Council establishing a European maritime single window environment and repealing Directive 2010/65/EU, signed on 20 June 2019, which replaces Directive 2010/65/EU of the European Parliament and of the Council of 20 October 2010 on reporting formalities for ships arriving in and/or departing from ports of the Member States and repealing Directive 2002/6/EC, *OJ* 29 October 2010, L 283/1.
37 X., 'Los Angeles data monopoly fears raised', www.portstrategy.com, 12 November 2018.

5 Conclusion: Botport law is feasible

Automation, robotisation, digitalisation, artificial intelligence, data mining and other hi-tech developments will undoubtedly continue to transform the port landscape over the coming years and decades. Although evolution will almost inevitably be gradual, a future scenario in which unmanned ships will deliver goods to unmanned land vehicles and barges in unmanned ports is not inconceivable or even unrealistic. From a busy workshop for human beings, the port will itself become a machine, a Botport.

As ports become smarter, many organisational and operational matters have to be rethought. Some typical port-related professions, such as that of port worker, may slowly disappear. Others, such as that of pilot or VTS operator, may have to undergo at least a transformation.

Because port activities are mainly regulated at national or local level, no major updating of international rules is needed. This is different from the legal regime of unmanned shipping as such, in which context account must be taken of an extensive body of international and European (and of course also national) rules, which are based on the presence on board of a ship's crew.

For many port-related activities, no specific regulation applies at all, and general contract and liability law suffices. As port-related activities become unmanned, specific existing rules on human actors (job access, qualifications, labour law, duties and responsibilities, liabilities etc.) may simply become inoperative. Specific rules on port-related activities which are set to disappear could of course be repealed.

In sum, the trend towards smart ports does not seem to encounter fundamental regulatory obstacles, or at least it can be concluded that it will be easier to adapt the regulatory framework for ports to technological developments than that for maritime shipping.

CHAPTER 8

Autonomous vessels and third-party liabilities

The elephant in the room

Professor Barış Soyer[*]

1 Introduction

The use of technology to operate underwater vehicles remotely for military and scientific purposes has been a remarkable success and embraced for more than five decades.[1] Building on the success enjoyed with regard to the development of the technology concerning remote controlled underwater vehicles, various research projects have been undertaken in the last decade or so with a view to developing autonomous surface vessels which can be employed for commercial purposes. Perhaps the most influential project designed to develop a technical concept for the operation of autonomous merchant vessel and assess its technical, economic and legal feasibility was the Maritime Unmanned Navigation through Intelligence Networks (MUNIN) project,[2] partially funded by the European Union.[3] The MUNIN project was a concept study which aimed to identify the most critical technological, operational and legislative factors that might be obstacles to the realisation of autonomous shipping. The project, which ended in August 2015, has provided a great insight for the future development of autonomous vessels.

Similar studies, mainly driven by engineering and IT firms, have been launched since then with the encouragement and financial support of some Nordic countries. Some of these studies utilised lessons learned from remote operations in industries such as aviation, space exploration and defence, resulting in a design that uses interactive smart screens, voice recognition systems, holograms and surveillance drones to monitor and assess on-board operations and conditions around the vessel.[4] The ultimate aim of these projects is to produce a viable model which can be subjected to actual sea trials. We witnessed the realisation of this objective when in December 2018 Finnish state-owned ferry operator, Finferries (in collaboration with Rolls-Royce), tested

---

[*] Director of the Institute of International Shipping and Trade Law, Swansea University.
[1] For example, in the 1970s and 80s the Royal Navy used "Cutlet", a remotely operated submersible, to recover practice torpedoes and mines. Similarly, remotely operated vehicles have been used to locate many historic shipwrecks, including the RSM Titanic; see, www.whoi.edu/page.do?pid=83577&tid=3622&cid=130989 (last tested on 31 December 2018).
[2] See, www.unmanned-ship.org/munin/(last tested on 31 December 2018).
[3] EU's 7th Framework Programme, governed by the agreement SCP2-GA-2012–314286.
[4] See, www.iims.org.uk/rolls-royce-reveals-its-vision-for-future-shore-control-centre-for-unmanned-ships/(last tested on 31 December 2018).

the navigation of the world's first fully autonomous ferry, the *Falco*, in the archipelago south of the city of Turku. The *Falco* is a 53.8 metre double-ended car ferry, and during the test, it navigated autonomously for about a nautical mile and a half. Similarly, Yara and Kongsberg entered into partnership to build the world's first autonomous and zero emission ship, the *YARA Birkeland*. The vessel, which will operate in the territorial waters of Norway as a 120 TEU container feeder vessel, will function initially as a manned vessel, moving to remote operation in 2019; it is expected to be capable of performing fully autonomous operations from 2022.

At this stage, it is not possible to predict with precision the vessel model that various corporations are working towards and will ultimately be able to introduce to the commercial market in the years to come. However, it is safe to assume that an autonomous vessel (i.e., one that is able to make navigational decisions and determine actions by itself), will be developed incrementally. In the early stages, it is very likely that a vessel which has different degrees of autonomy (e.g., a hybrid model vessel) will be manufactured. Such vessels might, for example, have autonomous navigational ability but retain a skeleton crew to take over the controls in certain conditions (e.g., when navigating in congested waters or whilst docking); or they might be controlled and operated by a remote controller in certain circumstances (e.g., in case of a system failure or pre-programmed software not coping with the conditions prevailing).

Turning to the academic legal debate on the subject so far, the main discussion has focussed on the regulatory framework—that is, to what extent existing technical rules (concerning safety, environment, and training) and watch-keeping standards could accommodate the development of autonomous vessels.[5] This is understandable, as autonomous navigation in high seas and oceans can only be a reality if such vessels operate in compliance with safety rules stipulated in international rules such as the International Convention for the Safety of Life at Sea 1974 (SOLAS) and International Regulations for Preventing Collisions at Sea 1972. The International Maritime Organisation (IMO) has also adopted a similar starting position. In May 2018,[6] its Maritime Safety Committee established the Maritime Autonomous Surface Ships (MASS) Working Group to undertake a scoping exercise with a view to identifying which of the existing international instruments dealing with maritime safety should be amended and what new instruments should be developed to facilitate the operation of autonomous vessels in international waters.[7]

However, so far no comprehensive discussion has been carried out in academic circles on liability issues emerging from the operation of autonomous vessels. It is submitted that this is a debate that is as important as the suitability of a regulatory framework in the context of developing autonomous vessels, essentially for two reasons. First, if there is fundamental uncertainty about the underlying liability rules, once such vessels are put

---

5 See, E. van Hooydonk, "The Law of Unmanned Merchant Shipping—An Exploration" (2014) 20 The Journal of International Maritime Law 403–423; R. Veal & M Tsimplis, "The Integration of Unmanned Ships into the Lex Maritima" (2017) Lloyd's Maritime and Commercial Law Quarterly 303–335 and L. Carey, "All Hands off Deck: Legal Barriers to Autonomous Shipping" (2017) 23 The Journal of International Maritime Law 202–219.

6 MSC 99.

7 It is expected that the work of the MASS WC will be completed by the end of 2020.

into commercial operation, the cost of uncertainty will be inevitably passed on to insurers, who will reflect this uncertainty with an increase in the premiums charged for liability insurance.[8] This rate increase could potentially raise the operational costs, wiping out the benefits that are expected (i.e., reduction in crew wages and fuel costs) from the development of this technology. Second, inability to predict their liability costs and subsequent profits might deter manufacturers from investing in the development of autonomous vessel technology. Aside from product liability issues, if there is a chance that manufacturers could face claims from third parties in case of a collision, when a problem in the algorithms give rise to an incident and they will have no prospect of limiting liability for such claims, this increases the risk of the underlying investment. In that case, the manufacturers would like to see higher returns to justify the added risk they expose themselves to, or they might pull out of this market altogether.

The purpose of this chapter is to debate the nature of the liability regime that vessels operating in an autonomous mode should be subjected to. It is submitted that the current fault-based liability regime might not be the ideal one, taking into account the technological aspects of autonomous shipping, public perception on the matter, and the role that law is expected to play when it comes to developing new technologies.

2 Proposed liability regime for third-party claims

2.1 Imposing a "strict liability" regime

Generally speaking, negligent navigation at sea gives rise to a claim in tort of negligence requiring the innocent party to prove that he has suffered the damaged complained of, and also that the negligence of the defendant had some causal effect in bringing about the damage suffered.[9] In exceptional instances, however, the claimant does not need to prove actual negligence to succeed in a tort claim for damage done by a ship. As far as English law is concerned, for example, under s. 74 of the Harbours, Docks and Piers Clauses Act 1847, the owner of a ship[10] which damages the harbour, dock, pier, quays, or works, is answerable to the undertakers for the damage done by such ship or by any person employed about her.[11] Likewise, under some international regimes, a strict liability regime is imposed for certain types of damages (i.e., pollution damage).[12]

---

8 See, M.G. Geistfeld, "Legal Ambiguity, Liability Insurance and Tort Reform" (2011) 60 DE PAUL L REV 539, at 559–56.

9 See, *The Tempus* [1913] P 166 at 172, per Evans, P.

10 It has been held by the House of Lords in *BP Exploration Operating Co Ltd* v. *Chevron Shipping Co (The Chevron North America)* [2001] UKHL 50; [2003] 1 AC 197 that reference to "owner" in this section is a reference to the proprietor or true, registered owner and does not include any charterer, not even a bareboat charterer.

11 See also s. 56 of the same Act with regard to wreck removal liability.

12 See, Art III of the Civil Liability Convention 1992 which applies to vessels constructed or adapted for the carriage of oil in bulk. By virtue of Art I.5, oil means "any persistent hydrocarbon mineral oil such as crude oil, fuel oil, heavy diesel oil and lubricating oil, whether carried on board a ship as cargo or in the bunkers of such a ship." See also, the International Convention on Civil Liability for Bunker Oil

It is submitted that an international regime that establishes a strict liability regime for the responsible party[13] will be appropriate in cases where the vessel is autonomously operated. It is suggested that five reasons justify this standpoint:

 i) In case of autonomous vessels, the size of the total software package is likely to be enormous considering the number of eventualities that can arise when navigating in different types of waters, and naturally the structure of this package will be very complicated. It will possibly be divided into sub-systems and smaller entities inside a large amount of different devices communicating with each other.[14] Therefore, things can go wrong for a whole host of reasons, ranging from basic programming errors to software bugs and poorly-designed algorithms. If a fault-based liability system is adopted, this could be detrimental to third-party claimants; as the judicial process of apportioning fault between different parties involved in the design of this technology (i.e., manufacturers of sensors, hardware producers, and programmers) will be time-consuming, complicated, and expensive, given the need to use several technical experts. If, on the other hand, a "strict liability" regime is adopted, third-party claimants (e.g., a manned vessel involved in a collision with an autonomous vessel) will be able to recover their loss from a responsible party without delay. No doubt, in case of a recourse or contribution action by the responsible party to others involved in the production of the vessel (e.g., software producers or censor manufacturers), it will be necessary to identify the degree of fault; but at least by that stage, third-party claimants will be out of the equation, so that they are not adversely affected from any lengthy and fact-specific litigation.
 ii) It is inevitable that algorithms used in autonomous vessels will reflect the ethical values of the person who designs them. For the designer, a really difficult question is programming how the autonomous vessel should act in a situation where only really poor alternatives are left. For example, should the autonomous vessel intentionally collide with another vessel or instead sail aground in a rocky area, risking massive oil pollution damage to the environment?[15] Ultimately, it will be the man-made software which makes

---

Pollution Damage 2001 which is designed to provide a strict liability regime for bunker oil damage caused by vessels other than tankers.

13 Which party is the most appropriate party to assume such liability will be discussed in the following part.

14 For a general overview of technology that can be the basis of the development of autonomous ships, see, T. Hogg & S. Ghosh, "Autonomous Merchant Vessels: Examination of Factors that Impact the Effective Implementation of Unmanned Ships" (2016) Australian Journal of Maritime & Ocean Affairs 206.

15 A similar question has been posed in the context of autonomous cars, known as "the trolley problem". This is an ethical debate evaluated in depth by J. J. Thomson, "The Trolley Problem" (1984–85) 94 Yale L J 1395. The hypothetical scenario indicates that there is a runaway trolley barrelling down railway tracks. Ahead on the tracks, there are five people tied up and unable to move. The trolley is headed straight for them. The decision-maker in the story is standing some distance off in the train yard, next to a lever. If he pulls the lever, the trolley will switch to a different set of tracks on which one person is tied up. There is a never-ending dilemma over which is the most ethical thing to do. Do nothing, and the

the system do what it does; but if the programmer opts for the former option, this will create rather difficult ethical considerations for the court in determining the degree of fault in the context of a "fault-based" liability system. Conversely, a strict liability regime will protect the interest of third-party claimants by enabling them to recover their loss without further consideration, especially in a case where they were deemed not to be worthy of protection as a result of the ethical values adopted by the software designer.

iii) It has been raised as a concern that there might be instances where machines with artificial intelligence do not perform in a way that is consistent with their designers' intentions.[16] It is possible that truly intelligent machines will learn to adapt the instructions they initially receive from humans to circumstances not directly forecast at the time of their creation. And perhaps these machines will learn to internalize values that are not the ones their creators tried to embed.[17] If this holds true, allocating fault on a traditional basis in an instance where an autonomous vessel has acquired capacity to act in a way that is contrary to the "rules" that it has been given by its programmer will be a very difficult, if not an impossible, task. In such an instance, a system of "strict liability" would be more appropriate to address the inadequacy of tort law to resolve questions of liability that may push beyond the frontiers of science and technology.

iv) Another dimension of the debate that needs to be carefully considered is the stance of the public on the use of autonomous vessels. The manufacturers will no doubt strive to ensure that such vessels do not pose any danger to other vessels or people on board them, or to other maritime property or environmental resources. However, it is also undeniable that regulators will not allow autonomous vessels to operate if there is significant public opposition to their use. Social risk acceptance is a complex issue and not necessarily related to the actual risk level posed by a piece of equipment.[18] Also, as indicated earlier, it might be difficult for humans to maintain control of machines that are programmed to act with considerable autonomy.[19] There are a number of mechanisms by which a loss of control may occur: a malfunction, such as a corrupted

---

trolley will kill the five people on the main track. Pull the lever, diverting the trolley onto the side track, and it will kill one person but will do so as a result of the deliberate action of the subject.

16 N. Bostrom, "The Superintelligent Will: Motivation and Instrumental Rationality in Advanced Artificial Agents" (2012) 22 Minds & Machines 71–85.

17 U. Pagallo, *The Law of Robots: Crimes, Contracts and Torts* (New York: Springer, 2013), pp. 115–145.

18 Interestingly, it was stressed in the MUNIN Report that not all commercial goods will be suitable for autonomous transport by sea; for example, hazardous cargoes (e.g., flammable, explosive, biological) will continue to require special considerations and possibly not be suitable for such carriage. See www.unmanned-ship.org/munin/(last tested on 31 December 2018).

19 On this matter, see generally, N. Silver, *The Signal and the Noise: Why So Many Predictions Fail—But Some Don't* (London: Penguin, 2013).

file or physical damage to input equipment; a security breach; or a flaw in programming. These make autonomous vessels a potential source of public risk on a scale that far exceeds the more familiar forms of public risk that are solely the result of human behaviour.[20] It is, therefore, submitted that employing a strict liability regime at times when such vessels operate autonomously might assist in gaining public support. A strict liability regime would undoubtedly endorse the assurance given to the public by manufacturers that the technology used in autonomous vessels is safe, by ensuring that an effective compensation regime is available to others who might be adversely affected in extreme cases where this technology fails.

v) Tort law is said to serve different functions.[21] That is the reason why each judgment of a court is likely to reflect a particular philosophical and policy bias; and in similar fashion, the judicial development of each type of tort has been rather different.[22] It is submitted that a "strict liability" in this context will not only serve the "protection of rights" function of tort law, which is very important considering the hazards that autonomous vessels can pose to human beings and other maritime property, but will at the same time provide incentive for manufacturers to make their products safer (deterrence effect). A liability system which is designed to ensure that manufacturers produce better quality products will no doubt assist in gaining "public" support for such vessels. It goes without saying that production of safer vessels will also reduce the risk of loss and liabilities, hence leading to a reduction in the cost of liability insurance.

2.2 Strict liability and related issues

Having deliberated why there is a need to introduce a strict liability regime for autonomous vessels, it is now necessary to evaluate various attributes of such a regime. As is often the case, "the devil is in the detail."

2.2.1 Exceptions

Even if autonomous vessels are introduced into the maritime world, it seems probable that such vessels will not at all times be relying on artificial intelligence for navigation. It is very likely that an autonomous vessel will be programmed in a way that control will be passed on to a skeleton crew on board or a remote controller on shore in certain circumstances (e.g., in case of an emergency). It makes little sense in those

---

[20] M. U. Scherer, "Regulating Artificial Intelligence Systems: Risks, Challenges, Competencies and Strategies" 29 (2016) Harvard Journal of Law & Technology at 366–367.
[21] See the contribution of T. Honore, "The Morality of Tort Law" published in D.G. Owen, *Philosophical Foundations of Tort Law* (Oxford: OUP, 1995), p. 73.
[22] Lord Wilberforce in *Broome* v. *Cassell & Co Ltd* [1972] AC 1027, at 1114, stressed that English tort law has committed itself to no single theory.

instances that the relevant party should be strictly liable to third parties, given that humans, either on board or on shore, will be in control of the operation of the vessel. So, it is submitted that the liability of the vessel in cases when she is under the control of an on-board or offshore operator should be "fault based".[23]

The position should be the same if an autonomous vessel is involved in a collision when she is not in operation (i.e., at anchorage). In that case, one cannot justifiably argue that the responsible party should face strict liability, given that his actions have not created any risk to navigation or other parties.

A more difficult question arises in a case when hackers manage to penetrate the cyber security systems of an autonomous vessel and take control, causing damage to third parties. Could this be an instance where an exception to the strict liability of the relevant party is introduced into the relevant legal code? This is a difficult question. In various strict liability regimes, the relevant party is often exempted from liability in cases where an incident is caused by an act or omission done with the intent to cause damage by a third party.[24] Taking a similar stance here could, therefore, be readily justified. However, introducing an exception to the liability of the relevant party in case of a cyber attack on an autonomous vessel could leave third parties vulnerable, especially if they have no insurance against cyber risks. The policy decision facing the draftsman in this context is whether the liability insurer of an autonomous vessel, or first-party insurer and liability insurer of the other vessel, is in a better position to assume liability for cyber breaches an autonomous vessel faces. It is submitted that the liability insurer of the autonomous vessel is likely to be the better option, for two reasons. First, the party who puts an autonomous vessel in navigation is well aware that, in case of a cyber attack, it is very difficult for the offshore controllers to intervene and take control of the vessel back. Therefore, the party responsible for an autonomous vessel is the party who creates a risk to the others engaged in navigation; so it is only fair that the risk is assumed by that party. Second, it is likely that the cost of liability cover for the responsible party in this case will be less than the cost of liability and first-party cover for the other vessel(s). Therefore, it is appropriate that the party responsible for the autonomous vessel remains strictly liable for losses and liabilities caused by cyber-attacks directed at that vessel.

It follows that the relevant party should also assume responsibility for any incident arising as a result of breakdown in communication. For example, imagine that the autonomous vessel is programmed in a manner to hand over control to the onshore operator when facing a difficult situation. However, connection with the vessel is lost and the online operator fails to assert effective control, causing a collision with another vessel. In that situation, even though the breakdown in communication might have nothing to do with the owner of the vessel, as the main risk creator, it makes sense that the responsible party remains strictly liable.

---

23 A similar solution has been adopted for automated cars in the UK by the Automated and Electric Vehicles Act 2018 (i.e., the liability regime is fault based when an automated car is controlled or needs to be monitored by an individual).

24 See, for example, Art III(1)(b) of the Civil Liability Convention 1992.

2.2.2 Channelling liability

Assuming that a strict liability regime is put in place, one of the most controversial issues will be determining the party which the liability should be channelled to.[25] One might be tempted to argue that the "manufacturer" of an autonomous vessel is the most suitable party for this purpose. This has an instinctive appeal at first sight. However, one should not lose sight of possible difficulties that can emerge. Given that an advanced level of technology is required to manufacture an autonomous vessel, it is very likely that several parties (e.g. shipbuilders, programmers, and sensor manufacturers), will cooperate in the construction process. The main question is, therefore, which corporation the liability will be channelled to. Also, channelling third-party liability to manufacturers would require them to carry acceptable liability insurance provided by a reliable insurance company. It is highly unlikely that P & I clubs would be willing to provide this kind of insurance; so manufacturers would need to seek this kind of cover from the commercial market. However, cover from the commercial market could be rather costly, considering that the current legal regime does not allow manufacturers to limit their liability for maritime claims from third parties.[26]

Conversely, there are various reasons why the registered owner might be a better option for channelling of liability purposes. First, this is in line with other areas of maritime law where a party that chooses to be involved in a potentially hazardous activity also assumes liability that might emerge.[27] Second, after an autonomous vessel is delivered by the manufacturer, the owner (or his agents/employees) will be expected to maintain and inspect systems critical for the vessel's autonomous navigation, for example by installing safety-critical software updates and regularly inspecting sensors. Given the fact that the owner's active involvement is vital for an autonomous vessel to operate safely, it should not come as a surprise if the owner is expected to assume strict liability when things go wrong. Last but not least, there is a very effective and well-established liability insurance system in place, provided by P & I clubs, available for shipowners; and extending the cover to autonomous vessels would not cause any significant turbulence. In fact, it can also be argued that spreading any potential liability through the P & I clubs mechanism would be a more cost-efficient way of dealing with liability insurance issues.

---

25 This would preclude third parties from bringing an action against any other party.

26 For example, Article 1 of the Convention on Limitation of Liability for Maritime Claims 1976 stipulates:

1. Shipowners and salvors, as hereinafter defined, may limit their liability in accordance with the rules of this Convention for claims set out in Article 2. This point will be discussed in depth at 2.2.5.
2. The term "shipowner" shall mean the owner, charterer, manager and operator of a seagoing ship.
3. Salvor shall mean any person rendering services in direct connexion with salvage operations ...."

27 For example, the registered owner of a tanker involved in carriage of oil is strictly liable to third parties for any loss and liability under the Civil Liability Convention 1992. Similarly, in the offshore sector, the operator usually assumes responsibility to third parties for losses and liabilities.

2.2.3 Recourse action

It will be, of course, open to the shipowner to bring a recourse action against a manufacturer or software developer for the liability he has incurred. Such an action is likely to be based on the tort of negligence, as all parties involved in the manufacturing process are expected to take reasonable care to avoid foreseeable damage.[28] What amounts to reasonable care will depend essentially on industry norms and guidelines. At this precise moment, no such guidelines exist. However, as the work of the IMO progresses in line with regulatory development, technical rules and standards (based on the performance standards and additional clarification requirements for component/software developers) will undoubtedly be developed. Such rules and guidelines will be valuable in the context of any recourse action.

In essence, in a recourse action the ship owner needs to demonstrate a fault of the manufacturer that is causative of his loss. However, a manufacturer will not be liable in tort for damage or injury arising from defects which could not be detected by due diligence on his part.[29] Also, in a case where negligent defect on the part of the manufacturer is deemed to have caused the accident, the manufacturer might nevertheless be exempted from liability if the ship owner has failed to carry out reasonable maintenance and inspection. So a programming defect, which could have been detected by reasonable inspection of the ship owner, will possibly not give rise to a tort action against the manufacturers.

2.2.4 Incidents between two autonomous ships

It follows from the discussion carried above that if two or more autonomous vessels are involved in a collision when both were navigating autonomously, the liability should be appropriated between them on an equal basis. This would make sense given that the owners of both vessels are assuming the same degree of responsibility by putting autonomous vessels in use. This kind of solution is not unfamiliar in maritime law. For example, section 187(2) of the Merchant Shipping Act 1995 stipulates that if the evidence is such that the liability cannot be apportioned with any certainty, then as a last resort, the liability should be apportioned equally.[30]

2.2.5 Limitation of liability

In maritime law, those exposed to liability, such as shipowners, salvors and their employees, charterers, managers and operators, are entitled to limit their liability. Unless international conventions that are in force are amended, manufacturers, such as software producers and programme designers, will not be able to limit their

---

28 *Donoghue v. Stevenson* [1932] AC 562.
29 *Taylor v. Rover Co Ltd* [1966] 1 WLR 1491.
30 See, for example, *The British Aviator* [1965] 1 Lloyd's Rep 271 (CA); *The Nordic Ferry* [1991] 2 Lloyd's Rep 591 and *The Bow Spring and The Manzanillo II* [2004] EWCA Civ 1007; [2005] 1 Lloyd's Rep 1.

liability[31] when a recourse action is brought against them by the shipowner for malfunction of parts manufactured by them. Whether the right of limitation of liability should be extended to such parties is a policy decision, but if it is not, one should bear in mind that the liability of a manufacturer of an autonomous vessel will be higher than the liabilities that a shipowner will face by third parties, given that the former might be partially or fully responsible to the replacement cost of an autonomous vessel in addition to liabilities that he will face in a recourse action.

Another point to consider with regard to limitation is the position of a shipowner. The right of limitation is not indefinite and might be lost in some instances. Under the Convention on Limitation of Liability for Maritime Claims 1976, for example, a person liable shall not be entitled to limit his liability "if it is proved that the loss resulted from his personal act or omission, committed with the intent to cause such loss, or recklessly and with knowledge that such loss would probably result."[32] Unless this test is amended, it is submitted that it will be virtually impossible to break the limits if a programming or software error causes a collision between an autonomous vessel and other vessels. In that scenario, it will be rather difficult, if not impossible, for third parties to demonstrate the personal act or omission of the shipowner. The outcome will probably be the same even if ship managers fail to upload software updates onto the system, as in most instances such a conduct will fall short of "recklessness"[33] required to break the limits.

3 Conclusion

It is understandable why the debate on autonomous vessels has so far focussed on to what extent existing technical rules concerning safety standards could accommodate the development of autonomous vessels. That is a natural starting point, as it will be rather difficult if not impossible to put autonomous vessels into commercial use in international and territorial waters of other states under the current international legal regime.

The work carried out so far suggests that the technology required to make autonomous navigation a reality will be developed in the next decade or so. However, even if regulatory obstacles are cleared, whether the shipping world will embrace autonomous ships will depend on various factors. Public acceptance of autonomous vessels will be an important consideration, of course. Will the general public be receptive to the idea of a chemical tanker navigating in international waters autonomously? Also, it is important that the infrastructure of ports around the world is upgraded to receive such vessels.

---

31 See Article 1 of the Convention on Limitation of Liability for Maritime Claims 1976. A similar outcome would follow under the International Convention relating to the Limitation of the Liability of Owners of Sea-Going Ships 1957.

32 Article 4. The same test also applies in other maritime conventions, such as International Convention for the Unification of Certain Rules of Law relating to Bills of Lading 1968 and Convention relating to the Carriage of Passengers and their Luggage by Sea 1974/2002.

33 Recklessness is understood to be "a state of mind stopping short of deliberate intention, and going beyond mere inadvertence". See R. v. Lawrence (Stephen) [1981] 1 All ER 974, at p. 978, per Lord Hailsham.

However, the most important consideration for shipowners will be whether such vessels will be commercially viable. It has been suggested that autonomous vessels will yield significant commercial advantages to ship operators by reducing fuel and operational costs and creating more cargo storage capacity.[34] It has also been argued that introduction of autonomous ships will reduce losses caused by human error, especially errors due to operator fatigue and basic operator errors.[35] However, it will certainly not be possible to eliminate human error completely. The human element will always be present because an autonomous vessel will be designed, programmed, and constructed by human beings. Also, it is not a deniable fact that the cost of an autonomous vessel will be much higher than the cost of a manned vessel. One of the most significant issues will be what liabilities operators of autonomous vessels would face. A disproportional increase in the liabilities that an autonomous vessel faces as opposed to the liabilities a similar manned vessel faces today will lead to a significant increase in insurance premium. It is also necessary to have a certainty on this matter so that insurers could calculate their potential exposure. This chapter advances a number of fundamental arguments on the issue; in particular it highlights the need:

  i) to introduce a liability regime for autonomous ships, ideally through an international convention;
  ii) to impose a strict liability regime when such vessels operate in an autonomous fashion;
  iii) to channel liability to the registered shipowner, not the manufacturer;
  iv) to leave the risk caused by cyber-attacks or losing connection with an autonomous ship on the shoulders of the shipowner; and
  v) to enable shipowners to have a recourse action against those responsible in the manufacture of an autonomous vessel.

---

34 See, www.unmanned-ship.org/munin/(last tested on 31 December 2018).
35 S Ahvenjärvi, "The Human Element and Autonomous Ships" [2016] Transnav 517, at 518.

CHAPTER 9

Shipping

Product liability goes high-tech

*Professor Andrew Tettenborn**

Few resolutions of the European Parliament begin with references to Pygmalion and Frankenstein's monster, or suggest with an apparent straight face that the time might have come to give intelligent machines legal personality. The 2017 resolution that did this[1] can safely be dismissed as a slightly silly *jeu d'esprit* by the overpaid and underworked. But there is nevertheless a grain of truth for shipping lawyers lying behind it. Machines and computer code, rather than master mariners and chief officers, are increasingly controlling shipping operations; it follows that shipping liability disputes will increasingly concern cases of machine malfunctions, software glitches and hardware hangups rather than direct human error. Hence this chapter, on product liability and the effect on it of the use of electronics and cyber-control in the shipping world.

1 Product liability, ships and digitisation

To anyone from an EU background, product liability traditionally evokes thoughts of strict liability under the Product Liability Directive of 1985.[2] This is of some relevance in the marine context, but (as will appear) only in a rather constricted way. It will briefly appear towards the end of this chapter, after the main part, which will concentrate on traditional product liability based on negligence.

In cases not concerning new technology, there is no serious doubt that on principle the general rules of negligence-based product liability apply at sea as they do elsewhere.[3] Thus shipbuilders whose negligence results in damage to other property can be sued by the owners of the latter provided the loss is not too remote and causation is otherwise established,[4] and the same goes for the

---

* Professor of Commercial Law, Institute of International Shipping and Trade Law, Swansea University.
  1 The European Parliament resolution of 16 February 2017 with recommendations to the Commission on Civil Law Rules on Robotics (2015/2103(INL)).
  2 Council Directive on the approximation of the laws, regulations and administrative provisions of the Member States concerning liability for defective products, Dir. 85/374.
  3 See C. Miller & R. Goldberg, *Product Liability* (2nd ed) Para.9.41; *Marsden's Collisions at Sea* (14th ed), paras.12–29 – 12–37.
  4 *The Esso Bernicia* [1989] AC 643 (refusal to strike out a claim against the builders of a tug following the stranding of a supertanker that caused widespread damage and massive pollution).

manufacturers[5] and suppliers[6] of components. The availability of such a claim, moreover, takes on additional significance since it can give rise not only to a direct claim but also contribution proceedings. Hence the owners of a vessel found at fault in a collision claim can where necessary seek contribution from shipbuilders or component manufacturers in so far as the latter could have been sued by the original claimant.[7] Conversely, limitations on general product liability also apply, such as the bar on tort claims against manufacturers or suppliers for damage to the manufactured item itself.[8]

These underlying principles are likely to survive any encroachment of digitisation (unless some international agreement can be reached, which seems unlikely). Hence except for claims for pure economic loss, and claims for damage to the ship from components fitted on board her at the time of acquisition by the claimant, suits based on negligence-based product liability will remain not only a possibility but a probability. But the practicalities are likely to change to some extent. One reason is that liability in negligence under the general principle in *Donoghue v Stevenson*[9] can be difficult to establish where there is a likelihood of intermediate examination or testing of a product.[10] This is likely to be highly relevant when it comes to any kind of electronic control system: most companies will not entrust the fate of $50 million worth of capesize bulk carrier or even $100,000 worth of containerised goods to such a system without pretty exhaustive testing and evaluation. Secondly, there may be other practical changes caused by the progressive replacement of people by code and EDI. This is likely to affect at least three fields in particular.

One is cargo documentation, identification and delivery. On principle this is ideal for digitisation. Repeated physical movements of paper over long distances are currently a nightmare for ship, cargo and financier alike; their supplanting by instantaneous transfer and reading of e-documents is an obviously progressive step. Admittedly attempts to digitise bills of lading, documents of title and other transport paper have hitherto had mixed success, and have not received anything like universal trust.[11] But the advent of effective blockchain and distributed ledger technology[12] may well change this by making such documents sufficiently reliable

---

5 *Bow Valley Husky (Bermuda) Ltd v St John Shipbuilding Ltd* [1997] 3 SCR 1210 (claim by the owner of an offshore facility against a component manufacturer for failure to warn of the flammability of its product).

6 *Andrew Weir Shipping Ltd v Wartsila UK Ltd* [2004] EWHC 1284 (Comm); [2004] 2 Lloyd's Rep 377 (a duty to warn case). In a few old cases some scepticism appeared about the liability of such people: e.g. *Grant v Australian Knitting Mills Ltd* [1936] AC 85, at 107 (per Lord Wright) and *Riverstone Meat Co Pty Ltd v Lancashire Shipping Co Ltd* [1961] AC 807, at 869 (per Lord Keith). But these dicta should now, it is suggested, be regarded as outdated.

7 Some difficulties may arise in so far as the shipowner bought the vessel or component from the builder or maker, since there may well be an exemption clause protecting the latter from liability. But no such difficulty arises with claims by other shipowners not in privity with builders or makers.

8 *Hamble Fisheries Ltd v Gardner & Sons Ltd* [1999] 2 Lloyd's Rep 1.

9 [1932] AC 562.

10 See *Clerk & Lindsell on Torts* (22nd ed), paras.11–37 – 11–39.

11 BOLERO, essDOCS and e-title are the best known: none has achieved anything like universality.

12 Although "blockchain" and "distributed ledger" are often used synonymously, technically the former is a subset of the latter. "Distributed ledger" is any system in which a ledger and changes to it are

and tamper-proof to persuade shipowners to rely on them and P&I interests to provide cover,[13] and to convince congenitally sceptical financiers to lend on the basis of such documentation.[14] Similarly, the process of keeping track of containers – a major concern with container vessels laden with 20,000 TEUs now nothing out of the ordinary – has quietly gone digital. And whatever the teaching, so dear to law professors, about the need for goods to be released only against a paper bill of lading, it is worth noting that the trucker taking cargo away from the terminal will these days likely have obtained it by producing a PIN or other electronic authorisation.[15]

Secondly, there is the care of cargo, as contrasted with that of the vessel itself. Aspects of this are already increasingly automated. Examples include continuous monitoring of temperature levels in reefer transport, and conversely the regular testing of the atmosphere around bulk cargoes liable to overheating or spontaneous combustion as a standard fire precaution. Similarly, for delicate cargoes like fruit, containers are increasingly more than boring metal boxes. They are often now decidedly smart devices,[16] with sophisticated contraptions to monitor, and sometimes indeed spontaneously to make changes to, the atmosphere within them on the fly. Yet again, stowage plans and their execution are now to a large extent automated, hence (one hopes) not only maintaining good trim and the logistics of loading and discharge, but also avoiding errors like the stowage of delicate or flammable cargoes next to engine-room bulkheads.

Thirdly, and much more in the future, there is the process of navigation itself; the day-to-day operations of getting under way, stopping, manoeuvring, docking, watchkeeping, routing, dealing with hazards and collision avoidance. Although the entirely unmanned cargo ship in commercial service is still very much a future project,[17] there have been successful experiments;[18] and there is already a definite

---

distributed over a number of participants and not dependent on any centralised server or database. "Blockchain" is a distributed electronic ledger system in which each ledger is readable by all participants and all ledgers can be securely and indelibly updated virtually simultaneously, with all additions and their timing being permanently preserved. See I. Bashir, *Mastering Blockchain: Distributed Ledger Technology, Decentralization, and Smart Contracts Explained*, Ch.1.

13 A container shipment from China to Canada was successfully completed by Israeli shipowners Zim using blockchain technology developed by Wave to supply documentation in November 2017: see *Marine Log*, 21 November 2017 (www.marinelog.com/index.php?option=com_k2&view=item&id=27709:zim-completes-pilot-of-blockchain-based-paperless-bills-of-lading&Itemid=257, accessed January 2019).

14 In May 2018 a shipment of soya beans from Argentina to buyers in Malaysia was experimentally performed and financed entirely through blockchain technology developed by R3. The banks involved were HSBC and ING. See "HSBC claims first trade-finance deal with blockchain", *FT*, 13 May 2018.

15 A process that has already exercised the courts: *Glencore International AG v MSC Mediterranean Shipping Co SA* [2017] EWCA Civ 365; [2017] 2 Lloyd's Rep. 186.

16 On the legal implications of which, see F. Stevens, in B. Soyer & A. Tettenborn (eds), *Maritime Liabilities in a Global and Regional Context*, Chap 5.

17 Though a seductive one for owners. Even at Third World rates crewing makes up over 30% of ship costs; with Western seafarers it can be over 60%.

18 In June 2017 Svitzer, a Maersk towage subsidiary, in collaboration with Rolls-Royce, successfully applied remote control to undock a tug, turn it, sail it a short distance and then re-dock it. Further trials are planned. See *Tug Technology and Business*, 19 April 2018. It is planned that the first operational crewless autonomous cargo ship, the *Yara Birkeland*, will launch in 2020: *The Verge*, 24 July 2017.

prospect of increasing numbers of these processes being automated and crews being correspondingly reduced gradually towards skeleton numbers.

Will these matters cause product liability considerations to become more important in shipping litigation? In some cases, it must be admitted that the answer is often going to be no. In so far as the carrier's seaworthiness obligation is concerned, for example, the carrier is already liable under the Hague and Hague-Visby Rules for the negligence of independent contractors to whom he entrusts measures to ensure it,[19] so the fact that he relied on an apparently competent supplier of electronic controls will not avail him if in fact the latter was negligent and as a result the vessel was unfit to carry the cargo safely. In such a case, third party liability will only be relevant if either the carrier is bankrupt and bereft of P&I cover,[20] or there is a need to escape limitation under the LLMC 1976.

On the other hand, in other areas the effect may be noticeable. Outside the field of unseaworthiness many other aspects of liability – for example, collision, injury to crewmen and many cases of liability under the terms of specific charters[21] – currently depend on ordinary vicarious liability for fault: that is, on whether employees have been negligent in the course of their employment. But in so far as employees are replaced by computers and algorithms, this solution is thrown out of balance. There is no such thing as a negligent computer; it follows that if owing to a computer malfunction something goes wrong the shipowner, unlike the employer of a negligent crewman, is liable only for personal fault (for example, a showing that they failed to supervise or operate the device properly, or had means of knowing that there was something wrong with it). Stress will therefore shift from the owner's P&I club to those on shore responsible for constructing the system and the accompanying machinery, and those writing the code for it. Secondly, even where owners do remain liable, the involvement of shore-based producers may give further scope for third party or contribution proceedings by them against others who might have been held liable.[22] Third, it is also true that a growth in the scope of third party claims by cargo may provide an escape in collision cases from the "several liability" rule. Cargo claims against the non-carrying vessel arising out of an incident in which both vessels are at fault are available only to the extent of the proportionate fault of that vessel:[23] cargo claims against third parties are not so limited.

The fourth relevance of third party liability may be practically the most important, however. This is limitation, particularly relevant in the case of large claims against

---

19 *Riverstone Meat Co Pty Ltd v Lancashire Shipping Co Ltd* [1961] AC 807. The position is probably the same under the Hamburg Rules because of the general liability for the fault of "servants and agents" in Art.5.1, and certainly the same under the Rotterdam Rules because of Art.18.

20 Itself becoming a more remote possibility since the EU Directive 2009/20/EC requiring all vessels calling at EU ports, and all EU registered vessels, to carry cover.

21 As in cases like *The Antonis P Lemos* [1985] AC 711 (owners' negligence in delaying loading); or see e.g. Clause 13(2) of the Baltime 1939 form (charterer's negligence).

22 An instance might be where a computer glitch caused a shipowner to hand over goods to a non-bill-of lading-holder thus becoming strictly liable to the latter. Assuming any problems of a duty of care could be got over, there would be a theoretical possibility of a claim against the person responsible for the defective code.

23 Under the rule in s 187(1) of the Merchant Shipping Act 1995.

the owners of small ships. The LLMC 1976 allows shipowners to limit and extends this right to some people connected with them: the special case of salvors aside, these are the "owner, charterer, manager or operator" and their respective employees.[24] But that is the limit of protection. Except possibly where entire control of an autonomous vessel has been delegated (for example to an onshore control centre), in which case the delegate might be classed as an "operator", none of these words seems applicable to a third party producer or provider of control services. It seems to follow that, absent any change to the LLMC 1976, product liability claims brought against such persons are not covered by it. But this is subject to the next paragraph: will courts be prepared to allow claimants to take advantage of this, or will they regard it as an illegitimate attempt to circumvent a wholesome regime?

2 Product liability, duty of care and public policy: the problem of the Nicholas H decision

The difficulty here arises from the House of Lords' decision in *The Nicholas H*.[25] There, it will be remembered, a thoroughly unseaworthy vessel sank with her entire cargo of lead and zinc. Cargo sued not only her owners for the relevant limitation amount, but also her classification society NKK for its entire loss, alleging that the latter had been at fault in allowing her to go to sea unseaworthy in the first place. The claim against NKK was dismissed as untenable; and while this was partly put on the basis of a lack of any undertaking of responsibility[26] and on the need to protect class from bearing a responsibility it was never intended to,[27] an important strand of the reasoning was that allowing such suit would allow cargo to give the go-by to the complex scheme of liabilities and defences (and limitations of liability) under the Hague-Visby rules.[28]

How far can this decision be taken? On one view the reasoning in it extends to almost any shipping-related claim against any third party anywhere, including a product liability suit: after all, in nearly all such cases there will be a potentially subvertible limitation or other regime applicable.[29] It is suggested, however, that *The Nicholas H* is unlikely to be construed so widely. For one thing, in that case stress was laid on one particular feature. This was that what was at stake was a responsibility – to take care to ensure safe carriage – that lay primarily with the carrier and had been egregiously broken by it. The complaint against NKK was by

---

24 See Arts 1(2), 1(4).
25 [1996] AC 211. For a useful discussion see K. Tan, "Of Duty", (1996) 112 LQR 209.
26 Ibid, at p 242.
27 Ibid, at pp 240–241. On this aspect see A. Tettenborn, "The Liabilities of Classification Societies – More Ackward Than It Looks?" in D.R. Thomas (ed), *Liability Regimes in Contemporary Maritime Law*, Chap.7.
28 Ibid at p 240 (Lord Steyn: allowing suit by cargo would "disturb the balance created by the Hague Rules and Hague-Visby Rules as well as by tonnage limitation provisions, by enabling cargo-owners to recover in tort against a peripheral party to the prejudice of the protection of shipowners under the existing system").
29 Apart from the Hague-Visby regime, in a time or voyage charter there will be the terms of the charter itself, not to mention the apportionment provisions of the Inter-Club Agreement; outside carriage there will be the general right of owners and charterers to limit under the LLMC 1976.

comparison ancillary: its alleged sin was a mere negligent failure to ensure the carrier lived up to its own obligations, and to that extent made any case against it rather less compelling.[30] This feature is not generally present with defective hardware or code; a carrier making use of this to control an autonomous vessel is attempting to fulfil its primary obligation, not shirking it. Furthermore, in support of this view it is worth remembering that in one case the House of Lords has allowed a product liability claim to proceed in a case where there was clearly a right to limit. In *The Esso Bernicia*,[31] a VLCC was damaged following a mismanoeuvre by a tug and proceeded to demolish a jetty, the destruction being great. A product liability action against the builders of the tug was allowed to proceed. Although this case was decided some years before *The Nicholas H*, and it was a case where limitation would clearly have applied, its correctness has never been seriously called into question.

3 Technology, code and product liability

There is no doubt that defective electronic and computer hardware, like any other physical control equipment, fall fair and square within the field of product liability: if they fail as a result of negligent production or distribution, then liability will follow as a matter of course. Software and code at first sight look different. They are not tangible, save possibly when embodied on a CD, DVD or external hard drive, and it seems do not obey the ordinary rules of personal property.[32] No doubt this is why works on product liability spend some time arguing about what a product is and whether software liability is really product liability at all.[33] However, in the commercial context the point does not really matter, for three reasons. First, while it is true that on a purchase of software an issue can arise as to whether this is a sale of goods creating presumptively strict liability or a sale of services carrying merely a duty of care,[34] this is a largely academic issue in the commercial context because bespoke terms will almost invariably pre-empt it anyway. Secondly, while the "product or not" point theoretically does matter as regards strict liability claims, the exclusion from the European product regime of all suits for pure economic loss and business property damage means that in most cases it will be irrelevant. Thirdly, as regards negligence liability, while the actual decision in *Donoghue v Stevenson*[35] was indubitably a product liability case, the principle it established covers supply of services just as much as physical products.

---

30 See [1996] AC 211, at 237.

31 [1989] AC 643.

32 For example, they were held to be outside the law of lien in the carefully-reasoned decision in *Your Response Ltd v Datateam Business Media Ltd* [2014] EWCA Civ 281; [2015] QB 41.

33 E.g. C. Miller & R. Goldberg, *Product Liability* (2nd ed), Chap.9; *Clerk & Lindsell on Torts* (22 ed), paras.11–09 – 11–10, 11–51.

34 See cases like *St Albans D.C. v. International Computers Ltd* [1996] 4 All E.R. 481 and *Southwark LBC v IBM UK Ltd* [2011] EWHC 549 (TCC); 135 Con. L.R. 136; and K.Moon, "The Nature of Computer Programs: Tangible? Goods? Personal Property? Intellectual property?" (2009) EIPR 396.

35 [1932] A.C. 562.

We will therefore be dealing largely with claims based on fault, not against owners, charterers or cargo owners, but against other third parties involved in the deployment of electronic means of control. Essentially, therefore, we will be talking about the potential liability of those concerned with the production of control mechanisms: manufacturers of hardware and circuitry, writers of software and distributors and operators of control systems. With blockchain and distributed leisure systems, claimants are likely to train their guns on the writers of the underlying software and those responsible for communication of encrypted information between the various participants. With systems based on a central server there will obviously be a larger range of defendants, since then anyone responsible for the production or setting up of the central server will also be in the firing line.

4 The areas of particular relevance: cargo documentation, cargo care and navigation

4.1 Cargo documentation

Some of the biggest advances as regards digitisation have, as pointed out above, been made in the area of cargo documentation: bills of lading, traceability of containers, the formalities necessary for handover to the consignee and so on. What are the prospects for product liability claims here against those responsible for the system? This being the area of documentation and record-keeping, we are (it is suggested) thinking here in terms of the effects of e-malfunctions causing goods to be mislaid, lost or misdelivered. As regards systems based on a central register, typical instances might be negligently-caused glitches, or vulnerabilities to hacking in either the central server or the satellite servers through which cargo owners connect to the centre. (An example of the latter would be a defect allowing evildoers to obtain passwords, combinations or PIN codes allowing the collection of goods by impostors). With blockchain-based technology the issue is less likely to arise, at least as regards vulnerabilities, since the need for evildoers to compromise vast numbers of distributed databases simultaneously is the precise reason why blockchain is so secure in the first place. But claims are still conceivable, as are allegations of negligence leading to misbehaviour by the software lying behind the blockchain, or the hardware used by a particular user.

Occasionally such negligence may cause physical damage to cargo or vessel (or both). One example might be deterioration of the contents of a container of meat after a negligently-introduced software glitch causes it to be mislaid for a time, or fire damage caused where a computer failure leads to flammable materials being misstowed next to a hot bulkhead. Where this is so, it is suggested that there is no difficulty on principle, since the ordinary rule in *Donoghue v Stevenson*[36] presumably applies. There is little doubt that this is loss within the ambit of the duty broken (i.e. to supply effective electronic documentation relating to goods): assuming that fault and causation are proved, liability ought to follow as a matter of course. Indeed, it is arguable that with a commodity which is normally as

---

36 [1932] AC 562.

meticulously produced and tested as software and electronic control mechanisms, there may be room in some cases for an inference of negligence in order to ease life for the claimant. Just as the courts have held that if a fairly new tyre bursts at speed negligent manufacture can be inferred,[37] one might say the same about an otherwise unexplained software glitch: absent a convincing explanation, someone connected with the production process must have blundered.

Most of the time, however, the loss arising from this sort of event will be financial: costs resulting from delay, loss of the use of goods, investigation expenses and so on. By contrast with cases of physical damage, it seems clear that presumptively no action in tort will lie here, since pure financial losses, however foreseeable, are not generally recoverable under the rule in *Donoghue v Stevenson*.[38] The only way to recover them would be to show something in the nature of an assurance from the defendant computer control provider to the claimant cargo owner that could be construed as an acceptance of responsibility towards the latter; but this is likely, to say the least, to be an uphill task.

One matter is unclear in this respect: what about negligence causing the disappearance or theft of goods? Which side of the physical damage/economic loss divide does this lie on? Imagine, for example, that incompetently-written computer code allows thieves to obtain the PIN code to goods covered by a bill of lading and drive away with them:[39] or that a negligent failure in blockchain security allows an electronic bill of lading somehow to get into the wrong hands and have goods collected against it. Does theft count as equivalent to destruction, or as mere economic loss? It seems the latter is more likely;[40] but one cannot be certain – which is a pity, especially for insurance and P&I interests, since the sums turning on the distinction may well be substantial.

4.2 Care of cargo

As we mentioned above, many of the incidental tasks of cargo care in the course of carriage are now automated, from atmosphere control to ventilation to fire prevention. As and when vessels become more autonomous, moreover, such controls are likely to become increasingly integrated with control of the vessel generally and thus dependent on the products of shore-based providers of electronic control systems. What happens then if, owing to negligence by those responsible for their

---

37 See *Carroll v Fearon* [1998] PIQR P 416; also *Baker v KTM Sportmotorcycle UK Ltd* [2017] EWCA Civ 378; [2018] ECC 35 and *Clerk & Lindsell on Torts* (22nd ed), para.11–55.

38 See *Clerk & Lindsell on Torts* (22nd ed), para.11–19 and cases such as *Simaan General Contracting Co v Pilkington Glass Ltd (No.2)* [1988] QB 758, *Hamble Fisheries Ltd v Gardner & Sons Ltd* [1999] 2 Lloyd's Rep1 and *Barking & Dagenham LBC v GLS Educational Supplies Ltd* [2015] EWHC 2050 (TCC).

39 Compare the facts in *Glencore International AG v MSC Mediterranean Shipping Co SA* [2017] EWCA Civ 365; [2017] 2 Lloyd's Re. 186.

40 Hence in *Bailey v HSS Alarms Ltd, The Times*, June 20, 2000, the Court of Appeal held a burglar alarm monitoring company liable for negligently failing to prevent theft, but only because there was a high degree of proximity between it and the victim. Another way of reaching the same answer is to say that in any case the law is hesitant in the absence of an assumption of responsibility to impose general duties to guard against deliberate evildoing by third parties, including thieves: see cases such as *Smith v Littlewoods Organisation Ltd* [1987] AC 241.

production, the atmosphere control mechanisms in a smart container break down, affecting the bananas inside; or the monitoring software in a vessel fails to pick up indications of a power supply failure to a container of frozen lamb?

On principle claims of this sort, based as they nearly always will be on physical damage or destruction of cargo, are likely to be straightforward. Even if there are further claims for expenses caused by loss of use or other financial losses, these are again unproblematical in so far as they are the foreseeable result of damage or destruction. Assuming therefore that causation and fault are proved, duty of care is unlikely to raise difficulties and liability is on principle straightforward.

It might be argued that in many cases of this sort the decision in *The Nicholas H* could provide an obstruction in so far as a claim of this kind against a provider of control mechanisms duplicates a claim against the carrier itself. It has to be remembered that a version of the Hague or Hague-Visby Rules will in the vast majority of cases be applicable to the contract of carriage, either by force of law or by incorporation; and the duty under Art.III rule 2 of the rules to "properly and carefully load, handle, stow, carry, keep, care for and discharge" the cargo is a non-delegable duty under which the carrier is already liable for the negligence of any independent contractor.[41] If so, does a claim against the latter not suffer from the objection that all it does is provide an extra defendant who is unable to limit liability? This is true: nevertheless, it is submitted that it is not conclusive. Unlike *The Nicholas H*, this is not a case where the defendant's alleged fault is merely ancillary to the carrier's own breach: on the contrary, it is constitutive of it. Despite the lack of any right to limit, it lies ill in the mouth of a negligent defendant to object to liability merely because he has caused the person employing him to be liable independently of any fault in the latter.

4.3 Navigation

We come finally to the case which attracts most of the headlines: product liability as it might affect autonomous navigation and automated vessel management. Assuming these will increasingly be used, which seems a racing certainty, what happens if we then encounter behaviour that might in the case of a traditionally-manned vessel amount to navigational fault? The point matters particularly here because, in contrast to liability for providing an unseaworthy ship and failing to care properly for cargo, most cases of navigational fault involve straight negligence, with no question of non-delegable duties or liability for independent contractors. So in, for example, straightforward collision cases, under the present law the shipowner himself is free from liability in so far as the collision was due to the fault of an apparently competent independent contractor.[42] Since, there is (as pointed out

---

41 *Hourani v Harrison* (1927) 28 Lloyd's LlL R 120; see too *Riverstone Meat Co Pty Ltd v Lancashire Shipping Co Ltd* [1961] AC 807, at 838 (per Lord Simonds) and *Leesh River Tea Co v British India SN Co* [1967] 2 QB 250, at 278 (per Salmon LJ).

42 See *Marsden's Collisions at Sea* (14th ed), paras.12–06 – 12–08. It is not thought that the slight relaxation of the independent contractor rule in *Woodland v Swimming Teachers Association* [2013] UKSC 66; [2014] AC 537 will have any practical effect here.

above) no such thing as a negligent employed computer, it follows that in the brave new world of autonomous ships a claim against the third party may well on occasion be the only one available to the victim.[43]

In general, it is submitted that in cases like this product liability claims against providers of control systems are straightforward as a matter of law, assuming they are claims (as is likely) for damage to property or personal injury rather than for simple loss of profits or pure economic loss. The possibilities are widespread. Negligently-caused malfunction of computer controls can readily cause accidents giving rise to injury, whether to crew, passengers, salvage operatives or ordinary bystanders. They can equally well cause collisions, with accompanying damage to other vessels, or explosions damaging cargo, port installations and property on shore. Subject to the practicalities of proof, defendants shown to be at fault will find it difficult to avoid liability for losses and damages of this sort.[44]

There is one qualification, however, that needs to be discussed in this connection: claims by the victims of pollution, either from oil carried as cargo, bunker fuel or (assuming that the HNS Convention will be in force by the time autonomous vessels are in regular use, which seems a racing certainty) hazardous substances generally. Claims for pollution of this kind are all dealt with by separate self-standing regimes: namely the Civil Liability Convention of 1992, the Bunkers Convention of 2001 and the HNS Convention of 2010. All create a measure of strict liability in the shipowner, backed by P&I cover[45] and (in the case of the Civil Liability and HNS Conventions) independent funds. All, importantly, contain a measure of channelling of claims through the shipowner, and restrictions on parallel claims against third parties. The possibility of whether product liability claims also remain available to pollution victims is nevertheless important: even if they are guaranteed recovery against the owner, the issue remains significant to the question whether the owner can in turn bring contribution proceedings.

This question depends on the terms of the channelling provisions. As regards English law, those relating to oil pollution are contained in s. 156 of the Merchant Shipping Act 1995, prohibiting any claim by the pollution victim against, among others, any servant or agent of the owner, and any other person "employed or engaged in any capacity on board the ship or to perform any service for the ship".[46] Concerning HNS Convention liability, there is, as yet, no English

---

43 It is a nice question, which we have no space to go into here, whether a change to this, to make owners liable for the negligence of third party controllers, would run foul of the provision in the 1910 Collision Convention, Art.3, which states: "If the collision is caused by the fault of one of the vessels, liability to make good the damages attaches to the one which has committed the fault".

44 Compare *Hindustan SS Co Ltd v Siemens Bros & Co Ltd* [1955] 1 Lloyd's Rep 167, where a problem in an engine room telegraph caused a vessel to engage full ahead and hit a tug and part of Avonmouth dock. A *Donoghue v Stevenson* claim against the telegraph manufacturer failed, but only for lack of proof of fault.

45 Compulsory in all three cases: Civil Liability Convention, Art VII, Bunkers Convention, Art 7 and HNS Convention, Art 12.

46 See s 156(2)(b).

legislation;[47] but Art. 7(5) of the Convention, which will form the basis of any legislation that is passed, is in similar terms.

How might these affect product liability claims? Since a software producer or component manufacturer is unlikely to be regarded as a "servant or agent" of the owner unless contracted by him, the question is whether he falls in the category of those "engaged ... to perform any service for the ship". The point is an open one but it is suggested that the marginally better solution is that the exception does not apply to a person simply making or preparing some device or software to be supplied for use in connection with the ship, as against doing actual work on the vessel. If so, then in so far as an oil or chemical spill from a vessel is due to a computer or control glitch, it is suggested that the possibility of direct liability remains.

5 Strict liability

At the beginning of this chapter, we said that we would be concentrating on negligence liability. The subject of strict product liability under the 1985 Product Liability Directive,[48] as transcribed by Part I of the Consumer Protection Act 1987,[49] is nevertheless worth a brief treatment, as it may sometimes be relevant.

As is well-known, the Directive creates a strict liability for damage caused by any defect present in a "product" at the time of manufacture;[50] liability attaches automatically to the manufacturer and to any importer into the EEA.[51] A defect for these purposes is anything meaning that "the safety of the product is not such as persons generally are entitled to expect".[52] In the context of control mechanisms, the effect of the Act can be fairly simply summed up as follows. Any bug or glitch that caused the system to malfunction in an unsafe way and thereby caused damage would be covered, as would any design feature that compromised safety, such as a shipboard sensor that was unable to pick up converging objects until it was too late to avoid a collision.[53]

The reason for the limited applicability of strict liability under the Directive, despite its apparently wide ambit, is twofold. First, the EU strict liability scheme,

---

47 Power to pass it is contained in the Merchant Shipping Act 1995, s 182B, but it has not yet been exercised.
48 Council Directive on the approximation of the laws, regulations and administrative provisions of the Member States concerning liability for defective products, Dir. 85/374.
49 See generally *Clerk & Lindsell on Torts* (22nd ed), paras.11–45 – 11–89.
50 See Consumer Protection Act 1987, s 2(1).
51 See s 2(2).
52 See s 3(1).
53 The definition of a defect under the 1987 Act is admittedly complex: see in particular *A v National Blood Authority* [2001] 3 All E.R. 289; [2001] Lloyd's Rep Med 187, *Wilkes v Depuy International Ltd* [2016] EWHC 3096 (QB); (2017) 153 BMLR 91 and J. Eisler, "One Step forward and Two Steps back in Product Liability: The Search for Clarity in the Identification of Defects" (2017) CLJ 230. But thankfully these complications are unlikely to affect its maritime applications.

unlike that obtaining in most US jurisdictions, including Admiralty,[54] is restricted to claims for personal injury and damage to domestic property.[55] Suits for damage to commercial assets are thus entirely excluded. It follows that in the maritime context the EU rule can only ever be relevant to claims for injury to workers and bystanders, or to damage to such things as domestic apartments or dwellinghouses. Essentially, therefore, the only time the Directive will be relevant is where a collision or shipboard explosion causes industrial or bystander injuries, or where a major harbour incident or explosion causes damage to private property on shore.[56]

Secondly, unlike negligence liability it is strictly limited to damage caused by defective "products". Although there is no doubt that one-off "products" are included, services, however valuable or marketable, which do not meet this criterion are not. This immediately raises problems over precisely the computerised control systems that are involved with automated shipping: is a defect in such a system a defect in a product or a service?

The position appears to be this. A "product" in the 1987 Act is defined as "goods".[57] In so far as there is a failure of hardware due to a defect existing at the time of manufacture (for instance a defective circuit board or sensor component), there will thus clearly be liability. So too if hardware, such as a sensor, fails because firmware embedded in it has a glitch: the hardware will, it seems clear, be regarded as one composite (and defective) whole. By contrast, it seems clear that if code is simply written on a computer screen and then transmitted, this must be regarded as a service and not a product; it will therefore not attract strict liability.[58]

In so far as there is a defect in software embodied in a DVD or USB stick, and damage occurs following use of that medium, whether at sea or on shore, the

---

54 Where the tendency is to say it applies to all personal injury and property damage external to the defective item itself. See in particular the bald terms of the *Restatement 3d of Torts*, § 1: "One engaged in the business of selling or otherwise distributing products who sells or distributes a defective product is subject to liability for harm to persons or property caused by the defect"This reflected the earlier law: for a discussion see e.g. R. Force, "Maritime Products Liability in the United States", 11 (1986) The Maritime Lawyer 1, 48. An example of such strict liability is *Pan-Alaska Fisheries, Inc. v. Marine Const. & Design Co.*, 565 F2d 1129 (1977). The extension to Admiralty was confirmed in e.g. *Lindsay v. McDonnell Douglas Aircraft Corp*, 460 F2d 631, at 635 (8th Cir. 1972) ("We further conclude that federal maritime law should and does apply the doctrine of strict liability in tort ...."); see too *Pan-Alaska Fisheries, Inc. v. Marine Const. & Design Co.*, 565 F2d 1129, at 1134 (1978).

55 See Consumer Protection Act 1987, ss 5(1), 5(3).

56 See generally A. Tettenborn, "Maritime Consumers – The Consumer Protection Act and Shipping Law" (1988) LMCLQ 211; also C. Miller & R. Goldberg, *Product Liability* (2nd ed), para.9.41.

57 See s 1(2)(c). The definition in the Directive, it should be noted, is "all moveables". It can just be argued that because the civil law notion of moveables can encompass intangibles this is wider, and hence that software is included in it.

58 C. Miller & R. Goldberg, *Product Liability* (2nd ed), para.9.101 makes the point that products must be capable of being "supplied" (see s.4(1)(b) of the 1987 Act), which it is difficult to apply to intangibles. The Act also envisages products being imported into the EEA (see s 2(2)(c)), which again is difficult to apply to intangibles. This view is also supported by the decision (admittedly in another context) in *Computer Associates UK Ltd v Software Incubator Ltd* [2018] EWCA Civ 518; [2018] 1 Lloyd's Rep 613, esp at [55]-[69], and earlier dicta by Sir Ian Glidewell in *St Albans D.C. v. International Computers Ltd* [1996] 4 All ER 481, at 493.

matter is less certain. There is certainly a physical object here; nevertheless it seems odd that the presence of a medium of negligible value compared to the code on it should make all the difference.[59] However, this may indeed be the case, on the basis that as a consumer protection measure the Directive and the 1987 Act based on it should be read as widely as reasonably possible, despite any anomalies this may throw up.[60]

6 Conclusion

Autonomous and computer-regulated shipping is here and growing in importance. The practical impact of product liability law on it may well be modest, if only because of an unwillingness to allow existing regimes to be supplanted, the limited ambit of the duty of care under *Donoghue v Stevenson*, and the restricted reach of the product liability provisions of the Consumer Protection Act 1987. Nevertheless the prospect is there, and needs to be noted by practitioners: not only those acting for claimants, but also those instructed by P&I clubs and other defendants, who (one hopes) are always on the lookout for someone else on whom to lay off any liability that might unfortunately attach to their client.

---

[59] As pointed out by Lord Penrose in the Scots case of *Beta Computers (Europe) Ltd v Adobe Systems (Europe) Ltd* [1996] CLC 821, at 828–829; see too C Miller & R Goldberg, *Product Liability* (2nd ed), paras.9.100–9.101.

[60] This seems to have been accepted in *St Albans D.C. v. International Computers Ltd* [1996] 4 All ER 481; see also *Computer Associates UK Ltd v Software Incubator Ltd* [2018] EWCA Civ 518; [2018] 1 Lloyd's Rep 613 at [55], accepting the anomaly but regarding it as inevitable.

CHAPTER 10

Who is the master now?

Regulatory and contractual challenges of unmanned vessels

Professor Simon Baughen*

1 Introduction

Unmanned ships are coming, and coming soon. Kongsberg's *Yara Birkeland* will be the world's first fully electric and autonomous container ship. It will be equipped with various proximity sensors, radar, lidar,[1] AIS,[2] camera, infra red camera and its connectivity and communication will be through maritime broadband radio, satellite communications and GSM.[3] Loading and discharging will be done automatically using electric cranes and equipment. Berthing and unberthing will be done without human intervention, through an automatic mooring system. The ship will sail within 12 nautical miles from the coast, between three ports in southern Norway. There will be three centres to handle emergency and exception handling, condition monitoring, operational monitoring, decision support, surveillance of the autonomous ship and its surroundings and all other aspects of safety. The planned time frame is for testing with a captain and small crew, placed in a container-based bridge, to start in the second half of 2018, delivery from the yard and testing of autonomous capability in 2019, with fully autonomous operation starting in 2020.

Where the *Yara Birkeland* leads, other autonomous ships are sure to follow, initially with small coastal and inland waterway vessels. Autonomous ships offer the attraction of reducing accidents, with an estimated 80% of maritime accidents being due to human error. They also offer a reduction in wage costs, estimated to form 30% of a shipowner's operating costs, by eliminating an on-board crew. They may also offer fuel savings through the reduction in weight by eliminating the accommodation structure. However, autonomous vessels bring risks, notably that of a loss of control through malicious hacking, and loss of communication with shore-side control in periods of bad weather coupled with a reduction in datalink capacity. There will also be additional operational costs, such as the provision of shore-based controllers (SBC) who will monitor the ship and navigate it remotely

---

* Member of the Institute of International Shipping and Trade Law, Swansea University.
1 Light, Detection and Ranging.
2 Automatic Identification System.
3 Global System for Mobile Communication.

during sections of its voyage, as well as taking over navigation through remote operation when the ship gets into difficulty if weather and traffic conditions change considerably. The lack of an onboard crew will mean that no maintenance work can be done during the voyage, resulting in increased time in ports for such work. The lack of an onboard crew will also rule out the use of heavy fuel oil which is maintenance intensive and requires the use of costlier marine diesel oil (MDO) or marine gas oil (MGO). Additionally, owners may need to use port agents to perform functions relating to loading and unloading of cargo, including issuing of bills of lading, which are currently performed by the master and crew.

Unmanned vessels will also pose challenges for compliance with the international regulatory framework established through the various conventions of the International Maritime Organisation (IMO). The IMO's Maritime Safety Committee (MSC) recently embarked on a regulatory scoping exercise on how safe, secure and environmentally sound Maritime Autonomous Surface Ships (MASS) operations may be addressed in IMO instruments.[4] It has set out the following four point scale for MASS operations.

1. Ship with automated processes and decision support: Seafarers are on board to operate and control shipboard systems and functions. Some operations may be automated.
2. Remotely controlled ship with seafarers on board: The ship is controlled and operated from another location, but seafarers are on board.
3. Remotely controlled ship without seafarers on board: The ship is controlled and operated from another location. There are no seafarers on board.
4. Fully autonomous ship: The operating system of the ship is able to make decisions and determine actions by itself.

In this chapter I propose to examine the challenges posed by the absence of an onboard crew on a cargo vessel. I shall examine the third scenario in the IMO's scale where there is no onboard crew but navigation is effected by a mixture of complete autonomy through voyage programming and human intervention through SBCs monitoring the vessel's progress throughout the voyage, undertaking some navigational operations themselves through remote operation, such as entering and leaving ports and dealing with complex situations on the open seas which the autonomous algorithms are unable to deal with. I shall be looking at the role of the master in the absence of an onboard crew. Can there still be a master through the SBC? Part one of this chapter considers this question in the light of the various

---

4 At the 99th Session of MSC on 16–25 May 2018 a correspondence group on MASS was set up to test the framework of this regulatory scoping with a view of reporting back to its next session, MSC 100 (3–7 December 2018). The Correspondence Group will test the methodology by conducting an initial assessment of SOLAS regulation III/17-1 (Recovery of persons from the water), which requires all ships to have ship-specific plans and procedures for recovery of persons from the water; SOLAS regulation V/19.2 (Carriage requirements for carriage of shipborne navigational equipment and systems); and Load Lines regulation 10 (Information to be supplied to the master). If time allows, it will also consider SOLAS regulations II-1/3–4 (Emergency towing arrangements and procedures) and V/22 (Navigation bridge visibility).

international regulations that govern ships. In part two this chapter will examine the question from the contractual perspective, with reference to the master's role under time and voyage charters.

2 Regulation and the master[5]

The term 'master' is not defined in any international convention. *The International Law of the Shipmaster* defines the master as 'a natural person who is responsible for a vessel and all things and persons in it and is responsible for enforcing the maritime laws of the flag state' – a definition which does not require such a person be on board the vessel under their command.[6] National laws provide various definitions. In the UK s. 313 of the Merchant Shipping Act 1995 defines 'master' as 'every person (except a pilot) having command or charge of a ship'. The definition does not require on-board presence and could therefore encompass the SBC as remote operator of the vessel. It would not cover completely autonomous vessels as there would no longer be a person in command or charge of a ship whose navigation would be entirely under the control of the artificial intelligence with which it had been programmed. Other national laws define 'master' in such a way as to require presence on board the vessel.[7]

2.1 Manning requirements

It will be for flag states to determine the acceptability of unmanned vessels. Under art. 91 of UNCLOS it is for every State 'to fix the conditions for the grant of its nationality to ships, for the registration of ships in its territory, and for the right to fly its flag'.[8] However, the focus on the position of flag states as regards unmanned vessels should not let us lose sight of the equally important position of port states. UNCLOS does not qualify the rights of states to regulate the admission of vessels to their ports.[9] In the absence of a satisfactory regulatory framework being established through the IMO it is likely that many states will deny admission to unmanned

---

5 This chapter will proceed on the assumption that an unmanned vessel will constitute a 'ship'. Professor Sozer, in a report attached to the CMI Working Group on Ship Nomenclature, <http://comitemaritime.org/wp-content/uploads/2018/05/Letter-to-Presidents-of-NMLAs-re-IWG-on-Vessel-Nomenclature-080316.pdf> accessed 3 September 2018, analysed the definition of the terms in almost 20 key maritime conventions, and none link the definition of ship to the presence of crew on board.

6 J.Cartner, R.Fiske and T.Leiter, *The International Law of the Shipmaster* (London: Informa 2009), 86.

7 The CMI recently sent out a questionnaire on unmanned vessels to the Maritime Law Associations (MLA) of 19 States. The MLAs of Brazil, China and Croatia stated that the master is defined as a person on board the ship. All 19 MLAs answered that neither the chief pre-programmer of an autonomous ship nor another designated person not immediately involved in the operation of the ship could constitute the master. See, 'Summary of responses to the CMI questionnaire. <www.comitemaritime.org/Unmanned-Ships/02715311533200.html> accessed 26 July 2018.

8 Subject to the existence of a genuine link between the State and the ship. Article 91(2) provides that "Every State shall issue to ships to which it has granted the right to fly its flag documents to that effect.

9 An unmanned vessel will almost certainly constitute a ship and as such under art. 17 of UNCLOS would have the right of innocent passage through the territorial sea.

vessels. The initial phase of unmanned vessels is likely to be coastal trading within the territorial sea of the flag state – as contemplated for the *Yara Birkeland*.

Article 94 of UNCLOS sets out the duties of the flag state on manning of vessels. Paragraph 3 requires every State to 'take such measures for ships flying its flag as are necessary to ensure safety at sea with regard, *inter alia*, to: (b) the manning of ships, labour conditions and the training of crews, taking into account the applicable international instruments;' Paragraph 4 provides that:

> Such measures shall include those necessary to ensure: ... (b) that each ship is in the charge of a master and officers who possess appropriate qualifications, in particular in seamanship, navigation, communications and marine engineering and that the crew is appropriate in qualification and numbers for the type, size, machinery and equipment of the ship.

Paragraph 5 requires the flag state in taking these measures '[t]o conform to generally accepted international regulations, procedures and practices and to take any steps which may be necessary to secure their observance'.

These accepted international regulations are contained in the IMO Conventions. SOLAS[10] Chapter V, regulation 14 requires that '[f]rom the point of view of the safety of life at sea, all ships shall be sufficiently and efficiently manned'. This does not prescribe any particular level of manning, and does not require the presence of a crew on board. It is left to the flag state to decide what constitutes sufficient and efficient manning. There is no express requirement in any of the above provisions for at least one seafarer to be on board and it would be open for the flag state to decide that there would be sufficient and efficient manning with no onboard crew, provided there is proper assumption of crew functions by the SBC. The British Maritime Law Association, giving the UK response to the CMI's recent questionnaire on unmanned vessels, stated that art. 94's requirements were not prescriptive and arguably permitted unmanned operation if the relevant ship's autonomous navigation system were sufficiently safe.

SOLAS Chapter V contains two regulations that may be problematic for unmanned vessels. First, Regulation 24 provides for reversion to manual steering in hazardous navigational situations when heading and/or track control systems are in use.

1. In areas of high traffic density, in conditions of restricted visibility and in all other hazardous navigational situations where heading and/or track control systems are in use, it shall be possible to establish manual control of the ship's steering immediately.
2. In circumstances as above, the officer in charge of the navigational watch shall have available without delay the services of a qualified helmsperson who shall be ready at all times to take over steering control.

---

10 Exemptions. Chapter 1. Reg 4(b) allows the flag state to exempt any ship which embodies features of a novel kind from requirements of Chapters II-1, II-2, III and IV. Flag administrations may accept equivalent solutions if satisfied that they are at least as effective as that required by SOLAS.

3. The changeover from automatic to manual steering and vice versa shall be made by or under the supervision of a responsible officer.
4. The manual steering shall be tested after prolonged use of heading and/or track control systems, and before entering areas where navigation demands special caution.

Secondly, Regulation 15 deals with the requirements for Bridge layout and contemplates a physical bridge on the vessel. The virtual bridge on shore for unmanned vessels falls outside the requirements. However, Regulation 3(2) of Part 3, exemptions, provides:

> The Administration may grant to individual ships exemptions or equivalents of a partial or conditional nature, when any such ship is engaged on a voyage where the maximum distance of the ship from the shore, the length and nature of the voyage, the absence of general navigational hazards, and other conditions affecting safety are such as to render the full application of this chapter unreasonable or unnecessary, provided that the Administration has taken into account the effect such exemptions and equivalents may have upon the safety of all other ships.

With an unmanned vessel, the existence of a virtual bridge on shore would constitute a 'condition affecting safety such as to make the full application of the chapter unreasonable or unnecessary'.

2.2 The International Regulations for Preventing Collisions at Sea, 1972 (COLREGs)

The COLREGS provide the navigational rules for vessels to follow with the aim of avoiding collisions. In the UK they are currently implemented by regulation six of the Merchant Shipping (Distress Signals and Prevention of Collisions) Regulations 1996, which provides:

(1) Where any of these regulations is contravened, the owner of the vessel, the master and any person for the time being responsible for the conduct of the vessel shall each be guilty of an offence punishable on conviction on indictment by imprisonment for a term not exceeding two years and a fine, or on summary conviction by a fine.

The rules apply 'to all vessels upon the high seas and in all waters connected therewith navigable by seagoing vessels' and would therefore apply equally to unmanned vessels as to manned. Compliance with the COLREGs could be programmed into the unmanned vessel's navigation software, but there will be a dynamic interaction in the navigation of the vessel between completely autonomous navigation in accordance with the voyage programming, and navigation by remote control by the SBC. If the SBC can be regarded as the master, they would only fulfil that role during their periods of remote navigation, and monitoring during autonomous navigation. Alternatively, they would be a 'person for the time being responsible for the conduct of the vessel'. If there is a breach of COLREGs during a period of autonomous navigation, due to a defect in the navigational software or defective voyage programming, the SBC would probably not commit an offence, unless there was a failure to intervene and assume remote control of the vessel on becoming aware of the impending breach of the regulation.[11] A further question would be whether the software manufacturer would have committed an offence as a person 'for the time being responsible for the conduct of the vessel'.

Three particular regulations pose challenges for compliance by unmanned vessels. First, there is Rule 2 'Responsibility' which provides:

(a) Nothing in these rules shall exonerate any vessel, or the owner, master or crew thereof, from the consequences of any neglect to comply with these rules or of the neglect of any precaution which may be required by the ordinary practice of seamen, or by the special circumstances of the case.

(b) In construing and complying with these rules due regard shall be had to all dangers of navigation and collision and to any special circumstances, including the limitations of the vessels involved, which may make a departure from these rules necessary to avoid immediate danger.

Rule 2 gives precedence to good seamanship over COLREG provisions. The rule presupposes the exercise of human judgment in the 'ordinary practice of seamen' and in the making of a decision to depart from the rule when necessary to avoid immediate danger. This could be satisfied if the operating system provides the SBC with the ability to make informed nautical decisions and allows the vessel to act on the SBC's remote instructions in good time. However, it would not be satisfied with a completely autonomous vessel.

Secondly, there is Rule 5 'Look-out' which provides:

Every vessel shall at all times maintain a proper look-out by sight and hearing as well as by all available means appropriate in the prevailing circumstances and conditions so as to make a full appraisal of the situation and of the risk of collision.

The reference to 'by sight and hearing' requires human agency, but does not require an onboard presence. A look out through an on shore virtual bridge manned by an SBC would satisfy this requirement. However, a completely autonomous vessel would not comply with Rule 5.

Thirdly, there is Rule 18 'Responsibilities between vessels' which provides that a power-driven vessel must give way to all other vessels (except a seaplane); a sailing vessel must give way to a vessel not under command, a vessel restricted in her ability to manoeuvre and a vessel engaged in fishing; and that a vessel engaged in fishing must give way to vessel not under command and a vessel restricted in her ability to manoeuvre.

Gogarty and Hagger have argued that manned vessels must give way to unmanned vessels as these are either 'not under command' or 'restricted in her ability to manoeuvre'.[12]

These terms are defined in Rule 3 as follows:

---

11 Unless the SBC was also the voyage programmer and they had incorrectly programmed the voyage.
12 B.Gogarty and M.Hagger, 'The Laws of Man over Vehicles Unmanned: The Legal Response to Robotic Revolution on Sea, Land and Air' (2008) 19 Journal of Law, Information and Science 73, 115.

(f) The term 'vessel not under command' means a vessel which through some exceptional circumstance is unable to manoeuvre as required by these rules and is therefore unable to keep out of the way of another vessel.

The reference to 'some exceptional circumstance' would not cover a vessel which by its nature is unable to manoeuvre as required by the rules, but probably would cover a situation where the vessel has lost communication with the shore. This would be subject to the unmanned vessel's ability to display the appropriate lights and signals in the event of a loss of shore communication.[13]

(g) The term 'vessel restricted in her ability to manoeuvre' means a vessel which from the nature of her work is restricted in her ability to manoeuvre as required by these rules and is therefore unable to keep out of the way of another vessel. The term 'vessels restricted in their ability to manoeuvre' shall include but not be limited to:
  (i) a vessel engaged in laying, servicing or picking up a navigation mark, submarine cable or pipeline;
  (ii) a vessel engaged in dredging, surveying or underwater operations;
  (iii) a vessel engaged in replenishment or transferring persons, provisions or cargo while underway;
  (iv) a vessel engaged in the launching or recovery of aircraft;
  (v) a vessel engaged in mine clearance operations;
  (vi) a vessel engaged in a towing operation such as severely restricts the towing vessel and her tow in their ability to deviate from their course.

The restriction in ability to manoeuvre derives from the nature of the vessel's work and not from the nature of the vessel itself and none of the specific instances would cover the ordinary operation of an unmanned cargo vessel. Accordingly, unmanned vessels will be subject to the same priority rules as apply to manned vessels.

2.3 The master's duty to render assistance

Three conventions impose a personal duty on the master to render assistance to persons in distress at sea. This raises issues as who, if anyone, will constitute the master, and what would be the content of the obligation in the case of an unmanned ship. Article 98 (1) of the 1982 UN Convention on the Law of the Sea ('UNCLOS') provides:

Every state shall require the master of a ship flying its flag, *in so far as he can do so without serious danger to the ship* (emphasis added), the crew or the passengers:

(a) to render assistance to any person found at sea in danger of being lost;

---

[13] Rule 27(a).

(b) to proceed with all possible speed to the rescue of persons in distress, if informed of their need of assistance, *in so far as such action may reasonably be expected of him* (emphasis added);

(c) after a collision, to render assistance to the other ship, its crew and its passengers and, where possible, to inform the other ship of the name of his own ship, its port of registry and the nearest port at which it will call.[14]

Chapter V, Regulation 33 of the 1974 International Convention on the Safety of Life at Sea ('SOLAS') provides:

> [T]he master of *a ship at sea which is in a position to be able to provide assistance* (emphasis added), on receiving a signal from any source that persons are in distress at sea, is bound to proceed with all speed to their assistance, if possible informing them or the search and rescue service that the ship is doing so.[15]

Article 11 of the 1910 Salvage Convention and Article 10(1) of the 1989 Salvage Convention provide:

> Every master is bound, *so far as he can do so without serious danger to his vessel* (emphasis added) and persons thereon, to render assistance to any person in danger of being lost at sea.[16]

The master's obligation to render assistance is not absolute and is qualified by the italicised wordings: 'in so far as he can do so without serious danger to the ship;' 'in so far as such action can be reasonably expected of him;' 'a ship at sea which is in a position to be able to provide assistance'; and, 'so far as he can do so without serious danger to his vessel'.

With an unmanned ship, the most that the SBC can do is to communicate the need for help to other vessels in the area and to the coastal authorities. Assuming the SBC can be regarded as the master for these purposes, their obligations cannot extend beyond this.

The same is true of the two assistance obligations imposed under UK law by ss. 92 and 93 of the Merchant Shipping Act 1995. In the event of a collision s. 92 requires the master to render 'such assistance as is practicable' to the other vessel. Section 93 requires the master 'on receiving at sea a signal of distress [from an aircraft] or information from any source that [an] aircraft is in distress' to "[p]roceed with all speed to the assistance of the persons in distress the master to assist aircraft in distress *unless he is unable*, or in the special circumstances of the case considers it unreasonable or unnecessary, to do so'".[17] The italicised words again indicate that the SBC duty of assistance would be limited to one of communicating details of the aircraft in distress to other vessels in the area and the coastal authorities.

---

14 Emphasis added.
15 Emphasis added.
16 Emphasis added.
17 Emphasis added.

Similar issues arise with regards to the master's powers and duties under the 1998 Convention for the Suppression of Unlawful Acts of Violence against the Safety of Maritime Navigation and its 2005 Protocol.[18]

2.4 The master's documentary obligations

A variety of documentary obligations fall on the master under various international conventions. MARPOL provides reporting obligations in the event of oil spills and requires the keeping of various record books. The IMO civil liability conventions in force – the CLC 1969 and 1992, the Bunker Oil Pollution Convention 2001 and the 2007 Nairobi Wreck Removal Convention – all contain mandatory insurance provisions with the requirement that a 'blue card' evidencing this be kept on board the vessel, as does EU Directive 2009/20/EC on the insurance of shipowners for maritime claims.[19] The UK's implementing legislation requires the certificate to be carried on board the ship and to be produced on demand by the master 'to any officer of customs and excise or of the Secretary of State and, if the ship is a United Kingdom ship, to any proper officer'. Failure to carry the certificate or to produce it as required renders the master liable on summary conviction to a fine not exceeding level 4 on the standard scale.[20] Unmanned vessels cannot comply with these regulations and provisions will need to be made to allow the provision of these certificates to be made electronically.[21]

2.5 Watchkeeping

Article III of the International Convention on Standards of Training, Certification and Watchkeeping for Seafarers, 1978, as amended in 1995, 1997 and 2010 (STCW) provides that 'The Convention shall apply to seafarers serving on board seagoing ships entitled to fly the flag of a Party …' which would rule out its application to unmanned vessels. However, Regulation VIII/2(2) provides an obligation on flag administrations to

> require the master of every ship to ensure that watchkeeping arrangements are adequate for maintaining a safe watch or watches, taking into account the prevailing circumstances and conditions and that, under the master's general direction: (1) officers in charge of the navigational watch are responsible for navigating the ship safely during their periods of duty, when they shall be physically present on the navigating bridge or in a directly associated location such as the chartroom or bridge control room at all times.

---

18 See Articles 8 and 8 bis of the 2005 Protocol.
19 The UK has implemented this through The Merchant Shipping (Compulsory Insurance of Shipowners for Maritime Claims) Regulations 2012, SI 2012/2267, implementing EU Directive 2009/20/EC on the insurance of shipowners for maritime claims.
20 See s 163(6).
21 The FAL Convention has made provision for the certificates it requires to be provided in electronic form but this does not affect the certification requirements in the IMO Civil Liability Conventions or in EU Directive 2009/20/EC on the insurance of shipowners for maritime claims.

This clearly requires a physical presence on the vessel for watchkeeping and as matters currently stand the flag state administration would not be able to comply with the regulation with an unmanned vessel.

In the UK the STCW is implemented through the Merchant Shipping (Standards of Training Certification and Watchkeeping) Regulations 2015.[22] Part 2 of the regulations is concerned with training and certification and applies to a seafarer serving on board a sea-going ship registered in the UK; but part 4, which covers safe manning and watchkeeping, apply to sea-going ships which are: (a) UK ships wherever they are; and (b) other ships when in UK waters. Part 4, regs 47–49, brings in the watchkeeping requirements in Regulation VIII/2 of the STCW which require a physical presence on the navigating bridge or a directly associated location such as the chartroom or bridge control room at all times. Regulation 46 also brings in documentary requirements as to manning. A UK ship must have in force a safe manning document issued by the Secretary of State in respect of the ship and the manning of the ship, which must be kept on board at all times.[23] The master must ensure that the ship does not proceed to sea unless, on board, there is a valid safe manning document issued in respect of the ship and the manning of the ship complies with that document. Neither requirement can be satisfied with an unmanned vessel.

However, regulation 50 provides that

> The Secretary of State may grant on such terms, if any, as may be specified, exemptions from all or any of the provisions of this Part for classes of case or individual cases, and may amend or cancel any exemptions so granted.

Presumably exemptions could be granted in both cases provided the Secretary of State was satisfied as to the on shore virtual watchkeeping arrangements for the unmanned vessel, and was prepared to accept an electronic version of the safe manning document which would be accessible at all times to the relevant maritime authorities.

2.6 Labour law and seafarers

The SBC may undertake many of the functions of the master, but their employment will be entirely shore bound. The International Labour Organisation's Maritime Labour Convention 2006 deals with the living and working conditions of seafarers, defined in art. 2(f) as 'any person who is employed or engaged or works in any capacity on board a ship to which this Convention applies'. Clearly, the convention will have no relevance to unmanned ships which have no crew on board. Similarly, the master's lien for wages and disbursements will not be available to the SBC. The lien presupposes some onboard presence on the vessel by the

---

22 SI 2015/782.
23 Merchant Shipping (Standards of Training Certification and Watchkeeping) Regulations 2015 (SI 2015/782), Part 4, Reg 46.

master as part of the crew.[24] The provisions in Part III of the Merchant Shipping Act 1995 which apply to 'masters and seamen employed *in* sea-going ships[25] (emphasis added)' will also have no application to the SBC who is not employed in a sea-going ship.

2.7 The master's civil liability

The master's conduct of the vessel may expose them to liabilities in tort for damage or loss of property or for personal injury or death. There are three provisions in international conventions that may protect the master from such liability, either in full or by limiting their exposure. First, art. III (4) of the 1992 CLC provides for responder immunity for the following parties:

(a) the servants or agents of the owner or the members of the crew;
(b) the pilot or any other person who, without being a member of the crew, performs services for the ship;
(c) any charterer (how so ever described, including a bareboat charterer), manager or operator of the ship;
(d) any person performing salvage operations with the consent of the owner or on the instructions of a competent public authority;
(e) any person taking preventive measures;
(f) all servants or agents of persons mentioned in subparagraphs (c), (d) and (e);
(g) unless the damage resulted from their personal act or omission, committed with the intent to cause such damage, or recklessly and with knowledge that such damage would probably result.

If the SBC is employed by the owner they would fall within (a). If the SBC is an independent contractor they would most likely fall within heading (a) as an 'agent of the owner', or within heading (b) as a person who, without being a member of the crew, performs services for the ship or an 'operator' under heading (c).

Secondly, art. 1(4) of the 1976 LLMC provides:

> If any claims set out in Article 2 are made against any person for whose act, neglect or default the shipowner or salvor is responsible, such person shall be entitled to avail himself of the limitation of liability provided for in this Convention.

---

24 See Clarke J in *The Ever Success* [1999] 1 Lloyd's Rep 824, 832:

> In my judgment the authorities show that a master or a seaman is entitled to wages and thus to a co-extensive maritime lien if he renders the service appropriate to his rank. That is as, say, master, chief engineer or seaman. He must be part of the crew of the ship, but need not necessarily render the service on board the ship or live on board the ship, but the service must be in a real sense referrable to the ship and the service must be rendered during a period when the particular claimant can fairly be said to be part of the crew of the ship.

The SBC can not be said to be part of the crew of the ship, as there is no crew.

25 Emphasis added.

If the SBC is employed by the shipowner, then they will be able to limit liability under the convention. If, however, they are an independent contractor they will not be a person for whose act neglect or default the shipowner or salvor is responsible, and will not, therefore, be able to limit liability.[26]

Third, art. IV(bis) of the Hague-Visby Rules provides protection for the servant or agent of the carrier if they are sued in respect of loss or damage to goods covered by a contract of carriage falling under the Hague-Visby Rules, by extending to them the benefit of the carrier's defences and limits of liability under the rules. This protection does not cover a servant or agent who is an independent contractor. If the SBC is employed by the owner they will be protected, but if they are an independent contractor they would have to rely on a 'Himalaya' clause in the bill of lading, whether the action be founded in contract or in tort.

2.8 Criminal law and the master

The master may face criminal charges in respect of his operation of the vessel before the courts of a coastal state. A notorious example of this is the prison sentence imposed by a Spanish court on Capt Mangouras, the master of the *Prestige*, in connection with the oil spill from the vessel when it broke up in Spain's EEZ in 2002. In the UK the master can incur liability in respect of a failure with regard to the failure to have on board, or to produce for inspection, the 'blue card' in respect of mandatory liability provisions. The master, together with the owner, is guilty of an offence if a ship which is in a port in the UK, or is a UK ship and is in any other port, is dangerously unsafe,[27] and also for failure to carry an oil record book in a UK ship.[28] Discharges of oil into the sea when done with intent, recklessly, or with serious negligence attract the highest penal sanctions, with the owner and master each liable for a fine of up to £250,000.[29] It should be noted that unmanned ships make it much harder for a port state to get hold of the functional equivalent of the master who may be located in a distant state.[30]

---

26 In *JD Irving Ltd* v. *Siemens Canada Ltd* (*The SPM 125*) 2016 FC 287 the Federal Court of Canada held that art.1(4) would afford limitation to a person only if the shipowner or salvor has vicarious liability for the actions of that person. The claim was brought against a firm of marine consultants to prepare stability calculations in respect of the loading of a cargo of large industrial equipment on and off the barge *SPM125*. As the shipowner would not be vicariously liable for the defaults of an independent contractor, the marine consultants were unable to limit their liability under the 1976 LLMC.
27 See s 98(1) of the Merchant Shipping Act 1995.
28 See s 142 of the Merchant Shipping Act 1995.
29 See Merchant Shipping (Prevention of Oil Pollution) Regulations 1996 (SI 1996/2154), Reg 36A, applying penalties to breaches of Regs 12, 13 and 16. The Regulations give effect to MARPOL and the stricter implementation of these regulations in a 2009 EU Directive.
30 See R.Veal and M.Tsimplis, 'The Integration of Unmanned Ships into the *lex maritima*' (2017) Lloyd's Maritime & Commercial Law Quarterly 303, 318, stating that:

> 'One option would be a representative of the unmanned shipping company in each country who would be criminally liable for the ship's actions, in addition to the shore-based 'master' and the owner. Such an arrangement could be effected by coastal states as a condition of entry of unmanned ships into their ports.'

Effectively this would entail the employment of a hostage in every port of call.

3 Maritime contracts and the master

The navigational role of the master will be shared between two human participants, the programmer of the software for the vessel's autonomous operation on the voyage, and the SBC who will monitor the vessel's progress throughout its voyage and undertake navigation by remote operation for certain sections of the voyage. The programmer may or may not be the same person as the SBC, and programming may be performed by employees of the shipowner or by an independent contractor providing navigational services to owners of unmanned vessel. The master also has non-navigational functions. The master supervises the loading, stowing and discharge of the cargo carried on the vessel. The master signs bills of lading. These functions will require physical presence at the ports of loading and discharge, so cannot be assigned to the SBC. Owners will need to engage port agents to fulfil these functions. In this second section, I shall consider how charter party forms will need to be adapted to accommodate the diffusion of the roles of the master to various land-based personnel. I shall take NYPE 2015 as a time charter example, and GENCON 1994 as a voyage charter instance.

3.1 NYPE 2015

Clause 2 imposes an obligation on owners that the vessel on delivery shall be seaworthy and in every way fit to be employed for the intended service, including the full complement of master, officers and ratings who meet the STCW requirements for a vessel of her tonnage. With an unmanned vessel these requirements will not be able to be satisfied even if the SBC could be regarded as the master, as the STCW requirements will not apply to onshore personnel. The owners' obligations as regards crew reappear in cl. 6 which requires the vessel to have a full complement of master, officer and ratings.

Other navigational obligations appear in cl. 12(b) obliging the master to comply with the reporting procedure of the charterers' weather routing service and to follow routing recommendations from that service provided that the safety of the vessel and/or cargo is not compromised. There is also cl. 38 which gives the charterers the right to give instructions to the master as to slow steaming and ultra slow steaming, and cl. 15 which provides for the charterers to furnish the master from time to time with all requisite instructions and sailing directions, in writing, in the English language, and for the master shall keep full and correct deck and engine logs of the voyage or voyages. Cl. 30, incorporating the BIMCO Hull Fouling Clause for charter parties, provides for cleaning always to be under the supervision of the master.

Clause 8 contains three important obligations involving the master which are fundamental to the contractual structure of a time charter. The master is to perform the voyages with due despatch. The master is to be under the orders and directions of the charterers as regards employment and agency.[31] Charterers are to

---

[31] The nomination of ports is subject to an implied warranty that the port is prospectively safe. The obligation to nominate a safe port will extend to nomination of ports that have the facilities, such as sufficient internet access, to accommodate unmanned vessels.

perform all cargo handling, under the supervision of the master.[32] It is possible that three distinct entities perform these functions: the voyage programmer; the SBC; the owners' agent at the loading and discharge port. The form could be amended by replacing the reference to the master with a simple reference to owners, or to owners and their agents.

The master's involvement with cargo operations appear at various places in the form. In addition to the supervision of cargo handling by charterers referred to in cl. 8, the master is entitled to refuse cargoes or, if already loaded, to unload them at the charterers' risk and expense if the charterers fail to fulfil their IMSBC Code or IMDG Code obligations as applicable.[33] The important matter of bills of lading is dealt with in cl. 31 which reiterates the familiar obligation of the master to sign bills of lading or waybills for cargo as presented in conformity with mates' receipts. This is not a function that the SBC could perform, given that paper bills of lading will still be required. Alternatively, the charterers or their agents may sign bills of lading or waybills on behalf of the master but this is subject to the owners' (or master's) prior written authority, always in conformity with mates' receipts. Provision of mates' receipts is probably not something that the SBC is going to be able to perform remotely and will fall to owners' port agents. The clause could be amended, as with cl. 8, to replace 'the master' with 'owners' agents'. Clause 27 provides for cargo claims as between owners and charterers to be settled in accordance with the Inter-Club NYPE Agreement 1996 (as amended 1 September 2011), or any subsequent modification or replacement thereof.

Similar amendments will also be needed to clauses giving the master discretion as regards entry into areas affected by war risks[34] and piracy[35] as well as cl. 37 which requires the master to notify charterers of stevedore damage to the vessel within 24 hours. The reference in the off-hire provisions in cl. 17 to 'time lost from deficiency and/or default and/or strike of officers or crew' becomes redundant unless redrafted to refer to 'servants or agents of the owners involved in the performance of the charter'. Clause 33(a) incorporates the 'both to blame collision clause' with its reference to 'any act, neglect or default of the Master, Mariner,

---

32 This will make charterers responsible for these operations. The addition of the words 'and responsibility' after 'supervision' will shift responsibility back to the shipowners.

33 See cl. 29 'Solid Bulk Cargoes/Dangerous Goods': 'The Master shall be entitled to refuse cargoes or, if already loaded, to unload them at the Charterers' risk and expense if the Charterers fail to fulfil their IMSBC Code or IMDG Code obligations as applicable'.

34 See cl. 34 'BIMCO War Risks Clause CONWARTIME 2013':

> The Vessel shall not be obliged to proceed or required to continue to or through, any port, place, area or zone, or any waterway or canal (hereinafter 'Area'), where it appears that the Vessel, cargo, crew or other persons on board the Vessel, in the reasonable judgement of the Master and/or the Owners, may be exposed to War Risks whether such risk existed at the time of entering into this Charter Party or occurred thereafter.

35 See cl. 39. BIMCO Piracy Clause for Time Charter 717 Parties 2013

(a) The Vessel shall not be obliged to proceed or required to continue to or through, any port, place, area or zone, or any waterway or canal (hereinafter 'Area') which, in the reasonable judgement of the Master and/or the Owners, is dangerous to the Vessel, her cargo, crew or other persons on board the Vessel due to any actual, threatened or reported acts of piracy and/or violent robbery and/or capture/seizure (hereinafter 'Piracy'), whether such risk existed at the time of entering into this Charter Party or occurred thereafter.

Pilot or the servants of the Owners in the navigation or in the management of the vessel'. This could still cover defaults of the SBC as the functional equivalent of the master but could be amended to so that it refers to 'the servants or agents of the Owners in the performance of this charter'. Other clauses in the form will be redundant with an unmanned vessel, such as that part of cl. 13 on the space available to charterers that refers to accommodation for supercargo, and the reservation of proper and sufficient space for the vessel's master, officers, ratings, tackle, apparel, furniture, provisions, stores, cl. 14 on charterer's right to put a supercargo onboard and cl. 43 on smuggling by the master, other officers and ratings.

3.2 GENCON 1994

The GENCON form refers to crew or master in the following places.

First, cl. 2 provides owners with a general exemption 'even from the neglect or default of the Master or crew or *some other person employed by the Owners on board or ashore for whose acts they would but for this Clause*, be responsible or from unseaworthiness of the vessel' (emphasis added).[36] The italicised words show that the exemption would continue to operate as regards errors by either the voyage programmer or the SBC.

Secondly, cl. 5(c) provides for the master to give charterers notification of stevedore damage as soon as is reasonably possible and to endeavour to obtain stevedores' written acknowledgment of liability. This is a function that could not be performed by the SBC and would have to be performed by owners' agents at the ports of loading and discharge.

Thirdly, cl. 6 provides for 'the vessel to give NOR if berth not available on vessel's arrival on or off the port. Master to warrant that she is ready in all respects'. The SBC could give this warranty of readiness.

Fourthly, cl. 10 requires bills of lading to be signed by the master or by the owners' agents. There would be no problem here with the absence of a conventional onboard master, as owners' agents at the loading port could still sign the bills.

Fifthly, cl. 11 contains the 'both to blame collision clause' which could be amended so that it refers to 'the servants or agents of the Owners in the performance of this charter'.

Sixthly, there are also three clauses involving the role of the master or owners in the event of strikes (cl. 16 'General Strike Clause'); war (cl. 17 'War Risks ("Voywar 1993")'); and ice (cl. 18 'General Ice clause'). The last of these contains a reference to the master's right to leave the loading port for fear of being frozen in, and this could be exercised by the SBC.

3.3 General average

With an unmanned vessel jettison is unlikely to be a general average event, and expenses under rule XI for the wages and maintenance of crew in, to and at a port

---

36 Emphasis added.

of refuge becomes otiose. The wages of the SBC during the vessel putting in to a port of refuge will not fall within this rule.

3.4 Salvage

The master appears in various places in the 1989 Salvage Convention. Art. 6(2) provides:

> The master shall have the authority to conclude contracts for salvage operations on behalf of the owner of the vessel. The master or the owner of the vessel shall have the authority to conclude such contracts on behalf of the owner of the property on board the vessel.

Should the SBC have this authority to conclude salvage contracts for the vessel owner? The provision is premised on there being an onboard master who is in a position to contract in an emergency. Once the master goes onshore, the need for this authority disappears. Owners can make salvage contracts as easily as the SBC. The master's duty of assistance under article 10 has already been mentioned. Other provisions refer to the 'master or owners' and would not pose any problem with the operation of an unmanned vessel.[37]

3.5 Bills of lading

This is the subject of another paper in the colloquium. In brief, the Hague and Hague-Visby Rules will operate as regards carriage of cargoes in bills of lading when carried in unmanned vessels. It is the contract of carriage between the carrier and the shipper, the fact of carriage by sea, and the existence, or contractual contemplation, of a bill of lading that determines the applicability of the rules. The nature of the ship in which the goods are carried is of no import.[38] Similarly COGSA 1992 will also operate as regards the vesting of rights and obligations under bills of lading, waybills and ship's delivery orders.[39]

---

37 Arts.8, 15 and 19.
38 The one change will be in relation to the operation of art. IV(2)(a), which provides the carrier with a defence in the event of loss or damage being caused by 'Act, neglect, or default of the master, mariner, pilot, or the servants of the carrier in the navigation or in the management of the ship'. The absence of an on-board crew might be thought to remove this exception when the goods are being carried by an unmanned vessel. However, it is possible to regard the SBC as the functional equivalent of the master and therefore the carrier would still be able to rely on the exception in respect of loss or damage caused by any errors of navigation on their part. If the SBC is not regarded as the 'master' then they could constitute a 'servant of the carrier', although if the SBC is not employed by the carrier but is an independent contractor this would not be the case. It is doubtful whether negligence by the voyage programmer would fall within the exception as such negligence would render the vessel unseaworthy. Establishing the vessel's seaworthiness will now need to take in both onboard and shore-based conditions.
39 The sole reference to the master in COGSA 1992 is in s 4: 'A bill of lading which – (a) represents goods to have been shipped on board a vessel or to have been received for shipment on board a vessel; and (b) has been signed by the master of the *vessel or by a person who was not the master but had the express, implied or apparent authority of the carrier to sign bills of lading*, shall, in favour of a person who has become the lawful holder of the bill, be conclusive evidence against the carrier of the shipment of the goods or, as the case may be, of their receipt for shipment' (emphasis added). The italicised words show that the section will operate even when the bill is not signed by the master.

3.6 Piracy

An unmanned vessel becomes effectively immune to attack by pirates. Control of the vessel may be obtained through hacking and taking control of its voyage software. This will not constitute piracy which is defined in art. 101 of UNCLOS as:

> (a) any illegal acts of violence or detention, or any act of depredation, committed for private ends by the crew or the passengers of a private ship or a private aircraft, and directed: (i) on the high seas, against another ship or aircraft, or against persons or property on board such ship or aircraft; (ii) against a ship, aircraft, persons or property in a place outside the jurisdiction of any State;

This virtual means of taking control of a vessel will not involve any action 'by the crew or the passengers of a private ship or a private aircraft'.[40]

3.7 Pilotage

A pilot is a navigational advisor but the vessel remains under the command of the master and the shipowner is vicariously liable for any negligence on the part of the pilot, whether the pilotage be compulsory or not. The AAWA project contemplates that on entering or leaving a port the SBC will either choose to 'take teleoperation type control or increase the supervision level of the vessel'.[41] It may, however, be the case that autonomous berthing will not be permitted by the port authority in which case some form of pilotage will be required.[42] This will involve a split in the remote operation of the vessel, assuming that the vessel cannot be boarded.[43] Luci Carey has identified various problems that this will entail:

> The master is the person who remains responsible for the safety of the ship. If the 'master' is the SBO in another country, communicating with a pilot who may not be familiar with the operation of an autonomous ship, does the master really have command? Does the pilot have control? These concepts do not sit easily with the operation of an autonomous ship. The issue here is control. A pilot cannot take control of an autonomous ship unless the pilot is either able to instruct the SBO or board the ship and operate it manually. This assumes the pilot has not only local knowledge but also knowledge of how the autonomous ship operates. What happens if communications are lost? Who is liable for any loss that is incurred? Therefore it is crucial to identify the person that is 'in command' in relation to an autonomous ship. If the pilot has control of the autonomous ship, it may not be possible for the SBO, who is not only

---

40 The term 'pirates' is defined in the Schedule to the Marine Insurance Act 1906 as including 'passengers who mutiny and rioters who attack the ship from the shore'. *Carver's Carriage by Sea* (12th ed., Sweet & Maxwell, 1971), par. 183, has the definition: 'Piracy is forcible robbery at sea, whether committed by marauders from outside the ship, or by mariners or passengers within it'. This was approved by Kennedy LJ in *Republic of Bolivia v. Indemnity Mutual Marine Assurance Co. Ltd.*, [1909] 1 K.B. 785, 802.

41 AAWA, 'Remote and Autonomous Ships – The Next Steps' (Position Paper, Rolls-Royce plc, 2016), 12. <www.utu.fi/en/units/law/research/research-projects/Pages/aawa.aspx> accessed 17 August 2018.

42 The AAWA project also suggests that either the SBC could become a licensed pilot for compulsory pilotage areas, or the autonomous ship could be given an exemption from the pilotage requirement. AAWA, 'Remote and Autonomous Ships – The Next Steps' (Position Paper, Rolls-Royce plc, 2016), 12.

43 At common law there could be no pilotage in this situation as pilotage only begins once the pilot is '*on board* (emphasis added) at a particular place for the purpose of conducting a ship through a river, road or channel or from or into a port'. See *The Adoni* [1918] P 14.

not on board beside the pilot but quite possibly in another country altogether, to wrest control back again in the event the pilot appears to be in error.[44]

If the pilot is in control, will the rule that the shipowner is vicariously liable for the pilot still apply?

4 Conclusion

Unmanned vessels will lead first to a fragmentation of the role of the master, and then to his disappearance. With level 3 autonomous operation, the SBC will be able to be regarded as the functional equivalent of the master for some purposes in that they are the human entity that is in command of the vessel's navigation through remote operation. However, it is unlikely that the SBC can be regarded as the functional equivalent of the master for all navigational purposes. Navigation of a vessel at level 3 involves three elements: (i) the voyage software; (ii) the programming of the voyage; and (iii) the remote monitoring of the voyage and the assumption of remote navigational control where needed by the SBC. The second and third of these elements involve human agency, but the demarcation between these two is an issue that needs to be addressed in determining 'who is the master now?'. Level 3 autonomy will see the 'part master'. Indeed, if the SBC is treated as the functional equivalent of the master, we will see a multiplicity of masters. The SBCs will be land-based. Assuming three shifts in a 24-hour period, you will have three persons in remote control of the vessel during a day. With a long voyage SBCs in another time-zone may also be used, which would bring the total number of potential masters up to six. Furthermore, each controller will probably be in remote control of more than one vessel in their shift. This is a far cry from the traditional practice of one ship, one master. When we reach level 4 with full automation, the master will disappear and become the 'past master'.

The CMI has produced a spreadsheet in its submission to the IMO identifying provisions in the IMO regulations that will need clarification or amendment to deal with unmanned vessels, and identifies numerous provisions with the comment 'interpretation of the master'.[45] The issue of the documentation that needs to be carried on board vessels, such as the 'blue card' evidencing that mandatory liability insurance is in place, will also need to be addressed by allowing these requirements to be satisfied by electronic certificates. The STCW will need to be adapted to provide for training and certification standards for remote onshore controllers. There is also the need for the IMO to develop regulations on software security. BIMCO and the Comité International Radio Maritime, an organisation involved in the development of the marine electronics industry, have jointly prepared a proposed software maintenance standard that has been sent to the IMO for review. Its goal

---

[44] L.Carey, 'All Hands Off Deck? The Legal Barriers to Autonomous Ships'. (NUS Law Working Paper No. 2017/011. NUS Centre for Maritime Law Working Paper 17/0626). Available at <https://papers.ssrn.com/sol3/papers.cfm?abstract_id=3025882> accessed 17 August 2018.

[45] ANNEX 2 to the CMI IWG Submission to MSC 99th Session.

is to ensure software updates are secure and systematic for maintenance and to minimise hacking and malware problems.[46] The urgency of this issue was brought home by the disruption to Maersk's operation over ten days in the summer of 2017 as a result of collateral damage from the 'nopetya' programme which probably originated as a cyber attack by Russia on Ukraine by introducing malware into a popular Ukrainian accounting package called 'M.E.Doc'.[47]

Contractually, the master's role will also undergo substantial change. There will be no onboard master to sign bills of lading, to supervise cargo operations, or to receive instructions from time-charterers as to the vessel's employment. It is unlikely that these functions will fall to the SBC and owners will have to fulfil them through employing port agents. However, this should not provide a serious problem for the contractual forms used in chartering and carriage of goods. Owners' contractual obligations will remain the same, irrespective of who is navigating the vessel and who is signing bills of lading. There is much to be said for the removal of all references to the master in charters and bills of lading and replacing them with a reference to 'owners'.

---

[46] IMO was due to consider the standard at the NCSR meeting in February 2018. Pilot tests for the standard were carried out in 2017, and ISO has provisionally accepted the proposal. BIMCO said it expects a working group to complete the standard in 2021, when cyber security is due to become part of ISO standards.

[47] IMO has issued MSC-FAL.1/Circ.3 *Guidelines on maritime cyber risk management* and the Maritime Safety Committee, at its 98th session in June 2017, also adopted Resolution MSC.428(98) – *Maritime Cyber Risk Management in Safety Management Systems*. The resolution encourages administrations to ensure that cyber risks are appropriately addressed in existing safety management systems (as defined in the ISM Code) no later than the first annual verification of the company's Document of Compliance after 1 January 2021.

CHAPTER 11

Carrier liability for unmanned ships
Goodbye crew, hello liability?

*Dr Frank Stevens**

1 Introduction

In the early seventeenth century, a then common type of ship, the Venetian buss, was rapidly supplanted by another type, the cog. The reason? A buss required a crew of fifty, whereas a cog with the same carrying capacity had a crew of only twenty. In the eighteenth century, East Indiamen such as the Dutch *Amsterdam*[1] or the Swedish *Götheborg*[2] had crews of up to 200. Tea clippers such as the British *Cutty Sark*,[3] with similar cargo carrying capacity but almost twice the sail area, had a crew of 18 to 28. The German *Pamir*,[4] one of the last sailing cargo ships, with a much larger carrying capacity and a larger sail area than the *Cutty Sark*, had a crew of 22 on its 1949 voyage around Cape Horn (the last by a commercial sailing ship). The same evolution took place again in the age of motor vessels.[5] In the 1950s, a general cargo vessel would have a crew of 50 or more. Today, even the largest bulkers and container vessels have crews of around 20.

Shrinking crew sizes is nothing new, therefore. It has happened time and again in the history of commercial shipping, without resulting in or requiring amendments of the carriage or liability rules. What is new, however, is that technological progress now seems to make it possible to reduce the number of persons on board to zero. If that happens, what are, from a carrier's perspective, the legal consequences of this ultimate reduction of crew?

---

* Associate Professor, Erasmus University.
1 On its maiden voyage in November 1748, the *Amsterdam* (length 48 m, beam 11 m, 1,100 tonnes displacement) carried a crew of 203 sailors.
2 The *Götheborg*, launched in 1738, had a length of 47 m, a beam of 11 m and measured 788 GT. Its regular sail area consisted of 1,550 m² (18 sails), with a maximum sail area of 1,964 m² (26 sails). It carried a crew of around 130 sailors.
3 The *Cutty Sark*, launched in 1869, had a hull length of 65 m, a beam of 11 m and measured 963 GRT. It had 29 sails, with a total sail area of 2,973 m².
4 Built in 1905, the *Pamir* had a length of 114 m, a beam of 14 m, measured 3,020 GRT and had a total sail area of 3,800 m².
5 See, for example, J. M. Ross, *Human Factors for Naval Marine Vehicle Design and Operation*, Boca Raton: CRC Press, 2017, at p. 118; M. Stopford, *Maritime Economics*, London: Routledge, 2009 (3th Ed.), at p. 227; N. Wijnolst & T. Wergeland, *Shipping Innovation*, Amsterdam: IOS Press, 2009, Table 100 at p. 341.

In this respect, there is a distinction to be made between remotely controlled vessels on the one hand and fully autonomous vessels on the other.[6] Both types have in common that there is no crew physically on board during the voyage,[7] but a remotely controlled vessel is permanently monitored and controlled by a team of remote operators in a control centre on-shore, whereas in a fully autonomous vessel, it is the vessel's own control system that makes the decisions, without even onshore human intervention. There will, of course, be a human that decides on the voyage the vessel has to perform, and if things go wrong, the vessel will raise an alarm with human operators ashore, but standard operation during a voyage will be without human supervision or intervention.

2 The carriage law aspects of manning

2.1 Seaworthiness

A person whose business it is to carry goods by sea must do so with a seaworthy ship. At common law, this is an absolute duty, though under the Hague-Visby Rules the duty is only to exercise due diligence before and at the beginning of the voyage. 'Seaworthiness' is a very extensive concept, not limited to the features of the physical ship herself, but also extending to the qualities of the crew. Indeed, in the Hague-Visby Rules this is expressly confirmed in Article 3.1(b): the carrier is bound to exercise due diligence, *inter alia*, to properly man the ship.

Where this may at first sight seem an obvious obligation, there is actually no necessity for it. The Hague-Visby Rules are concerned with the carriage of goods, and define the carrier's rights and obligations in this respect. The carrier's basic obligation is to carry the goods to their destination and to deliver them in the same condition they were in when handed over to him in the port of loading. If he fails to do so, he is presumed to be liable. But how, or by what means, the carrier satisfies that obligation is in essence not important. As long as the goods arrive at their destination in the same condition, it does not matter whether the carrier did so with a modern, state-of-the-art ship or with an old vessel out of some museum, with 20 crew on board or only five. This approach was explicitly adopted in the Hamburg Rules.[8] These do not expressly require the carrier to make his ship

---

6 There are many different ways in which levels of autonomy can be defined and determined. A well-known set of levels was developed by Sheridan and Verplanck in 1978 (T. Sheridan & W. Verplanck, *Human and Computer Control of Undersea Teleoperators*, Cambridge, Massachusetts Institute of Technology, 1978). Both the SARUMS and MUNIN research projects have developed their own taxonomy, and the autonomous vehicles sector has yet another set of taxonomies. For the purposes of this paper, however, it is sufficient to simply distinguish between remotely controlled and fully autonomous vessels.

7 There could be hybrid systems, where vessels do carry a crew to look after passengers or cargo during the voyage, but with that crew not controlling the navigation of the vessel.

8 See the Report of the Working Group on International Legislation on Shipping on the work of its fourth (special) session (Geneva, 25 September – 6 October 1972), A/CN.9/74, para. 30:

> ... the Drafting Party had considered that a general rule based on presumption of fault made it unnecessary to list the most important obligations of the carrier in article 3 (1) and (2) of [the Hague-Visby Rules] since, according to the general rule, the carrier would have to perform all of his obligations under the contract of carriage with due care.

seaworthy or to properly man it; they only provide that the carrier is liable if the goods are lost, damaged or delivered late. The first CMI draft of what was later to become the Rotterdam Rules also limited itself to stating the carrier's general obligation, without repeating certain aspects of that obligation as positive duties. That approach was quite quickly abandoned, however, as many delegates nevertheless preferred to spell out the carrier's duties.

Moreover, it is trite law that seaworthiness (both in general and as it relates to manning in particular) is a relative concept, not an absolute one. The Hague-Visby Rules do not impose a minimum number of crew, and the carrier is not obliged to provide a crew that can safely bring the ship and the cargo through any difficulties whatsoever. The obligation is only to provide a crew that is reasonably suited for the intended use or service. It is clear, therefore, that the seaworthiness and manning obligations are simply means to an end, and not an end in themselves.

It is generally accepted that the simple fact that a crew member makes a mistake or is negligent does not mean that the vessel was unseaworthy.[9] Human beings are, after all, fallible, and the seaworthiness obligation has never been understood to mean an absolute warranty that no accidents would happen on the ship. Furthermore, the fact that a person does not hold the proper certificate or that the crew is insufficient in numbers does not, without more, lead to a conclusion of unseaworthiness. A seaman who is not properly certificated may still be perfectly competent,[10] just as a crew that is numerically too small can still get the job done if all its members are competent and efficient.[11] Also, an issue that can (easily) be fixed during the voyage does not make the ship unseaworthy. In 1997, for instance, the *MV Cita* ran aground on the Isles of Scilly when the mate fell asleep on watch, probably owing to overtiredness.[12] The German Supreme Court, upholding the Hamburg Court of Appeal, held that although overtiredness of a crew member could make a vessel unseaworthy, that was not the case when matters could easily have been put right by organizing the watch schedule in such way that the mate

---

9 So held in England: *The Makedonia* [1962] 1 Lloyd's Rep. 316, 336 ('It is quite true, and I must have it much in mind, that you cannot convert casual negligence into inefficiency by simply substituting one word for another. There is a wide gulf between the two and it must be crossed before casual negligence becomes inefficiency sufficient to support a charge of improper manning'). See too *Manifest Shipping Co. Ltd. v Uni-Polaris Shipping Co Ltd (The Star Sea)* [1997] 1 Lloyd's Rep. 360, 374 ('We do entirely accept (as the judge in his judgment recognised) that one mistake or even more than one mistake does not necessarily render a crew member incompetent. Anyone can make a mistake without the conclusion being drawn that he has either a "disabling want of skill" or a "disabling lack of knowledge'); also *The Eurasian Dream* [2002] EWHC 118 (Comm); [2002] 1 Lloyd's Rep. 719 at [129] and *Macieo Shipping Ltd v Clipper Shipping Lines Ltd (The Clipper Sao Luis)* [2001] C.L.C. 762 at [28]. So too in Belgium: CA Ghent 19 March 1998, [1998] E.T.L. 419, holding that mistakes by the engineers in handling engine problems, which ultimately led to a complete engine breakdown, did not prove incompetence, when the engineers had sufficient experience, both in general and with the specific type of engine installed. And also in the Netherlands: Hoge Raad (Supreme Court), 28.03.2003, S&S 2005, 133 (ECLI:NL:HR:2003:AF2677) (*Quo Vadis*), deciding that an error of judgment of a master in appreciating the measures that had to be taken in light of adverse weather conditions did not, in itself, prove that the master was incompetent.

10 *The Empire Jamaica* [1955] P. 259 (affirmed, [1957] A.C. 386); *Macieo Shipping Ltd v Clipper Shipping Lines Ltd (The Clipper Sao Luis)* [2001] C.L.C. 762 at [28].

11 *Hongkong Fir Shipping Co. Ltd. v Kawasaki Kisen Kaisha Ltd. (The Hongkong Fir)* [1962] 2 Q.B. 26, 55 (Sellers L.J.).

12 The facts and an analysis of the causes can be found in the MAIB's Accident Report 3/98.

could get his much-needed rest.[13] A ship is only unseaworthy because of its crew if (members of) the crew are incompetent or inefficient[14] and a reasonably prudent owner, if he had been aware of this incompetence or inefficiency, would not have allowed the vessel to put to sea.[15] The level of incompetence or inefficiency required for an unseaworthiness finding has also been described as a 'disabling want of knowledge' or a 'disabling want of skill'.[16]

Findings of unseaworthiness related to the condition of the ship itself are not that uncommon; ships have been found unseaworthy for such issues as insufficiently fastened port holes, fractured shell plating, leaking rivets, unavailability of suitable tackle, inadequate bunkers, the dirty and partially blocked state of the cooling system, defective propellers, welding flaws in the crankshaft, etc.[17] In comparison, findings of unseaworthiness because of crew incompetence are quite scarce, certainly in recent years. In *The Hongkong Fir*[18] in 1961, the vessel was considered unseaworthy because the engine room staff was not sufficiently experienced and not sufficiently numerous to deal with the vessel's old engines, with the chief engineer being addicted to drink and repeatedly neglecting his duties to boot. In *The Makedonia*[19] in 1962, the ship was held unseaworthy because of the inefficiency of the chief and second engineers, whose incompetent handling of the bunkers led to an engine breakdown in mid-ocean. In *The Star Sea*[20] in 1996, the court held the vessel unseaworthy because the master did not have sufficient knowledge of how to operate the vessel's CO_2 system. And in *The Eurasian Dream*[21] in 2002, the ship was held to be unseaworthy because the master, who was new to car carriers, had not received sufficient information and training on the specific operations and risks of a car carrier.

This imbalance should probably not come as a surprise. Ships today are very complex pieces of machinery, with many items that can break down or be in a defective condition. The crew on the other hand is limited in number, there are

---

13 BGH 26.10.2006 (I ZR 20/04), *TranspR* 2007, 36, at [27]-[28].
   The Court further held that the organisation of the watch schedule is a matter for the Master and that the owner did not need to give instructions in this respect.
14 In *The Makedonia*, Hewson J. preferred the term 'efficiency' to the term 'competence', because he (correctly) pointed out that a person who is in principle competent can still be inefficient, e.g. because of a lack of motivation, drunkenness or drug abuse, physical unfitness etc (see *The Makedonia* [1962] 1 Lloyd's Rep. 316, 334).
15 See *Clifford v. Hunter* (1827) 1 M & M 103; *Rio Tinto Co. Ltd. v. Seed Shipping Co.* (1926) 134 L.T. 764, (1926) 42 T.L.R. 381; *Hongkong Fir Shipping Co. Ltd. v Kawasaki Kisen Kaisha Ltd. (The Hongkong Fir)* [1961] 1 Lloyd's Rep. 159, 168 (Salmon J) (decision upheld at [1962] 2 Q.B. 26).
16 *Standard Oil Co of New York v Clan Line Steamers Ltd (The Clan Gordon)* [1924] A.C. 100, 120–121 (Lord Atkinson).
On the different types of inefficiency, see also K. Bachxevanis, "'Crew Negligence' and 'Crew Incompetence': Their Distinction and Its Consequence" (2010) 16 J.I.M.L 102; R. White, "The human factor in unseaworthiness claims" (1995) L.M.C.L.Q. 2013: 221, 226–228.
17 See in general, S. Girvin (2011), *Carriage of Goods by Sea*, OUP (2nd Ed.), at [24.06]-[24.07]; G. Treitel & F. Reynolds, *Carver on Bills of Lading*, Sweet & Maxwell, 2011 (3rd Ed,.Sweet & Maxwell, 2011), at para.9–015.
18 [1962] 2 Q.B. 26.
19 [1962] 1 Lloyd's Rep. 316.
20 [1997] 1 Lloyd's Rep. 360.
21 [2002] EWHC 118 (Comm); [2002] 1 Lloyd's Rep. 719.

rules and regulations on training and certification, and incompetence or inefficiency tends to show,[22] if maybe only after some time. With regard to the question whether an unmanned ship can nevertheless be 'properly manned' for the purposes of the Hague-Visby Rules, a distinction is to be made between remotely controlled vessels and fully autonomous ones.

Remotely controlled vessels have a team of shore-based remote operators that are in charge. Such operators, even if they are not physically on board the vessel, could conceivably still be considered as her crew of the vessel, and thus covered by the proper manning requirement of Article 3.1(b) of the Hague-Visby Rules. Even if they are not considered to be crew, however, it goes without saying that the operators must be properly trained for the job, and it is submitted that their competence and efficiency would still be covered by the general seaworthiness requirement of Articles 3.1(a) and 3.1(b) combined. This means that the remote operators must have a proper knowledge both of the remote control system itself and of the characteristics and limitations of the remotely controlled ship. They will also need to have proper knowledge of shipping and navigation in general, including for example such matters as COLREGS. In the STCW, the maritime industry has an international convention that sets the standards for the training and certification of crew members. However the STCW, by Article III, only applies to seafarers serving on board seagoing ships, and thus would not apply to shore-based controllers. Remotely-controlled ships, once they progress beyond the experimental stage, will be interacting with manned ships and ships remotely controlled from other countries. At that point, an international convention on the training and certification of shore-based remote controllers might prove useful or even necessary. For such a convention, the STCW will undoubtedly be a useful source of inspiration. Until that time, however, it will be up to the owners of remotely controlled ships to determine what level of competence they require of their shore-based operators.[23] In that regard, it should be stressed that, as with the crews on board ships, the standard is not perfection. The remote controllers only need to be reasonably suited for their job, and the established test for on board crews remains perfectly applicable. If it turns out that a shore-based controller was, in fact, not competent or not efficient, would a reasonably prudent shipowner, if he had known the relevant facts, have allowed the ship to put to sea under the control of that operator?

An interesting question in this respect is whether remote operators need actual sea-going experience in order to be efficient. Experience on traditional manned ships would certainly be a plus, or might even be indispensable in the first stages of remotely-controlled ships, but will probably become less important once such ships have become tried and tested systems. Remote operators will obviously always need to be trained, but that training does not necessarily include service on board manned vessels. There is the practical issue that if remotely-controlled and

---

22 Compare *The Makedonia* [1962] 1 Lloyd's Rep. 316, 338 ('If [these engineers] were inefficient in the ways I have described when the effects of their inefficiency were shown, they must have been inefficient with regard to those matters before').

23 Obviously complying with possible national rules and legislation on the matter.

fully autonomous vessels become the norm, there might be few manned vessels left on which a future operator can gain experience; but even leaving aside such practical limitations, the developers of remote control systems should also be able to develop adequate training programs and systems. After all, NASA's control centre does not exclusively rely on astronauts who have actually been into space.

A further question is whether remote operators should be limited to one vessel only, or whether a single operator could control several vessels simultaneously. Depending on the way the control system and control centre is designed and set up, it might well be possible for a single operator to be in charge of several vessels – at least when everything goes according to plan. If, however, an emergency develops on one of the vessels, the operator will need to concentrate his attention on her, and there will need to be back-up or reserve operator capacity to take over the others, especially if there arises a simultaneous emergency on one of those. Again, however, the standard is not that the control centre team should be able to deal with every possible combination of likely and unlikely malfunctions. The control centre team must be reasonably equipped – as far as training, equipment, back-up, etc. goes – to deal with reasonably foreseeable situations.

Furthermore, the standard is not perfection for the shipowner either, but – at least under the Hague-Visby Rules – only due diligence. The shipowner thus satisfies his duty under Article 3.1 if he acts diligently in selecting, and then training and informing, the shore-based operators. In the recent crew-related unseaworthiness cases, one of the issues has often been that the ship owner failed to provide required information to the master or the chief engineer, who were as such not necessarily incompetent, but were rendered inefficient because they did not have all the information they needed.[24] Shore-based controllers will also need to be provided with all necessary information and training on the remote control system itself, on the remotely-controlled ship, etc. Under the Hague-Visby Rules, however, the shipowner only needs to exercise due diligence before and at the beginning of the voyage. In the days the rules were drafted, that limitation made sense. Once a ship had put to sea, there was little her owner could do until she called at the next port. With advances in communication technology, that ratio has largely disappeared. It is hardly surprising, then, that the Rotterdam Rules would extend the seaworthiness obligation to cover the entire voyage. If a ship is remotely controlled by shore-based operators, the reason to limit the due diligence obligation to the beginning of the voyage is completely absent. The shore-based operators are permanently under the control of the shipowner and can be replaced at any time. If, during the voyage, it becomes apparent that an operator is incompetent or inefficient, the shipowner would thus under the Rotterdam Rules be obliged to replace him if he could reasonably do so. The Rotterdam Rules are currently not in force, however, and may never be. It is submitted, though, that even under the Hague-Visby Rules the temporal restriction on the due diligence obligation should not be

---

24 This was so in *The Star Sea* [1997] 1 Lloyd's Rep. 360 (insufficient information on the vessel's CO_2 system) and *The Eurasian Dream* [2002] EWHC 118 (Comm); [2002] 1 Lloyd's Rep. 719 (insufficient information on the operations and risks of a car carrier).

a valid excuse for the ship owner not to act with regard to the remote operators, if he has a reasonable possibility to do so. If it turns out, for example, that one of the shore-based operators has an alcohol or drugs issue that impacts his efficiency, it is hardly conceivable that the shipowner would be within his rights in waiting until the ships reaches the next port before he takes action. In civil law countries, the ship owner's duty to act notwithstanding the 'before and at the beginning of the voyage' language of Article 3 of the Hague-Visby Rules could be based on the general duty to perform contracts in good faith, and even in the UK, an implied term might be read into the contract of carriage that inefficient operators will be replaced as soon as their inefficiency becomes apparent.[25] Another possible avenue might be to qualify the ship owner's inaction in a case where he could have taken corrective action as a failure to properly care for the cargo, which under the Hague-Visby Rules is a continuous duty persisting throughout the entire voyage.

Fully-autonomous vessels, by contrast, do not have any crew at all, onshore or offshore. There might well of course still be humans involved at certain moments, for example when something breaks down or when the ship finds herself in conditions that exceed her operating parameters, but these persons are more like today's specialised third-party repairmen. They are called in as and when required, but can hardly be considered to be part of the ship's crew. The obvious question then is whether a ship with no crew at all can still be considered 'properly manned' for the purposes of the Hague-Visby Rules. The answer, it is submitted, is positive. 'Proper' manning is indeed a relative and a goal-based requirement. The proper manning requirement was not written into the Hague-Visby Rules by representatives of the seafarers' labour unions to ensure employment for seafarers. For the Hague-Visby Rules, there must only be such crew as is required to safely sail ship and cargo to their destination. If it is shown, through experiment or actual experience, that unmanned ships are reasonably suitable to do so, the manning requirement in Art. 3.1(b) should not stand in the carrier's way. Here also, it must be stressed that the standard is not perfection. In other words, it is not so that carriers can only start using fully autonomous cargo ships if the developers of such ships can guarantee that there will never be incidents that result in cargo loss or damage. The standard is 'reasonably suited', and the carrier must only exercise due diligence. The due diligence in this regard would lie in the selection of the system(s) used, the appraisal of the reliability and robustness of those system(s), their protection against hacking and cybercrime, etc.

The more complex technology and software becomes, however, the larger the possibilities of malfunctions, software errors, etc. It is entirely possible, therefore, that if fully autonomous vessels become a commercial reality, there will be incidents with cargo loss or damage caused by the vessel's own control system. In that case, the vessel may, in hindsight, be unseaworthy. The carrier, however,

---

25 See, for example, *Yam Seng Pte Ltd v International Trade Corporation Ltd* [2013] EWHC 111; [2013] 1 Lloyd's Rep. 526, where Leggatt J pointed out that terms may be implied in a contract where necessary to give it business efficacy (para.[132]), and further stated that 'there are (...) standards of commercial dealing which are so generally accepted that the contracting parties would reasonably be understood to take them as read without explicitly stating them in their contractual document' (para.[138]).

may have exercised due diligence, in which case he will not be liable for the consequences of the unseaworthiness. In other words, if the control system of a fully autonomous vessel malfunctions and causes loss of or damage to the cargo, the carrier will be exonerated, as long as he has exercised due diligence in selecting, installing and maintaining the control system. This may seem contrary to the (implied) promise of technology that everything will be better and safer, but from a legal point of view, it is a straightforward application of the Hague-Visby Rules. Unlike, for example, a road carrier under the CMR, who can never use the defective condition of his vehicle as a defence (Art. 17.3), a maritime carrier under the Hague-Visby Rules can do so, given the exercise of due diligence. There is, of course, no basis to distinguish between defects that relate to 'simple' technology (valves, pumps, engines, etc.) and defects that relate to complex technology (an automated control system). Under the Hamburg Rules, the burden on the carrier would probably be more difficult, as the carrier would have to prove that he took all measures that could reasonably be required to avoid the occurrence and its consequences (Art. 5.1). That, however, will often require that the carrier pinpoint what exactly caused the control system to behave in an unexpected or inappropriate way, which in a complex system may be very difficult (or at least prohibitively expensive) to establish. The Rotterdam Rules on the other hand have reintroduced the unseaworthiness defence (Art. 17.5).

With regard to the moment the due diligence must be exercised, this will primarily be before and at the beginning of the voyage. Once the vessel starts her voyage, she is on her own and makes her own decisions based on the algorithms that have been programmed into her. Nevertheless, even with fully autonomous ships there is likely to be some communication between the ship's systems and the shore (at the very least, an autonomous ship needs to be able to raise an alarm onshore if something does go wrong). If the people ashore are aware that something is wrong and are able to correct the situation remotely, it is arguable that they are under a legal duty to do so.

One of the concerns that has been voiced with regard to unmanned vessels is that it will become more difficult for the carrier or shipowner's opponent in claims and proceedings to obtain information. How will a cargo claimant, or the owner of the other vessel in a collision, etc. manage to find out which control system is used, how it was set up in general, what data and parameters were fed into it for this specific voyage, how the control system proceeded from those data and parameters to the decisions eventually made, etc.? With regard to the carriage of goods, however, that concern is less acute than in scenarios where the fault of the other side has to be proved (e.g. collision cases). Under all sea carriage conventions (Hague-Visby, Hamburg and Rotterdam Rules), if the cargo is not delivered at its destination in the same condition, the carrier is presumed to be liable. If the carrier then wants to argue that this is because the control system 'misbehaved' in a way that he could not reasonably have prevented, the burden of proof lies with the carrier. It is the carrier that will have to show what exactly happened and how those facts fit within the exemptions of the applicable convention.

2.2 Care for the cargo

In addition to his duty to use due diligence to make the ship seaworthy (under Article 3.1 of the Hague-Visby Rules), the carrier also has a duty to properly care for the cargo under Article 3.2. This latter duty, unlike the due diligence obligation, continues throughout the entire voyage. How can the carrier take proper care of the cargo, however, when there is no-one on board the ship?

The problem may not be as insoluble as it seems at first sight. The requirement to properly and carefully load, handle, stow, etc., the goods is, like the seaworthiness obligation, a relative obligation. The argument that to 'properly carry' goods is an absolute obligation, requiring the goods to be carried in such a way that they arrive at their destination in undamaged condition, come what may, was clearly rejected by the House of Lords in *Albacora S.R.L. v Westcott & Laurence Line*.[26] Instead, the House, in the shape of Lords Reid, Pearce and Pearson, held that properly carrying goods means carrying them in accordance with a 'sound system'.[27] A 'sound' system is a system that takes into account the information the carrier has (or should have had) about the cargo, general industry practice, etc.[28] Ultimately, the question is which measures a reasonably prudent carrier would have taken in light of the information he had (or should have had) about the carried goods. It is submitted, however, that for a system to be 'sound', the presence of a crew on board is not necessarily required. Everything will depend on the type and nature of the cargo, the measures required during the voyage (e.g. ventilation or heating) and the industry practices (and possibly new methods or techniques) that will develop.

Furthermore, much of the care for the cargo has already moved ashore. In his account of the 1949 voyage of the sailing cargo ship *Pamir*, William Stark relates how the crew spent two days manually hauling 180-lb[29] grain sacks from the forward hatch to the aft hatch, because the master felt that the ship was trimmed too much down by the head.[30] It is clear, however, that this is something from the past. There is simply no way that, for example, the crew of a container carrier could manually move containers from one stack to another while the vessel is at sea. Equally, when the lashings of general cargo (steel coils, rolling equipment, etc.) give way during heavy weather, there is virtually nothing the crew can do but hope that the loose cargo does not smash through the sides of the ship, and some damage control when the weather calms down. The stowage plan, which traditionally was prepared by the master or chief officer on paper,

---

26 1966 S.C. (H.L.) 19; [1966] 2 Lloyd's Rep. 53.

27 The term 'sound system' had already been used by Viscount Kilmuir LC in *GH Renton & Co Ltd v Palmyra Trading Corp. of Panama* [1957] AC 149, 166.

28 See *Albacora S.R.L. v Westcott & Laurence Line* 1966 S.C. (H.L.) 19; [1966] 2 Lloyd's Rep. 53; *The Flowergate* [1967] 1 Lloyd's Rep 1; *Gatoil International Inc v Tradax Petroleum Ltd* [1985] 1 Lloyd's Rep 350; *Volcafe Ltd v Cia Sud Americana de Vapores SA (trading as CSAV)* [2016] EWCA Civ 1103, [2017] Q.B. 915.

29 I.e. 81 kg.

30 W. F. Stark, *The Last Time Around Cape Horn: The Historic 1949 Voyage of the Windjammer Pamir*, Chapter VII, New York: Carroll & Graf, 2004.

is now predominantly prepared ashore with specialised computer software. The loading, lashing and securing of the cargo has been delegated to specialised shore-based companies. The master, and through him the carrier, is still liable for the correct loading, stowing, lashing etc. of the cargo, but the actual tasks in these respects are to a large extent no longer performed by the crew or indeed anyone on board the vessel. For those cargo duties, that are today already performed ashore, a move towards remotely-controlled or fully autonomous vessels would not change much.

In light of the evolutions described above, the role of the crew in the care for the cargo is shrinking or even disappearing.[31] That evolution is indeed also reflected in the case law on cargo claims. In *Klausen & Co A/S v Mediterranean Shipping Co SA*,[32] the court held that the crew should have noticed that something was amiss with the air temperature readings on a reefer container. Nevertheless, the claim was partially dismissed, because the court also found that even if the crew had noticed the anomaly, there was no proof that they could have done anything about it while at sea. In *The City of Berytus*,[33] where an entire cargo of secondhand cars had been destroyed by a shipboard fire, the Antwerp Court of Appeal found that the crew was not sufficiently familiar with the ship's firefighting equipment and was not well trained in firefighting, but nevertheless dismissed the cargo claim. The fire had actually occurred while the vessel was in the port of Antwerp, and several fire brigades were called in to fight it. Even those professional firefighters, however, did not manage to extinguish it and in the end had to let it burn out. It would appear, therefore, that the courts recognise that the crew's possibilities to take action are (very) limited, certainly when at sea.

It has sometimes been suggested, however, that the presence of a crew on board is necessary for such purposes as protecting the cargo against piratical attacks[34] or jettisoning dangerous cargo.[35] It would seem, though, that these concerns are rather far-fetched. It is undoubtedly true that on traditional manned ships, the crew does play a role in preparation against, and reaction to, attacks. On the other hand, traditional ships are vulnerable to pirate attacks precisely because they need to be accessible to the crew. There are doors to the superstructure, bridge and engine room; there are access hatches to the holds, and so on. Other infrastructure, such as railings that are required to create a safe working environment for the crew, is also a perfect anchor point for

---

31 See, for example, J. King, "Technology and the Seafarer" (2000) Journal for Maritime Research 48, 59:2.

    The role of the seafarer has changed over the last quarter century or so. By the 1970s it was becoming clear that the four principal functions of shipboard operation [navigation, cargo, maintenance, catering] had been effectively reduced to two: navigation and catering. The cargo function remained to the extent that loading, discharging and monitoring still involved the crew.

32 [2013] EWHC 3254 (Comm).
33 CA Antwerp, 4th Section, 06.03.2017, Docket N° 2015/AR/19.
34 See for instance Gaël Piette, "Les navires sans équipage", *D.M.F.* 2017, N° 797, 15, at p. 20.
35 Luci Carey, "All Hands Off Deck? The Legal Barriers to Autonomous Ships" (2017) 23 J.I.M.L. 202, at p. 205.

grappling hooks. An unmanned vessel with no need to accommodate people while at sea, could be designed and constructed in a way that would make it much more difficult for pirates to board her. Jettisoning dangerous cargo is also more of a theoretical than a practical concern. What indeed could the crew of the *Hanjin Pennsylvania* have done if they had realised that the calcium hypochlorite in one of the containers in the hold was subject to a self-accelerating process of decomposition, or that some of the containers had been stuffed with undeclared fireworks? And even if, by chance, containers of dangerous goods are stowed in an accessible location, to what extent is it realistic to expect the crew to manually handle and jettison them in cases of danger?

The crew still has important cargo-related duties when in port. Since those duties are performed when the ship is in port, however, they could equally be performed by (specialised) shore-based personnel, whether the vessel concerned is remotely-controlled or fully autonomous. When at sea, the crew's cargo duties mainly consist of (pre-planned) cargo management such as heating or ventilating the cargo, monitoring its condition, and responding to problems or emergencies. Actions such as heating or ventilation can also be performed remotely or can be fully automated. Monitoring can also be done remotely. Smart containers, for example, allow container and cargo owners to remotely monitor the condition of both the container itself and the goods inside it. A more difficult issue, however, is that an on-board crew may be able to correct problems or malfunctions, for example by resetting an instrument, or replacing a faulty sensor, valve, etc. If there is no crew on board, problems or malfunctions may be remotely detected, but it will no longer be possible to have a human take a look at the issue, or at least not with any degree of speed. The crew's possibilities at sea should not be overestimated, though. Crew members cannot be specialists in all types of machinery that are found on board a modern ship, and the ship cannot carry spares for all possible parts either. Furthermore, the fact that there is no crew on board during the voyage will be an additional factor in the design of the ship's cargo systems. In the future, those systems will have to be designed in such a way that they are sufficiently reliable to allow prolonged periods of unattended operation. The maritime industry, however, is not the only industry where systems must be very reliable because they are not easily accessible for maintenance or repairs. The space industry is a very obvious example, but the nuclear and chemical industries also come to mind, for example.

In conclusion, it is submitted that, in general, it is indeed possible for a carrier to have a 'sound system' of care for the cargo in place, even if there are no crew members physically on board during the voyage. There might, of course, be specific types of cargo that do require human supervision during the voyage, or cargoes for which the shippers or owners do not want to accept shipment on unmanned vessels, but those are likely to be the exceptions rather than the rule.

2.3 The nautical fault exception

Under the Hague-Visby Rules, the carrier must exercise due diligence to properly man the ship. Once he has done so, however, errors or mistakes of the crew members in her navigation or management then become a defence for the carrier. This is the well-known nautical fault exemption of Article 4.2(a) of the Hague-Visby Rules. This exemption made sense, or was at least defensible, when the original Hague Rules were drafted, but has come under increasing criticism with the advances in communication and other technology.[36] Both the Hamburg Rules and the Rotterdam Rules have abolished the nautical fault exemption. The Rotterdam Rules, however, are currently not in force. The Hamburg Rules are, but only in a limited number of countries. Many maritime countries still apply the Hague or Hague-Visby Rules, and will need to determine to what extent the nautical fault exemption applies to unmanned vessels.

Here again, as with the seaworthiness question, remotely-controlled vessels need to be distinguished from fully autonomous vessels. A remotely-controlled vessel has a team of operators who are shore-based, but nevertheless quite clearly 'servants of the carrier' within the meaning of Article 4 (2) (a) of the Hague-Visby Rules. Such shore-based servants are, of course, not new. Even in the past, the carrier always had some servants ashore. In order for the nautical fault exemption to apply, however, the neglects or defaults of the servants need to be in the navigation or the management of the ship. Traditionally, shore-based servants of the carrier had little influence on this, which was primarily or even exclusively the domain of the ship's crew, certainly once the ship had put to sea. With remotely operated vessels, that is no longer true. On the contrary, the navigation and the management of the ship will be fully transferred to the shore-based operators. If an operator is negligent or makes a mistake, there is no obvious reason why the nautical fault exemption would not be available to the carrier. The negligence or error will of course have to relate to the navigation or the management of the ship, as opposed to the management of the cargo, but chances are that a remote operator will be (much) more involved with remotely operating the ship than with remotely managing the cargo. The sometimes difficult distinguishing between the management of the ship and the management of the cargo might actually be easier with a remotely controlled vessel, and leaning more towards the management of the ship and thus the possibility for the carrier to invoke the nautical fault exemption. It is, of course, allowed to ask why the principal of a remote operator of a vessel should enjoy such exemption when the principals of other remote operators do not, but that is more a critique of the continuing viability of the nautical fault exemption in general than a legal reason why – in countries that apply the Hague-Visby Rules – this exemption would not apply to

---

36 See, for instance, P. Leau, "Dead in the Water: The Nautical Fault Exemption of the Hague-Visby Rules" (2015/16) 7 *Singapore Law Review, Juris Illuminae*; L. T. Weitz, "The Nautical Fault debate" (1998) 22 Tul.Mar.L.J. 581; A. Chao, "La faute nautique, une notion en perdition" (1991) *BTL* 367; P. Delebecque, *Droit maritime*, Dalloz (13th Ed.), No.745, Paris; S. Miribel, "Nouvelle 'faute nautique' confirmée, l'échafaud attendra …" (2014) *D.M.F.* 256 (note); N. Molfessis, "Requiem pour la faute nautique", *Mélanges Pierre Bonassies*, éd. Moreux, Presses universitaires d'Aix-Marseille, Aix-en-Provence, 2001, 207.

shore-based servants of the carrier that err while remotely navigating or managing the ship.

With fully autonomous vessels, however, the situation is more complex. Even if a vessel is fully autonomous, there will still be humans involved. Such ships do not decide on their own that they are going to go from Hamburg to New York, with an intermediate call at Antwerp. This kind of voyage and routing instructions will have to be entered into the autonomous system by a human operator. Conceivably, that operator could make a mistake with those instructions, which at a later stage cause loss or damage. If such a scenario plays out, the operator could be considered a servant of the carrier, dealing with the navigation of the vessel. This scenario does not seem very likely, though. The operator would only be inputting destinations, and the decisions on how to safely get from one point to the next would be made by the autonomous ship's control system. A more realistic and more dangerous scenario is that the control system has defects ('bugs' in software parlance) or limitations that cause loss or damage.

A first possibility in this respect is that the defective condition of the control system is not due to a fault in the legal sense of the term. When developing software, it is indeed impossible – just like in the drafting of contracts or legislation – to think of every possible eventuality that could happen. The simple fact that a piece of software does not 'behave' as it is afterwards determined that it should have behaved does not, in and of itself, prove that the software was badly designed or that the developers made mistakes. What is the legal position when the control system is 'defective', in the sense that it reacts to a given situation in an undesired way, causing loss or damage, but without the developers being legally to blame?[37] It hardly seems possible to consider the control system itself as a 'servant' of the carrier within the meaning of Article 4.2(a) of the Hague-Visby Rules. IT or robotic systems may function in a very independent or autonomous way, but they are not legal entities.[38] The nautical fault exemption would therefore seem unavailable to the carrier in this scenario. Provided the carrier used due diligence in selecting (and maintaining) the control system, he could argue that the defective condition of the system renders the ship unseaworthy, for the consequences of which he is not liable under Article 4.1.

The other possibility is that the control system is defective, in a way for which the developers are considered liable. They should have realized that their system would not do what it was expected to do and have taken steps to correct that situation. Initially, the system will have been developed by human programmers.[39] In principle, it is possible that the control system has been developed in-house by a ship owner and that the programmers are directly employed by the ship owner,

---

37 The error (identified in hindsight) is an error that a reasonably competent, careful programmer could also have made.

38 Although some have suggested that (in the future) a class of electronic legal entities could be created. See, for example, the European Parliament resolution of 16 February 2017 with recommendations to the Commission on Civil Law Rules on Robotics (2015/2103(INL)), para 59.(f).

39 Self-learning, self-adapting systems could mean that the system, as it exists and functions at a certain point in time, is actually no longer identical to the system as it was originally created.

but it seems much more likely that such systems will be developed by separate, specialised companies. In the latter case, the programmers are most likely not 'servants' of the carrier within the meaning of Art. 4 (2) (a) HVR.[40] In the former case they are, but it will often be difficult to claim that their activities relate to the navigation or the management of the vessel, as required for Article 4 (2) (a) HVR to apply. It is entirely possible, by the way, that their programming was performed months or even years before the voyage during which the loss or damage is caused. In most cases, therefore, it will not be possible for the carrier to invoke errors or mistakes of the programmers as nautical faults. As pointed out above, it does not seem possible, in the current state of the law, to see the control system itself as a 'servant' of the carrier. For fully autonomous vessels, therefore, the nautical fault exemption of the Hague-Visby Rules would seem to *de facto* disappear.

3 Conclusions

From a carriage law perspective, there would not seem to be major obstacles to the introduction of unmanned vessels. Such vessels, both remotely controlled and fully autonomous, can be seaworthy, i.e. reasonably fit to encounter the perils of the voyage and to carry her cargo safely on that voyage. In countries that apply the Hague-Visby Rules, however, the due diligence obligation may well be extended in time (or supplemented with a similar, implied obligation during the voyage). In countries that apply the Hamburg Rules or that will apply the Rotterdam Rules in the future, the due diligence obligation in any case extends to the entire voyage.

Proper care for the cargo does not seem an insurmountable hurdle either. Both carriers and cargo interests will need to build up experience and become familiar with the implications (and possibly limitations) of the new technology, but there is no reason why 'sound systems' to carry cargo on board of unmanned vessels could not be developed.

The nautical fault exemption, finally, would seem to survive for remotely controlled vessels, but will probably *de facto* disappear for fully autonomous vessels. In countries that apply the Hamburg Rules or that will apply the Rotterdam Rules, of course, the nautical fault exemption is or will in any case be abolished.

---

40 Art. 4 (2) (a) only includes 'servants' (*préposés* in the French text) of the carrier, and not 'servants or agents' as do other provisions. It is arguable, therefore, that the person concerned must be employed by the carrier. Stevedores, as independent contractors, are generally considered not to come within the scope of Art. 4 (2) (a). See G. Treitel & F. Reynolds, *Carver on Bills of Lading*, Sweet & Maxwell, 2011 (3rd Ed.), at [9–213]. See also R. Aikens, R. Lord & M. Bools, *Bills of Lading*, Informa, 2006, para.10.205; S. Girvin, *Carriage of Goods by Sea*, OUP, 2011 (2nd Ed), para.29.08.

PART 3

LEGAL TECH AND ITS IMPACT ON SHIPPING AND INSURANCE

CHAPTER 12

Impact of technology on disclosure in shipping litigation

Peter MacDonald Eggers QC[*]

1 Introduction

A central feature of the work of the Commercial Court for more than a century has been the determination of shipping disputes: disputes relating to charterparties and bills of lading, the carriage of goods and passengers by sea, collisions, salvage, and international trade. Such disputes often reflect problems which emerge as a result of novel situations and such situations arise because of the development of new methods of conducting business in the shipping industry, an industry which is global in its dimensions and which develops in line with new technologies.

One of the hallmarks of litigation in England is the disclosure (formerly, the discovery) of documents in the control of the parties to the litigation, requiring each party to inform the other party or parties of the existence of documents they have in their control, allow inspection of such documents and provide copies of such documents, even if those documents are adverse to the positions of the disclosing party.[1]

Shipping litigation may take a variety of forms. Some disputes may be limited in scope or small in value; others may be immense. A claim made by or against the owner or operator of a vessel will very often entail the necessity of determining the dispute in light of very substantial numbers of documents, in particular documents which relate to the operation and management of a vessel, but also the financial transactions of the parties to the relevant contract. In the 21st century, much of this documentation is electronic in form. Indeed, many companies operating support services for the shipping industry seek to operate paperless office environments (for example, insurance services).

When a shipping dispute is litigated, it follows that each of the parties will have to disclose the documents in their control, subject to questions of relevance and privilege. In the modern world, the parties' electronic disclosure obligations will depend on two central considerations. First, the manner in which the Court will regulate the disclosure of Electronic Documents. Second, the categories of documents held in an electronic form.

---

[*] Barrister, King's Bench Walk, Visiting Fellow of the Institute of International Shipping and Trade Law.
[1] Note the definition of adverse documents in para. 2.7 of the draft Practice Direction for the Disclosure Pilot for the Business and Property Courts:

> A document is "adverse" if it or any information it contains contradicts or materially damages the disclosing party's contention or version of events on an issue in dispute, or supports the contention or version of events of an opposing party on an issue in dispute.

2 Disclosure under the civil procedure rules

Until 1999, discovery of documents represented a considerable burden on the parties to much litigation in that the scope of documents to be disclosed was widely drawn, requiring each party to provide discovery of documents in their possession "relating to the issue in the action". In *Ventouris v Mountain* Bingham, LJ said:[2]

> Our system of civil procedure is founded on the rule that the interests of justice are best served if parties to litigation are obliged to disclose and produce for the other party's inspection all documents in their possession, custody or power relating to the issues in the action.

However, the significant breadth of such discovery (adopting the "unlamented"[3] *Peruvian Guano* test of relevance, which included disclosure of documents indirectly relevant in that they might lead to a train of inquiry to find more directly relevant documents)[4] was such that, given that every transaction which might give rise to a dispute involved more and more documentation, because of the ease of copying documents, the discovery obligations of the parties could be onerous. Indeed, in considering the question of privilege in respect of copies of documents, Bingham, LJ[5] referred to that time (1991) as "an age of indiscriminate photocopying". That was an age when business also started using personal computers, and instantaneous communications were achieved more efficiently than in the past through faxes and telex messages.

The relentless advance of technological change has introduced greater means for the quick and ready increase in documentation, by reference to further and more efficient instantaneous communications (emails and text messages), creation of documents (word processing), copying of documents (using scanning equipment), data processing (using computer mainframes), storage of documents (computer servers, databases, memory sticks, and ever-enlarging hard disks), the use of social media and voicemail (for the transfer and sharing of information). In addition, the means available for the purpose of communications and information transfer and storage are enhanced by the use of various devices, such as office servers, personal computers, laptops, tablets, mobile devices, etc.[6] The information is not only that contained in the content of the document, but also deleted, but otherwise preserved, data relating to the document in question[7] and metadata[8] (revealing details of the document's creation, revisions, such as the author, date of creation, and time spent in editing). In 2009, it was then estimated that over 90%

---

2 [1991] 1 WLR 607, at pp. 611–612.
3 *Zipporah Lisle-Mainwaring v Associated Newspapers Limited* [2018] EWCA Civ 1470; [2018] 1 WLR 4766, at [36].
4 *Compagnie Financiere du Pacifique v Peruvian Guano Co Ltd* (1882) 11 QBD 55.
5 [1991] 1 WLR 607, at p. 621.
6 C. Hollander, *Documentary Evidence* (13th ed.), (London: Sweet & Maxwell, 2018), para. 9–09.
7 C. Hollander, *Documentary Evidence* (13th ed.), (London: Sweet & Maxwell, 2018), para. 9–10.
8 Metadata is defined by para. 5(7) of the Practice Direction 31B to mean

> data about data. In the case of an Electronic Document, metadata is typically embedded information about the document which is not readily accessible once the Native Electronic Document has been converted into an Electronic Image or paper document. It may include (for example) the date and time of creation or modification of a word-processing file, or the author and the date and time of sending an email. Metadata may be created automatically by a computer system or manually by a user.

of all business documentation is electronic in form;[9] it is likely that this proportion is even greater today.

In 1999, with the adoption of a new civil procedure code (Civil Procedure Rules) in place of the old Rules of the Supreme Court, the default position for discovery in litigation became a test of relevance more circumscribed than that of the *Peruvian Guano* test, namely "standard disclosure", which – if ordered – required the production of documents which adversely affect the disclosing party's own case, which adversely affect another party's case, or which support another party's case.[10] Even though such a test required the disclosure of fewer documents, the problem of reviewing and searching for a cache of documents remained the same. The same file of documents had to be searched whether indirectly or directly relevant documents had to be disclosed. It should be noted that the Court may still order a wider scope of disclosure pursuant to CPR rule 31.5(7)(d), including making a "ship's papers" order in marine insurance cases pursuant to CPR rule 58.14.

Soon after the introduction of the new Civil Procedure Rules, rules were also developed for "electronic disclosure" following a report prepared by Mr Justice Cresswell in 2004.[11] A Practice Direction was developed to deal with electronic disclosure. It has been said by the Court that it is "gross incompetence" for legal practitioners not to know the rules governing electronic disclosure and practise in them.[12] That Practice Direction is now Practice Direction 31B – Disclosure of Electronic Documents ("the Practice Direction"), which has been in force since 2010.

The definition of "document" in CPR rule 31.4 is "anything in which information of any description is recorded". This is self-evidently a broad definition and encapsulates information contained in an unrestricted number of media, including electronic documentation.[13] Indeed, para. 1 of the Practice Direction states that the definition extends to Electronic Documents, which para. 5(3) defines to mean:

> any document held in electronic form. It includes, for example, email and other electronic communications such as text messages and voicemail, word-processed documents and databases, and documents stored on portable devices such as memory sticks and mobile phones. In addition to documents that are readily accessible from computer systems and other electronic devices and media, it includes documents that are stored on servers and back-up systems and documents that have been deleted. It also includes metadata and other embedded data which is not typically visible on screen or a print out.

Where the relevant document is a hard copy document, a "piece of paper", it will not be treated as an Electronic Document. However, where that document is scanned and uploaded into an e-disclosure database, even for the purposes of disclosure in the litigation in question, it will be treated as an Electronic Document.[14]

---

9 *Earles v Barclays Bank plc* [2009] EWHC 2500 (Mercantile); [2010] Bus LR 566, at [71].
10 CPR rules 31.5 and 31.6.
11 C. Hollander, *Documentary Evidence* (13th ed.), (Sweet & Maxwell, 2018), para. 9–02.
12 *Earles v Barclays Bank plc* [2009] EWHC 2500 (Mercantile); [2010] Bus LR 566, at [71].
13 *Sony Music Entertainment (Australia) Limited v University of Tasmania* [2003] FCA 532, at [48–54] (Australia).
14 *Re Atrium Training Services Ltd (In Liquidation)* [2013] EWHC 2882 (Ch), at [55–62]; rev'd on other grounds *Smailes v McNally* [2014] EWCA Civ 1299, at [23].

Such electronic documentation has to be reviewed to determine what documents should be disclosed. The Practice Direction, which has been described as "thorough and clear",[15] was introduced to regulate electronic disclosure in accordance with the overriding objective (para. 6(3) of the Practice Direction) and adopts the following general approach:

i) Electronic disclosure requires a closer degree of co-operation between the parties to the litigation.[16] The purpose of the Practice Direction is to encourage and assist the parties to reach agreement in relation to the electronic disclosure in a proportionate and cost-effective manner (para. 2 of the Practice Direction).

ii) The parties' lawyers must inform their clients that Electronic Documents are to be preserved, once litigation is contemplated (para. 7 of the Practice Direction).

iii) The parties and their lawyers must discuss the use of technology in the management of Electronic Documents and the conduct of proceedings, including the conduct of electronic disclosure and the presentation of documents to the Court (para. 8 of the Practice Direction).

iv) Before the Court's involvement at the first case management conference, the parties should discuss the approaches towards the preservation of Electronic Documents and carrying out searches (para. 9 of the Practice Direction).[17] This will require the parties exchanging information about the categories of Electronic Documents in their control, their computer systems, electronic devices and media containing relevant documents, the storage systems maintained by the parties and document retention policies. Further, the parties should discuss the parameters of electronic disclosure, including but not limited to limitations on disclosure, the use of keyword searches, the use of agreed software tools, the use of Data Sampling,[18] the methods to be used to identify privileged and other non-disclosable documents, and the possible use of neutral electronic repository for storage of Electronic Documents. In addition, it will require co-operation as to the format in which electronic disclosure is to be provided for inspection and copying.[19]

v) At the first case management conference, the parties will summarise the points on which they are agreed and not agreed (para. 14 of the Practice Direction). In the event of dispute, the Court should decide how best to approach such matters (para. 15 of the Practice Direction). Indeed, the Court will give appropriate directions at any time the parties are not agreed, or even if they are agreed, but the Court considers that the

---

15 *Triumph Controls UK Limited v Primus International Holding Co* [2018] EWHC 176 (TCC), at [15].
16 *Triumph Controls UK Limited v Primus International Holding Co* [2018] EWHC 176 (TCC), at [15].
17 *Earles v Barclays Bank plc* [2009] EWHC 2500 (Mercantile); [2010] Bus LR 566, at [70]; *Montpellier Estates Ltd v Leeds City Council* [2012] EWHC 1343 (QB), at [23].
18 Defined by para. 5(1) to mean *"the process of checking data by identifying and checking representative individual documents"*.
19 See also CPR rule 31.5(3)-(5).

agreed approach to electronic disclosure is inadequate (para. 17–18 of the Practice Direction).

vi) Technology should be used in order to ensure that document management activities are undertaken efficiently and effectively (para. 6(2) of the Practice Direction).

vii) CPR rule 31.7 requires the parties to carry out a reasonable search when providing standard disclosure.[20] The primary source of disclosure of Electronic Documents is normally reasonably accessible data (para. 24 of the Practice Direction). In accordance with para. 20–22 of the Practice Direction, the reasonableness of such search depends on (a) the number of documents involved, (b) the nature and complexity of the proceedings, (c) the ease and expense of retrieval of any individual or category of documents, including (i) the accessibility of Electronic Documents or data (emails on computer systems, servers, back-up systems or electronic devices or media, taking into account developments in hardware or software systems), (ii) the location of the Electronic Documents, (iii) the likelihood of recovering Electronic Documents, (iv) the cost of recovering and disclosing Electronic Documents, and (v) the likelihood that Electronic Documents will be materially altered in the course of recovery, disclosure and inspection, and (d) the significance of any document which is likely to be located during the search. These issues arise in particular with respect to the recovery or retrieval of documents from back-up data, which might be in a different or compressed format.[21]

viii) The means of undertaking the search must be discussed, agreed upon or decided, including whether the wholesale review of an entire cache of documents is required, the definition of the parameters of any search (by reference to the location of electronic files, the date of their creation, etc), the use of keyword searches (identifying the terms of such keywords),[22] or other forms of electronic search (*e.g.* dates of creation). See para. 25–27 of the Practice Direction.

ix) The disclosure of Electronic Documents in their Native Format (meaning "*the original form in which [the Electronic Document] was created by a computer software program*")[23] will include the disclosure of metadata. Any additional metadata sought by a party must justify such disclosure by reference to its relevance and the cost of disclosure (para. 28–29 of the Practice Direction).

x) Disclosure should be in a readily accessible form and disclosure data should be set out in a single, continuous table or spreadsheet, including certain specified information (para. 31 of the Practice Direction).

---

20 See *Fiddes v Channel 4 TV Corporation* [2010] EWCA Civ 516; *Smailes v McNally* [2015] EWHC 1755 (Ch), at [89–90].

21 *Digicel (St Lucia) Ltd v Cable & Wireless plc* [2008] EWHC 2522 (Ch); [2009] 2 All ER 1094.

22 Defined by para. 5(3) of the Practice Direction to mean "a software-aided search for words across the text of an Electronic Document".

23 Para. 5(8) of the Practice Direction.

xi) Electronic Documents should generally be made available for inspection in a form which allows the party receiving the documents the same ability to access, search, review and display the documents as the party giving disclosure (para. 6(4) of the Practice Direction). This will include the facilitation of the use of special technology not otherwise available to the receiving party (para. 35 of the Practice Direction).

xii) Electronic copies of disclosed documents should be provided in their Native Format, in a manner which preserves metadata relating to the date of creation of each document (para. 33 of the Practice Direction). In addition, a party should provide any available searchable Optical Character Recognition (OCR)[24] versions of Electronic Documents with the original (para. 34 of the Practice Direction).

Given its nature, perhaps the two most important considerations in connection with the governance of electronic disclosure is that of the volume of such documents and the cost of search, review, and disclosure. In *Digicel (St Lucia) Ltd v Cable & Wireless plc* Morgan, J considered the Cresswell Report in the context of the Part 31 Practice Direction on electronic disclosure then in force and said:[25]

> The Cresswell Report makes a number of points which it is useful to record. At paragraph 3.3, the report explains why the issues which arise in relation to disclosure of Electronic Documents are different from the issues which arise in relation to disclosure of paper documents. These reasons include the huge volume of documents which are created and stored electronically, the ease of duplication of Electronic Documents, the lack of order in the storage of Electronic Documents, the differing retention policies of the parties, the existence of metadata and the fact that Electronic Documents are more difficult to dispose of than paper documents.

This does not mean, at least in the context of a vast electronic archive, that the approach to disclosure must "leave no stone unturned",[26] but a more rigorous system should be adopted where the archive is more confined and/or where there is an identified target document.[27]

The nature of Electronic Documents reveals the need for an effective means of search. In *Goodale v Ministry of Justice*[28] the Senior Master of the Queen's Bench Division explained the problems:

> This judgment concerns a serious practical problem for the case management of disclosure which is now occurring on a regular basis. The reason is that, since certainly

---

24 Defined by para. 5(9) of the Practice Direction to mean "the computer-facilitated recognition of printed or written text characters in an Electronic Image in which the text-based contents cannot be searched electronically". As to the shortcomings of relying on OCR versions, see *Smailes v McNally* [2015] EWHC 1755 (Ch), at [32–37] and [64–97].

25 [2008] EWHC 2522 (Ch); [2009] 2 All ER 1094, at [38].

26 *Digicel (St Lucia) Ltd v Cable & Wireless plc* [2008] EWHC 2522 (Ch); [2009] 2 All ER 1094, at [46]; *Smailes v McNally* [2014] EWCA Civ 1299, at [42].

27 *Smailes v McNally* [2014] EWCA Civ 1299, at [42].

28 [2009] EWHC B41 (QB), at 1–4]. See also *Pyrrho Investments Limited v MWB Property Limited* [2016] EWHC 256 (Ch), at [5–15].

the beginning of this decade, increasing numbers of public bodies and private businesses, not to mention individuals, have gone over to creating, exchanging and storing their documentation and communicating with each other entirely by electronic means. The end result is that an enormous volume of information is now created, exchanged and stored only electronically. Email communication, word processed documents, spreadsheets and ever increasing numbers of other forms of electronically stored information (ESI) now often form the entire corpus of the documentation held by companies and individuals who become involved in litigation. So the incidence of paper disclosure is becoming less and less prevalent though in some cases it may still be critical, and the incidence of the disclosure of electronically stored information, or ESI as it is known, is becoming more and more so. What is more, the volume of the ESI, even in small organisations is immense, often, as in the case of email, because of the huge quantities of documents created (including wide-scale duplication) and the fact that the documents can exist in many different forms and locations so that they are not readily accessible except at significant cost. It is also commonplace for many individuals to have more than one email account – business, personal, web-mail (for example, Yahoo, Gmail, Hotmail etc.) When ESI is available, metadata (literally data about data) associated with it can easily be unintentionally altered by the very act of collection, which in some circumstances can have a detrimental effect on the document's evidential integrity. What is more, ESI can be moved about nationally and internationally, indiscriminately and at lightning speed. What is the problem with this in litigation? Disclosure is a tripartite exercise of search, disclosure, and inspection, and the problem, when it comes to ESI is often for a party to gauge the scope of a reasonable search for ESI under CPR Rule 31.7 and PD31(2). The problem is how the parties and (if disputed) the court determines what the scope of that search of ESI should be, how it is going to be made proportionate and how it is going to be carried out correctly first time, without the court having to order it to be done again, as has occurred, for example, in Digicel (St Lucia) Ltd and others v. Cable and Wireless Plc and Others 2008 EWHC 2522 (Ch) in which case Morgan J ordered the defendants re-do their ESI search exercise at an additional cost of something like £2 million. By contrast, except in unusual cases, in the case of paper disclosure, parties usually know what paper they have. Often the problem is merely locating it physically and going through it to produce the documents required by the standard disclosure test. The problem with ESI is that, because of the matters mentioned above in paragraph 1, parties often do not know how much ESI they have, or where it is. They might have an idea as to which servers it is on or which personal computers it is on, or which back-up tapes it is on, but without a great deal more information, it is very difficult for them to know how much documentation will be revealed by searches of the media on which their ESI is stored and how much it is going to cost to search it and what the end result is going to be. A further issue might be that not all forms of ESI are searchable. Therefore, it has to be accepted that any search is not necessarily conclusive as to whether a particular document exists. Equally often the parties do not know where to begin their searches. In the case, for example, of email, the relevant servers are often not in their possession and sometimes not even in the jurisdiction. An ill considered search for ESI may produce far too few documents for review but more likely will produce such volumes that human review of every document is neither proportionate nor practical. Because of this a substantial industry has developed to handle the identification, collection, reduction and organisation for review of ESI. Often, this is carried out electronically, with technology aiding and supplementing human review.

When considering what constitutes a reasonable search of Electronic Documents, the initial responsibility is left with the party's solicitor undertaking or prescribing the search, the Court may be influenced by the degree with which the solicitor is fully informed of the issues of the case and the consideration given by the solicitor to any decision made in the process, having regard to the solicitor's diligence and conscientiousness, although ultimately the decision is that of the Court.[29] Therefore, it is not sufficient for a solicitor (or in-house counsel) merely to take the word of the custodian of a personal computer or mobile device that no emails or relevant emails exist in that particular computer; rather, that solicitor (or in-house counsel) should undertake an independent search of that computer.[30] In addition, the Court has said that the search which is undertaken must be "a meaningful and effective search"; to this end, the Court may well require that such a search be carried out by a person with the relevant qualifications and experience to do so. In *Mueller Europe Limited v Central Roofing (South Wales) Limited*,[31] Coulson, J said:

> Pursuant to CPR Part 31, the court has power to order a search for particular documents; pursuant to new Practice Direction 31B, the court can order such a search in relation to documents held electronically. As a matter of principle, I conclude that, if an order to search for Electronic Documents can only be complied with if it is undertaken by somebody with expertise in that field, then the court has the jurisdiction to order that the search should be carried out by such a person; otherwise, the court will be making an order with which the party against whom it is made will never be able to comply. That would not be in accordance with the overriding objective. A party in this sort of litigation is assisted by a number of different people to comply with court orders, including its solicitor and its experts. Orders are made against that party where, in reality, actual compliance is required by the third party advisor; for example, the "unless" order against Ms. Longworth, the defendant's expert accountant, will be something with which she has to comply, although the order is ultimately against the defendant, and carries with it a sanction that would harm the defendant, not Ms Longworth. Similarly, I can see no reason why, in principle, an order should not be made against a party requiring a search of Electronic Documents, to be undertaken by a suitably qualified person on behalf of that party.

It is a critical feature of this process that, aside from the Court in the event of a dispute, the process of electronic disclosure is such that any particular document which is revealed by a search of Electronic Documents must allow the disclosing party the final decision whether or not to disclose the document, in accordance with the principles governing such disclosure. Accordingly, if the relevant process requires a party automatically to disclose a document, such a process is not mandated by the Practice Direction, except possibly in an exceptional case. In *CBS Butler Ltd v Brown*[32] Tugendhat, J, said:

> In my judgment, an order which would deprive the Defendants of the opportunity of considering whether or not they shall make any disclosure is (in the words of Hoffmann J) an intrusive order, even if it is made on notice to the defendant. It is contrary to normal principles of justice, and can only be done when there is a paramount need to prevent a denial of justice to the claimant. The need to avoid such a denial of justice may be shown after the defendant has failed to comply with his disclosure obligations, having been given the opportunity to do so (as in

---

29 *Digicel (St Lucia) Ltd v Cable & Wireless plc* [2008] EWHC 2522 (Ch); [2009] 2 All ER 1094, at [51].
30 *Earles v Barclays Bank plc* [2009] EWHC 2500 (Mercantile); [2010] Bus LR 566, at [69].
31 [2012] EWHC 3417 (TCC); [2013] TCLR 2, at [25–28].
32 [2013] EWHC 3944 (QB); [2013] Info TLR 263, at [38].

Mueller). Or it may be shown before the defendant has had an opportunity to comply with his disclosure obligations. But in the latter case it is not sufficient for a claimant such as the employer in Lock v Beswick, or the Claimant, to show no more than that the defendant has misused confidential information or otherwise broken his employment contract. The position is a fortiori where the claimant has not even shown that much. What a claimant must show is substantial reasons for believing that a defendant is intending to conceal or destroy documents in breach of his obligations of disclosure under the CPR

This is especially so where predictive coding is deployed, *i.e.* where the relevance of a document is determined on a points basis by software analysis rather than by human judgement.[33] Nevertheless, it may well be appropriate for reviews of Electronic Documents to be undertaken by electronic means; the Court has allowed such means in the appropriate case taking into account all relevant considerations.[34]

3 Disclosure pilot for the business and property courts in England and Wales

On 1st November 2017, a Pilot Scheme for a reformed disclosure procedure was announced. Subject to a ministerial approval, the Pilot Scheme will be adopted by the Business and Property Courts in England and Wales, with some exceptions in particular the Admiralty Court, as from 1st January 2019 for a two year period. For this purpose, a draft Practice Direction has been drafted for implementation during the operation of the Pilot Scheme.

The Pilot Scheme has the following features:

i) It requires a large measure of co-operation between the parties (para. 2.3).It adopts a similar definition of "*document*" to that in the existing Practice Direction:

> A "document" may take any form including but not limited to paper or electronic; it may be held by computer or on portable devices such as memory sticks or mobile phones or within databases; it includes e-mail and other electronic communications such as text messages, webmail, social media and voicemail, audio or visual recordings. In addition to information that is readily accessible from computer systems and other electronic devices and media, the term "document" extends to information that is stored on servers and back-up systems and electronic information that has been "deleted". It also extends to metadata, and other embedded data which is not typically visible on screen or a print out.
>
> (para. 2.5–2.6)

ii) The parties are required to preserve documents for disclosure once proceedings are commenced or when it is apparent that such parties may become party to such proceedings (para. 3–4).

---

33 *Pyrrho Investments Limited v MWB Property Limited* [2016] EWHC 256 (Ch), at [16–24, 31]; *Brown v BCA Trading Limited* [2016] EWHC 1464 (Ch), at [10–11].

34 *Pyrrho Investments Limited v MWB Property Limited* [2016] EWHC 256 (Ch), at [33]; *Brown v BCA Trading Limited* [2016] EWHC 1464 (Ch). See also C. Hollander, *Documentary Evidence* (13th ed.), (Sweet & Maxwell, 2018), para. 9–20.

iii) Unless the Court otherwise orders or the parties otherwise agree, when a party serves its statement of case, it must also disclose the key documents on which it has relied in support of the claims or defences advanced in its statement of case (and including the documents referred to in that statement of case) and the key documents that are necessary to enable the other parties to understand the claim or defence they have to meet. This is referred to as Initial Disclosure. Initial Disclosure does not require the parties to undertake a search beyond that required to produce the Initial Disclosure (para. 5).

iv) Either party may request Extended Disclosure, which will be decided by the Court at the first case management conference. Such Extended Disclosure must be reasonable and proportionate having regard to the overriding objective (para. 6).

v) Where a party requests Extended Disclosure, a List of Issues for Disclosure arising from the statements of case must be prepared and the parties must prepare a Disclosure Review Document (para. 7, 10).[35]

vi) Extended Disclosure may take the form of one of five Disclosure Models (para. 8):[36]

(1) Model A: Known Adverse Documents: Disclosure of known adverse documents, which is defined by para. 2.8 to mean

> documents (other than privileged documents) that a party is actually aware (without undertaking any further search for documents than it has already undertaken or caused to be undertaken) both (a) are or were previously within its control and (b) are adverse.

(2) Model B: Limited Disclosure: Disclosure of the key documents on which they have relied (expressly or otherwise) in support of the claims or defences advanced in their statement(s) of case, and the key documents that are necessary to enable the other parties to understand the claim or defence they have to meet; and known adverse documents. This model does not require the parties to undertake a search beyond that required for the purpose of preparing a statement of case.

(3) Model C: Search-Led Request-Based Disclosure: The Court may order a party to give disclosure of particular documents or narrow classes of documents relating to a particular Issue for Disclosure, by reference to requests set out in the Disclosure Review Document. The Court may order the parties to undertake a search for such documents.

(4) Model D: Narrow Search-Based Disclosure: A party shall disclose documents which are likely to support or adversely affect its claim or defence or that of another party in relation to one or more of the

---

35 See Appendix 2 to the Pilot Scheme draft.
36 Similar, but not identical, options currently exist under CPR rule 31.5(7).

Issues for Disclosure (which is similar to standard disclosure). Such disclosure may include Narrative Documents (defined by para. 1.11 of Appendix 1 to mean "a document which is relevant only to the background or context of material facts or events, and not directly to the Issues for Disclosure"). The Court may order the parties to undertake a search for such documents.

(5) Model E: Wide Search-Based Disclosure: A party shall disclose documents, including Narrative Documents, which are likely to support or adversely affect its claim or defence or that of another party in relation to one or more of the Issues for Disclosure or which may lead to a train of inquiry which may then result in the identification of other documents for disclosure (because those other documents are likely to support or adversely affect the party's own claim or defence or that of another party in relation to one or more of the Issues for Disclosure) (*i.e.* the *Peruvian Guano* approach). For this model, each party should undertake a search. This model should be used only in exceptional cases.[37]

vii) The parties may seek guidance from the Court by way of a discussion with the Court in advance of or after a case management conference, concerning the scope of Extended Disclosure or the implementation of an order for Extended Disclosure (para. 11).

viii) Save where otherwise agreed by the parties or ordered by the Court, a party shall produce (1) disclosable Electronic Documents to the other parties by providing electronic copies in the documents' native format, in a manner which preserves metadata; and (2) disclosable hard copy documents by providing scanned versions or photocopied hard copies. Electronic Documents should generally be provided in the form which allows the party receiving the documents the same ability to access, search, review, and display the documents (including metadata) as the party providing them. A party should provide any available searchable OCR versions of Electronic Documents with the original, unless they have been redacted (para. 13).

The Pilot Scheme, if successful and ultimately implemented, may result in a fundamental shift to the conduct of disclosure in shipping litigation. However, Models C, D, and E may well require a review of large quantities of documents, even if some of the disclosure provided is more limited than in the past.

4 Electronic documentation in shipping disputes

Many commercial disputes concern the consideration of documents which relate to (a) the parties pre-contractual exchanges, (b) the contractual documentation, (c) the performance of the contract, (d) the breach of contract, (e) the articulation of the parties' dispute, and (f) the parties' financial position. There may well be other categories of

---

37 See C. Hollander, *Documentary Evidence* (13th ed.), (Sweet & Maxwell, 2018), para. 7–43.

relevant documentation. Much of this documentation is reflected in hard copy documents and email exchanges.[38] Such documents might be copied or stored or transferred in a variety of media or storage systems, including servers, computer hard disks, and mobile devices. Shipping disputes equally conform to such patterns and many disputes will involve the disclosure of such documents from such sources.

In addition, there are a number of technological advances in the management and operation of commercial shipping operations which require additional consideration in light of the parties' electronic disclosure obligations, including:

i) The vessel's own computer systems and servers, including cloud computing systems.
ii) The vessel's communication systems and records.
iii) The vessel's navigation and propulsion systems, which extends to autonomous surface navigation systems.
iv) The vessel's cargo control and manipulation systems.
v) The vessel's system of monitoring and management of fire and flooding protection.
vi) The vessel's tracking and monitoring systems and radio-frequency identification technology.
vii) The vessel's photographs and imaging.[39]
viii) The vessel's Voyage Data Recorder (VDR), which may include information as to the vessel's position using GPS, speed logs, gyro compass headings, radar or AIS (Automatic Identification System), ECDIS (Electronic Chart Display and Information System), bridge audio records, VHF radio communications, echo sounder readings, main alarms, hull openings, watertight and fire door status, hull stress, rudder operation, engine/propeller, thrusters, and anemometer and weather vane readings.
ix) The shipowner's and manager's servers and computers.
x) Electronic data interchange information for commercial transactions, *e.g.* electronic bills of lading, warehouse warrants/receipts.[40]

5 Conclusion

Lawyers are surely coming to grips with the complications associated with providing disclosure of Electronic Documents, whose very nature are changing faster today than they did in the past. The Business and Property Courts are adopting

---

38 In *Fairstar Heavy Transport NV v Adkins* [2013] EWCA Civ 886; [2013] 2 CLC 272, at [36], Mummery, LJ said:

> An important feature of e-mails, as with other Electronic Documents, is that there is no original physical document to be delivered up. The principal can only see the content of an e-mail if it is displayed on a screen or if it is printed out on paper by the printer.

39 *Kairos Shipping Ltd v ENKA & Co LLC* [2016] EWHC 2412 (Admlty); [2016] 2 Lloyd's Rep 525, at [21–25].

40 *Glencore International AG v MSC Mediterranean Shipping Co SA* [2017] EWCA Civ 365; [2017] 2 Lloyd's Rep 186.

measures which seek to ensure that the otherwise time-consuming and costly burdens of providing disclosure are managed in accordance with the dictates of the litigation and the overriding objective, but will still need to be conversant in the rapid technological changes introduced in the shipping industry.

Many shipping disputes are still determined on the basis of the review and disclosure of paper documents and email exchanges. It is unclear to what extent the full measure of a party's electronic documentation is being reviewed and disclosed, having regard to the above-mentioned procedures already adopted, and the provisional measures soon to be adopted, by the Court and the possible sources of such documentation. It may be that the disclosure strictly required in shipping litigation could result in more expansive bundles of documents being used in court and arbitral proceedings. It is for this reason that notions of proportionality should be adopted in controlling such disclosure. The right proportion, as with many cases, relates to issues of the volume of documentation, the ease of access, the cost of retrieval and review, the degree of potential relevance of the documents to a dispute, the complexity and value of the relevant claims, and the relative benefits and disadvantages of such disclosure overall. The electronic nature of documentation expands the nature of the exercise; it requires active case management to control that expansion, in shipping litigation and indeed all commercial litigation.

CHAPTER 13

Insurance and artificial intelligence
Underwriting, claims and litigation

*Simon Cooper**

1 Introduction

Artificial Intelligence (AI) represents both the biggest challenge and the biggest opportunity for the insurance industry for decades. It is set to fundamentally change the way in which the industry operates.

AI is an elastic term which can incorporate a number of different elements including big data, smart contracting, robotics, chatbots, telematics, gamification and the deployment of algorithms to facilitate the underwriting, claims and distribution processes. In insurance, these technologies are usually grouped together under the umbrella term, Insurtech.[1] What differentiates AI from earlier automated process is that it is autonomous; that is to say it is capable of making independent decisions on a basis of its own choosing and of learning from its own experiences.

Blockchain technology is often also included under the Insurtech heading. The primary objective of this Chapter is to discuss:

i) The current deployment of AI in the insurance industry and the plans for the near future;
ii) Some of the challenges which the use of Insurtech raises both for the insurer and the insured; and
iii) Some of the legal challenges that arise more generally from the use of AI and how those challenges might impact both the buyers and sellers of insurance.

It should be noted that Insurtech is growing at an extraordinarily fast rate and the comments and observations that follow should be read accordingly.

2 Insurance underwriting

Insurtech is being deployed broadly in two areas of the underwriting process: the personalisation of underwriting and the elimination of repetitive tasks and

---

* Ince Gordon Dadds LLP
1 For a general analysis on the concept, see: www.mckinsey.com/industries/financial-services/our-insights/insurtech-the-threat-that-inspires (last tested 31 March 2019).

unnecessary delays. Essentially, personalisation involves the gathering and deployment of highly specific 'source data' relating to the putative insured, the analysis of this data in the context of the relevant big data pool and the application of algorithms to this material to provide a fast but targeted policy proposal. These techniques also increase the insurer's ability to provide insureds with the kinds of insurance products that they want.

As discussed further below, the use of AI to eliminate repetitive tasks and improve efficiency can be seen in the marine insurance market and across commercial insurance generally. In contrast, the personalisation of insurance through AI has been limited largely to personal lines and SME business. It is inevitable, however, that its use will be broadened into commercial insurance, including the various marine classes, in the near future.

2.1 Usage based insurance

One of the major innovations which Insurtech has introduced is Usage Based Insurance (UBI),[2] which can be used to develop more personalised insurance products. This process is intended to improve significantly the insurance offering to individuals and, in due course, to corporations including ship operators and cargo owners.

Pay as you drive (PAYD) insurance is at the forefront of this process. New products have emerged to provide insurance to motorists driving less than a set mileage, perhaps 7,000 miles, a year. The insurance is priced on the basis of a fixed cost for the car's stationary risk, such as fire and theft, and a flexible element which is based on the number of miles driven each month. This information is collected through the use of telematics which involves a 'black box' in the car to relay information to the insurer in real time. Drivers can see the cost of their insurance as it is incurred and are also able to obtain an advanced indication of the cost of a particular journey.

It is interesting to note that Norwich Union (now part of Aviva) attempted to introduce a similar UBI product for motorists in 2006 but withdrew it in 2008. The slow take up of telematics by car manufacturers was blamed by the insurer for the failure of that scheme but it was also suggested that drivers' concerns about privacy meant that there was a reluctance to accept a telematics black box into the car. Ten years later, it seems that those objections have been largely overcome.

UBI enables insurance to be tailored not only by reference to how far an insured drives but also by reference to *how* the insured drives (known as 'pay how you drive' or PHYD insurance). This involves the use of telematics to monitor variables such as the speed at which the insured drives on different kinds of road, whether the insured brakes or accelerates sharply, whether he or she takes breaks on long drives, how much time they spend on motorways and where and when they drive. Again, this information can be transmitted from a black box in the car

---

2 For a general discussion on the concept, see: www.insurancebusinessmag.com/uk/guides/what-is-usagebased-insurance-116604.aspx (last tested 31 March 2019).

to the insurer. It is then compared with relevant big data resources to set a premium. Risk management measures can also be built into the process by indicating to the insured what is required to lower the premium and challenging the insured to meet those criteria through 'gamification' techniques in order to 'level up'.

Clearly this involves the collection and analysis of personal data from a large group of individuals and sources to see, for example, where an individual travels and at what times of day and days of the year are the most dangerous. This information can then be correlated against locations, times and dates of raised accident risk. There are obvious data protection issues which arise from this but also, perhaps, wider issues relating to privacy and consumer caution and concern about the amount of their data held by large corporations with the potential for misuse or loss, for example following a cyber incident.

UBI may also be open to abuse – for example – can the telematics tell when the insured is driving the car, when another named driver is at the wheel or when the car is being driven by someone who is not covered under the insurance? It is likely, therefore that some form of genetic code – a finger print or iris scan – will also be required to validate the UBI data (bringing with it additional privacy issues).

Although currently UBI is deployed largely in the motor sector (in relation to both individuals and fleets), it is easy to see how UBI technology may be transferred to other markets. Marine insurance seems particularly suitable in this regard, both in relation to hull and machinery cover and cargo insurance. For example, with the movement of each vessel or container tracked in real time and insurance adjusted to reflect not only distance travelled but also location and even weather conditions, pricing can become more transparent and insurance needs more targeted. In addition, although some of the features of UBI products, such as the ability to obtain advanced information about the insurance cost of making particular journeys, may seem unnecessary and unduly complex in the consumer context, scaled up they can have enormous benefits in commercial insurance by increasing the transparency of the insurance cost of individual voyages.

In relation to cargo, telematics could enable insurers to achieve a more accurate picture of where particular cargos are located, how they are stored and speed of travel.

The insurance of commercial drones is another example of how this type of insurance might work in practice. Insurers have combined with tech companies to identify and quantify risk for individual drone flights. This is achieved by aggregating data including hyper-localised weather, population density and proximity to high risk areas (which, in the case of drones, would include airports). An algorithm can then analyse this data and other data points to quantify the risk of a particular flight. One can see how this technology might be transposed to the marine sector.

It would be wrong, however, to think that this new technology is limited to various means of transport. It is also being applied actively to life and health insurance. Again, this involves the capture of specific data relating to the insured and the comparison of that data with relevant big data collected from other individuals. The use of AI technology can also improve the accuracy of data used to underwrite health insurance by providing information about how much we *actually* drink, smoke and exercise as opposed to what we say we do. Wearable telematics devices can communicate this information to the underwriters so that policies can be designed accordingly.

As with levelling up under motor insurance, 'gamification' may be used to enhance these processes. As the name suggests, gamification involves the inclusion of some gaming elements in the insurer/client relationship, for example by giving the insured targets to achieve in order to reach a new level of cover or premium. This approach is particularly relevant in the life and health sector where the attainment of Fitbit targets can be monitored. As well as strengthening the relationship between insurer and insured, gamification can introduce risk management elements into these insurance products.

2.2 Risk management

As noted above, many Insurtech assisted insurance products in the fields of life & health and motor insurance, can include an element of risk management through the use of telematics and gamification to monitor and hopefully improve the health or driving practice of the insured. The potential for risk management through the use of AI, however, extends much further than these classes. For example, the Internet of Things (IoT) can be used to monitor pipe leaks in real time for property risks or to see when workers are becoming fatigued and therefore at greater risk of an accident for liability insurance. Similarly, AI analysis of supply chains can enable businesses to identify contingent business interruption risk and to take steps to mitigate against it.

2.3 Anti-selection

While UBI insurance will benefit the healthy insured, one can see that there is a danger that the use of more precise data may result in less affordable insurance for less healthy insureds. This in turn may lead to regulatory challenges in relation to potential discrimination. In the UK, an insurer's ability to discriminate on the grounds of disability or age is already circumscribed by the Equalities Act 2010 and it would of course be necessary to ensure that any UBI or broader AI underwriting process continued to comply with that legislation. As noted, particular regulatory issues will also arise in connection with the use of sensitive personal or 'special data'[3] for these purposes and the transparency (or lack thereof) as to the purposes for which data is being used.

More controversially is the possibility of applying advanced analytics to genetic data to assist insurers by modelling an insured's susceptibility to genetic disorders and to assess health insurance risks and price accordingly. In the UK, this area is subject to the Code on Genetic Testing and Insurance[4] which is a voluntary

---

3 Under GDPR particularly restrictive rules apply to the processing of special data which includes data concerning an individual's ethnicity, health, sex life or sexual orientation.
4 https://assets.publishing.service.gov.uk/government/uploads/system/uploads/attachment_data/file/751230/code-on-genetic-testing-and-insurance.pdf (last accessed on 31 March 2019).

agreement between the Government and the ABI. One wonders, however, whether a similar code might eventually be necessary in the context of data gathered by the use of telematics in the context of UBI which may in the future be able to make very accurate predictions with regard to the life or health expectancy of particular individuals. Already insurers are looking at technology which will analyse an insured's 'selfie' using different facial data points to determine how quickly an individual is ageing, body mass index and whether they smoke. This information is then used to predict life expectancy.

2.4 Robotic process automation

The introduction of robotic process automation (RPA) and use of big data means that information can be gathered, underwriting decisions made and policy documentation issued much more quickly than in the past. This is achieved by using the RPA and chatbots to interrogate the insured in respect of key variables and to process that information and take the necessary underwriting decisions. Many of us will be familiar with a similar process in connection with the purchase of our motor or home insurance. The difference here, however, is that the process can be entirely automated by using RPA and the analysis of big data provides a far more accurate and sensitive basis for setting premium for particular risks on the basis of the source information provided by the insured. Clearly this can have major advantages for the shipping industry and, in particular, for cargo interests, by improving underwriting speed and efficiency and by reducing paperwork and, therefore, costs. Importantly, some of these facilities are available on line 24 hours a day so that insurance can be obtained at any time.

In summary, the key elements of all of these developments are the ability to use technology to obtain highly personalised data, combine it with relevant 'big data' and apply to that machine learning and algorithms to arrive in quick time at a bespoke risk assessment. Initiatives of this nature will become increasingly common as the full impact of the Internet of Things is realised. We can expect to see increasing use of location based sensors such as smart thermostats and geographical information systems (GIS) relaying information to insurers in real time to facilitate more accurate underwriting.

2.5 Blockchain and the verification of data

Many commercial transactions require the existence of relevant insurance contracts to be verified. For example, cargo insurance may involve numerous interested parties including owners, operators, cargo owners, mortgagees and banks. As traditionally structured, the sale of goods and their transhipment overseas involves a significant amount of paper work including commercial invoices and bills of lading which provide the basis upon which the insurer will issue a policy of insurance to the shipper and its banker. That banker must then transfer the documentation to the bank in the receiving country and the consignee will pay against those shipping documents. This transfer process can take up to a week during which time the goods may be sitting in port incurring charges, causing congestion and tying up assets. Insurers in Japan have developed a solution to this process based on Blockchain which will allow all of the parties to the transaction to view and verify the paper work in real time thus significantly speeding up the shipping process by removing the requirement for the physical transfer of documents between banks.

Similarly, marine hull insurance may involve cover for multiple, mobile assets in different regions around the world. The underwriting and the operation of insurance for these assets involves collecting and verifying a range of data, such as asset values, location and loss histories and the making of that data available to the different interests involved in the insurance process. This can be a lengthy process (with the risk of inaccuracy or uncertainty) but the use of Blockchain technology can significantly simplify and speed up the process, while at the same time providing the necessary degree of transparency and reliability.

A programme introducing these capabilities has been launched recently by a coalition of technology groups, insurers and a 'pilot' insured.

Although the original programme was limited to the compilation and 'locking' of a register of assets for a worldwide shipping company, it is expected to be extended into other markets including global logistics, aviation and energy. It is also likely to have a role in property insurance, in particular where it provides cover over multiple jurisdictions and requires the accurate listing of property in numerous different locations together with transparency with regard to premium allocation among those different locations. Global captive programmes are particular suitable for this kind of technology and it is already being rolled out in that context.

This use of Blockchain to verify the existence of insurance can have other applications too. For example, the broker Marsh, in conjunction with IBM, has developed a platform to streamline the process by which a company can verify that a contractor has the insurance they claim to possess.

2.6 Reinsurance

The use of AI is not limited to insurance but is also being adopted in the placement of reinsurance programmes. Here, the technology, and not least Blockchain, can be used to ensure the consistency of data available to all parties to a reinsurance while simultaneously improving the quality of that data. AI can facilitate reinsurers' ability to analyse the performance of their portfolios and to identify areas for potential improvement. It also allows a more accurate and efficient analysis of contract wordings to insure that they are consistent, without anomalies and meet the needs of both parties.

Finally in the reinsurance sector, AI is also being developed to better align reinsurers' risk appetite and the reinsured's requirements at a pre-contractual stage.

2.7 New risks and new opportunities

In addition to developing new techniques for assessing and underwriting existing risks, AI means that increasingly insurers are being asked to provide cover for the new technology itself. Indeed, across commerce as a whole, AI and associated technology is perceived by corporations as the 7th most pressing business risk – higher than political risk and climate change.[5] Furthermore, as responsibility and decision making shifts from humans to algorithms, new liability challenges arise for insurers.

Interconnectivity and the Internet of Things, which are vital in driving the AI revolution, bring with them a significant increase in the vulnerability of autonomous, self-learning machines to failure or an attack exploiting the numerous data points such technology requires. This will increase the demand for cyber insurance but, at the same time, the lack of data and the difficulty in predicting how and where AI will be deployed and operate is likely to make cyber risk more difficult for insurers to analyse and price.[6] Other products which will be in demand include new forms of business interruption insurance which do not require physical damage to trigger cover. It should also be borne in mind that improved AI is likely to lower the cost of developing malware and other forms of cyber-attack thus potentially increasing the frequency and sophistication of AI and cyber related losses.

3 Claims handling

AI can have a huge impact on the speed and manner in which insurers process claims.

One of the world's leading insurers confirmed recently that it will be deploying AI in deciding personal injury claims, with the expectation of cutting processing times from hours to seconds. Other insurers will be following suit in the not too distant future. New tech driven companies such as Lemonade Inc. are also entering the market with promises to process home insurance claims in seconds and pay them in minutes. Indeed, Lemonade claims to have resolved a loss in four seconds recently.

It is interesting to consider for a moment how these changes might be affected by two other recent developments: the introduction into English law of the right of an insured to claim damages for the late payment of its claims and the coming into effect of the GDPR.

Under s.13A Insurance Act 2015, it is an implied term in all English law insurances entered into after 15 May 2017 that the insurer will pay claims within a reasonable time. If that term is breached by the insurer's unreasonable delay, the insured can sue for breach of contract. The deployment of AI in the claims process is, of course, intended to speed up settlements and avoid delay. One wonders, however, what will happen if computer systems fail, either because of a technical

---

[5] Allianz Risk Barometer 2018.

[6] For an analysis on cyber insurance, see, S. Cooper "Cyber Risks, Liabilities and Insurance in the Marine Sector" published as Chapter 8 in B. Soyer & A. Tettenborn, *Maritime Liabilities in A Global and Regional Context* (2019, Informa Law from Routledge, Oxford), 103–117.

'glitch' or as the result of a virus or malware such as the recent 'WannaCry'[7] bug. Failure of an insurer's computer system and the consequent loss of claims information may well not qualify as 'reasonable delay' in the handling of claims, especially if not all the appropriate security measures had been observed by the insurer. If all appropriate measures have been taken, however, an insurer may be able to avoid any liability to damages by claiming that the delay in settling the claim was 'outside its control'.[8]

In addition, any damages that an insurer is obliged to pay as a result of such a failure may not be covered under any specialised cyber policy which the insurer itself had purchased. In circumstances where there is coverage, however, one can see that, without appropriate exclusions, a cyber insurer or reinsurer may face significant aggregation problems if, as with WannaCry, the malware hits a number of targets at the same time.

Detecting fraudulent claims is a major issue for insurers with recent industry figures showing approximately 113,000 fraudulent claims with a value of approximately £1.3bn detected in 2017.[9] It is no surprise, therefore, that Insurers are developing algorithms which use big data and machine learning to identify the markers of a fraudulent claim. Claims are then tested against these markers by the AI so that suspicious activity can be subjected to closer examination. It is to be hoped that this process is not jeopardised by the requirements of the GDPR to control the processing of personal data and inform data subjects of the purposes for which their data is being used. It seems inevitable, in any event, that fraudsters are developing their own complex algorithms to trigger unjustified claims payments and so, from this point of view at least, AI may be a double edged sword.

Interestingly, the EU is currently trialling AI powered lie detector technology principally for use in border control. Such technology may well have an application in the future handling of claims. Before that can happen, however, it will be necessary to ensure that issues such as inadvertent bias in the programming of the algorithm and the inevitable privacy issues are appropriately addressed.

4 Dispute resolution

Experience suggests that even with the most advanced AI there will be disputed claims, some of which will lead to litigation or other forms of dispute resolution such as arbitration or mediation. Here too, AI will have a role to play. New litigation prediction models for insurers are being developed with the intention of removing some of the uncertainty from dispute resolution. This new technology is

---

[7] The WannaCry ransomware attack was a May 2017 worldwide cyber-attack which targeted computers running Microsoft Windows by encrypting data and demanding ransom payments in Bitcoin. The attack has been estimated to have affected more than 200,000 computers across 150 countries, with estimates of total damage ranging from hundreds of millions to billions of dollars.

[8] Under section 13A(3) of the Act the insurer has a defence to any claim for damages for delay in paying the claim if the delay was reasonable. Section 13A(3)(d) provides that reasonable delay may include delay caused by factors outside the insurer's control.

[9] Association of British Insurers news release 22 August 2018.

designed to assist in assessing both the chances of success in defending claims, the likely quantum of successful claims and potential costs issues – including the reliability of cost estimates, the potential cost exposure to the other party and the likelihood of cost overruns. This information should enable insurers to arrive at a much more reliable cost benefit analysis of any dispute and to adjust their strategy accordingly.

There are a number of projects of this nature across the market reflecting cooperation between lawyers, technology providers, statisticians and academics. While they will certainly face technological, mathematical and regulatory challenges (for example in relation to GDPR and laws aimed at countering discrimination) these models represent part of the continuing drive to increase efficiency, reduce costs and eliminate frictional damage in the processing and settlement of claims. Without these changes, the threat to traditional insurance models will undoubtedly continue to increase.

At present, these tools are being developed principally with the resolution of high volume insurance claims in mind since it is easier to develop statistical models and predictive AI for this type of business. Nonetheless, predictive modelling is also expected to have an application for high value complex claims. Here the value of the claim may justify a wider data base including the analysis of information relating to particular Courts and individual judges. As far as complex marine and cargo claims are concerned, however, there seem likely to be limitations on this technology, not least in dealing with international disputes. Will, for example, a predictive algorithm have access to sufficient meaningful data to make a meaningful prediction, with any degree of accuracy, of how a Miami Court will approach the interpretation of JELC clauses?

5 Some problems

The growing use of AI is not without its pitfalls for buyers and sellers of cover as well as for brokers and other intermediaries.

5.1 The insurer

For the insurer, the huge volume of often 'special data'[10] assembled to facilitate technologies such as UBI will require very careful handling. A failure to safeguard this material, or to obtain the necessary consents for its use, can expose the insurer to severe financial penalties.[11] Perhaps more importantly, however, the loss or abuse of this data is likely to have a devastating impact on the insurer's reputation and commercial position. In addition, information of this kind is particularly attractive to cyber criminals and, at a time when even sophisticated operators are vulnerable to attack, managing this risk will require constant vigilance from the insurer and its service providers.

---

10 Special data is defined in Art.9 of the GDPR as personal data revealing racial or ethnic origin, political opinions, religious or philosophical beliefs, or trade union membership and the processing of genetic data, biometric data for the purpose of uniquely identifying a natural person, data concerning health or data concerning a natural person's sex life or sexual orientation.

11 Up to €20million or 4% of annual turnover under the Data Protection Act 2018.

Just as significantly, it will be important to manage the machine learning aspect of both underwriting and claims handling to avoid either direct or indirect discrimination on the grounds of race, gender, disability or location. For example, AI deployed in the underwriting process may note that males are more likely to have a motor accident than females or that individuals of a certain ethnicity are more likely to have cars stolen. If the AI starts to adjust premiums taking this information into account, there is a clear danger that it will place the insurer in breach of anti-discrimination laws. This breach may be as a result of indirect as well as direct bias, for example where the premium is increased for people living in an area which has a high concentration of a particular ethnicity, it is important, therefore, that insurers continue to exercise control over what their Insurtech is actually doing! Indeed, a recent focus paper by the EU's Fundamental Rights Agency[12] (FRA) draws attention to the fact that when algorithms are used in decision making there is a potential for breach of the principle of non-discrimination contrary to Article 21 of the EU's Charter of Fundamental Rights. The FRA therefore recommends, among other things, that potential biases and abuses created by the algorithm should be recognised, that the quality of data should be checked and that the way in which the algorithm was built should be capable of explanation.

Traditional insurers also face a profound threat to their business model from so called 'disrupters' – new businesses such as Lemonade which seek to bypass traditional insurance underwriting and distribution structures by making personalised insurance available quickly using a combination of AI, algorithms and chatbots to allow customers to download and use an app to purchase policies on smart phones and social media or packaged with other products. So far, however, the larger insurers have been able to respond to this challenge by joining with the startups to offer their own new models to their clients. In the circumstances, it is probably not the case that insurers face an existential threat to their existence, although it certainly is true that they are being required to show a capacity for innovation and flexibility with which the industry has not always been associated.

One final threat to insurers arises not so much from what they are doing themselves but from what their clients are doing. The increasingly wide spread use of AI means that insurers' clients may well be facing losses and liabilities of a kind which was rare or even non-existent in the past. Just as with cyber exposures, these risks may not be factored into traditional insurance policies such as all risk policies or package policies for large businesses. It may well be the case, however, that there is no relevant exclusion in the policy either so that insurers find themselves facing losses which were not anticipated and which they have not been included in their underwriting assessments. This is similar to the threat of 'non-affirmative' cyber insurance[13] which the industry has only recently begun to tackle and it will require careful analysis by insurers if it is to be managed successfully.

---

12 #*Big Data: Discrimination in data supported decision making.* FRA May 2018.
13 Non-affirmative cyber insurance is the cover provided, often inadvertently, for cyber related losses under non-cyber policies.

5.2 The insured

While AI should provide the insured with quicker and more focused insurance cover, and more convenient means of purchasing it, there are pitfalls. In particular the use of AI will make it much easier for insurers to identify subprime risks and there is clearly a danger of anti-selection or 'writing down' which will make it much harder for insureds with particular or unusual characteristics to obtain cover. Ultimately, this may require regulatory change to address – although the international nature of the industry and the impact of Brexit on the application of EU laws may mean that this is not forthcoming in the short term at least.

5.3 The intermediaries

One of the perceived advantages of AI is that it will create more direct contact between insured and insurer enabling the insurer to broaden its offering to its client and to respond more precisely to the client's needs thus helping to reduce the kind of indiscriminate marketing which can be both wasteful and unpopular. Existing distribution networks will be bypassed to remove unnecessary friction and cost from the insurance buying process allowing insureds to access the insurance provider more efficiently to secure the type of cover they need when they need it.

A blend of chatbots, AI and machine learning may be used to analyse and identify customer needs and to propose insurance solutions. This technology can be integrated into non-traditional platforms such as laptop computers and social media. This will mean that, like insurers, brokers and other intermediaries will find their business model under attack. While in the short term this may be an issue principally in the mass market, it is inevitable that it will also find a role in commercial placements. The coincidence of such a development with the greater scrutiny of the role of intermediaries from regulators threatens to create a perfect storm which will require intermediaries, like insurers, to adapt to survive.

6 Legal challenges

The use of AI raises a number of legal issues but perhaps the most difficult in the context of insurance is the question of liability. In order to properly underwrite the policies that they issue, as well as to enable them to resolve claims and analyse their own exposure, insurers will need to understand not only where the liability rests for damage caused by malfunctioning AI but also who is liable for damage caused by the decisions taken by AI. In cases in which errors by the developer or manufacturer of the AI can be shown to have resulted in the AI malfunctioning, issues of liability would appear at first sight to be relatively straight forward. As the decisions taken by AI systems become further removed from direct programming and increasingly based on machine learning principles, however, it may be difficult to identify the precise cause of a particular AI decision or the source of any damage. A system which learns from information it receives from the world, can operate independently from its operator and in a way that its designers did not or could not have anticipated. Who will be liable if the AI's actions are inexplicable or cannot be traced back to human error?

Various ideas have been put forward to address this issue. For example, it has been suggested that a suitably adapted version of the laws relating to animals could be applied to AI machines. An alternative suggestion has been to apply the law that relates to non-human legal entities – in other words, to recognise that AI is a legal personality in its own right just as companies are legal entities in their own right. Perhaps the draw back with that approach, however, is that at the end of the day the acts of a company can be attributed to a person or group of people and a company can only be criminally liable, for example, if an individual acting on behalf of the company can be identified. By contrast, the acts of AI may not necessarily be capable of being traced back to a person.

Given these difficulties, it seems likely that some form of legislation will be required to determine a system for apportioning liability in the event of an AI generated loss. The EU has begun to address this issue through the European Parliament's resolution and recommendations to the Commission contained in the *Civil Law Rules of Robotics* passed in February 2017. This document invites the Commission to consider two approaches to liability; a strict liability approach or a risk based liability approach. The latter would focus on 'the person who is able … to minimise risks and deal with negative impacts'.[14]

The EU paper also considers the possibility of a compulsory insurance scheme which would take into account '… all potential responsibilities in the chain [of causation].'[15] These recommendations are now under consideration by the European Commission.

In the UK, the House of Lords Parliamentary Select Committee on Artificial Intelligence has published a paper: *AI in the UK: ready, willing and able?* Which, among other topics considers the issue of liability. The paper concludes:

> In our opinion, it is possible to foresee a scenario where AI systems may malfunction, underperform or otherwise make erroneous decisions which cause harm. In particular, this might happen when an algorithm learns and evolves of its own accord. It was not clear to us, nor to our witnesses, whether new mechanisms for legal liability and redress in such situations are required, or whether existing mechanisms are sufficient.[16]

The paper goes on to recommend that the Law Commission of England & Wales be asked to 'establish clear principles for accountability and intelligibility'[17] as soon as possible.

The UK Government has also been looking at the possibility of legislating in the field of AI, although in their case only with regards to autonomous vehicles. The *Automated and Electric Vehicles Act* 2018 (AEVA), which came into law in July 2018, provides that the insurers will be liable for any loss or damaged caused by an autonomous or electric vehicle. This means that the driver/passenger in such a vehicle will not

---

14 European Parliament resolution of 16 February 2017 with recommendations to the Commission on Civil Law Rules on Robotics (2015/2103(INL)) paragraph 55.
15 Ibid paragraph 57.
16 *AI in the UK: ready, willing and able?* HL Paper 100 paragraph 317.
17 *Ibid*, Conclusion paragraph 56.

be faced with the possibility of having to make a complex product liability claim against the vehicle's manufacturer or developer. Insurers will be able, however, to exclude liability in certain circumstances in which the vehicle's software has been altered by the insured or has not been updated.[18] The AEVA also provides for a fund equivalent to the MIB to cover uninsured losses caused by autonomous vehicles. Interestingly, the drafters of the Act appear to assume that insurers will be able to pursue subrogated claims against whosoever caused the AI malfunction. This solution, while perhaps pragmatic, seems simply to kick the causation-can further down the road.

A number of countries, including the UK, Bermuda, Hong Kong and Australia, have created 'regulatory sandboxes' to facilitate the controlled development of regulation in the Insurtech field. Bermuda, for example, allows startups a year to develop out of the sandbox before becoming fully regulated.

One final point to mention is the question of whether AI can be programmed in such a way that it inflicts damage to one person or object instead of another – the so called 'trolley bus problem'. For example, could an AI vehicle be programmed to prioritise the life of its passengers over that of a pedestrian? An approach of that nature was hinted at by a major German car manufacturer recently but they back tracked very quickly when it was pointed out by the Federal Ministry of Transport and Digital Infrastructure that making such an decision on the basis of a pre-programmed set of criteria was likely to be illegal and that the Government intends to introduce regulations to that affect.

7 Summary

In summary, AI will revolutionise all aspects of insurance from underwriting to claims handling to dispute resolution and distribution. This process is already underway but its full extent is difficult to predict. Traditional insurance models face fundamental challenges but at least the early indications are that they are beginning to recognise and respond to those challenges.

I am not sure that the same can be said of governments. While some early steps have been taken to address the legal and regulatory issues that AI will generate, it is very far from clear, where that particular journey will end.

---

18 AEVA 2018 s.4.

INDEX

AAWA project 145
agents, use of 45, 50–51, 52, 55, 100, 126, 130, 142
AIS (Automatic Identification System) 77, 78, 129, 176
algorithms: artificial intelligence 178; autonomous shipping 108; blockchain 13, 14, 15; collision avoidance systems 77; encryption 38, 39–40; insurance 180, 182; and liability 108, 121–122; potential for discrimination 187; product liability 119; seaworthiness 155; smart contracts 4
Amazon 14, 17, 100
anti-competitive effects 11
anti-selection (insurance) 181–182, 188
antitrust 11–12
Antwerp 48, 49, 50, 60, 90, 94, 103, 157
AP Møller-Mærsk 10
arbitration clauses 85
artificial intelligence: autonomous shipping 109, 131; as business risk 184; and insurance 178–190; machine learning 182, 187, 188; Maritime Autonomous Surface Ships (MASS) 67; predictive coding in document search 173; self-adapting systems 160n38; smart ports 90; trolley problem 108n15, 190
asset registers 183
assignment 40
assistance to other ships 74, 135–137, 144
ASV Global 69, 77
asymmetric encryption 37–38, 40, 45
attornment 54
audit trails 18, 20
authentication 18, 20, 33, 36; *see also* identity verification
authority, acting outside 44, 46
authority to vary a contract 61
automated container terminals 100–101
automated mooring 100
automatic detection systems 96, 97

automatic mooring systems 129
autonomous shipping: carrier liability 148–161; jurisdiction issues 140; and maritime law 67–89; product liability 118–119, 124–126, 127; regulatory and contractual challenges 129–147; and the role of the master 129–147; and smart ports 91–94, 97, 98, 103; third-party liabilities 105–115
autonomous vehicles 189
autonomy assisted bridge (AAB) 68
auto-pilot 98; *see also* autonomous shipping
Aviva 179

ballast water treatment 7
bankers 17, 51, 52, 55, 57, 182–183
BankID 41, 42
Belgium 94, 150n9
Bermuda 190
big data 14, 178, 180, 182
bills of lading: blockchain 5–6; *Bolero Bill of Lading* (BBL) 11; customary trade practices 26; delivery of goods 33–34, 56–57, 118; delivery terms 48, 49; difference between US and UK law 32n75; digitisation 5–6, 117, 122; electronic signatures 40; exchanging for delivery orders 56–57; *Glencore v MSC* 50–52; *Himalaya* clauses 8, 140; international legal regimes 23; and the master 142, 144; negotiability 33, 50, 51; paramount clauses 8; Rotterdam Rules 29, 32; shipper-carrier relationships 23; shore-based controllers 142, 143, 147
BIMCO 19–21, 86, 141, 142n34, 146
Bingham, Lord 51, 166
biometrics 180
Bitcoin 6, 17, 40
black boxes 179
blockchain: electronic signatures 40–41; insurance 178, 182–183; and liability 117,

191

122; security risks 122; in the shipping industry 3–16; smart contracts 17–18; smart ports 101
blue cards 137, 140, 146
Bolero project 10–11
border control 185
both to blame collisions 142, 143
Botport law 90–104
breach of contract 61
Brexit 188
bulk carriage of commodities 10
bunker contracts 21
bunker fuel 86, 130
burden of proof 24, 125, 155
bystander injury 125, 127

cabotage 73
Canada 140n26
car insurance 179
care of cargo 123–124, 154, 156–158, 161
cargo documentation 117, 122–123, 142
cargo insurance 180, 182
cargo loss 23–25, 28–29, 47–63, 123–124, 140
carriage of goods by sea: domestic statues, judicial doctrines and customary trade practices 25–26; international conventions 23–28
carrier liability 24, 50, 124, 148–161
Central Commission for Navigation of the Rhine (CCNR) 94
certification, electronic 43, 137, 146
channelling liability 112, 125–126
charterparties 6, 8, 18, 19–21, 85, 141–142
charterers 19–20, 75, 107, 112, 113, 120, 122, 139, 141–142, 147
chatbots 178, 182, 187, 188
China 71, 100
choice of forum clauses 15, 16
choice of law clauses 15, 16, 85
ciphers 37
civil procedure rules for disclosure 166–173
cloud computing 176
Code on Genetic Testing and Insurance 181-2
collision avoidance systems 68, 77–78, 98
collisions: and autonomous ships 76–78, 83, 87, 111, 113, 114, 124–125, 142, 143; both to blame collisions 142, 143; product liability 117, 119
collusive behaviours 11
COLREGS (International Regulations for Averting Collisions at Sea 1972) 76–8, 87, 88, 89, 92, 106, 133–5, 152

Comité Maritime International (CMI) 31, 87, 91, 132, 146, 150
Commfides 41
company digital signatures 39, 44
company seals 39, 44
Company Security Officers (CSO) 79–80
condition of goods 149, 156
congestion 70
consignees 7, 28, 33, 49–50, 51, 54, 122
container transport: autonomous ships 69; digitisation of documentation 118; dockers 101; multimodal contracts 26–27; port-to-port basis 26; Rotterdam Rules 29; stowage 156; transport sharing devices/ apps 10
continuously unmanned ships (CUS) 68, 74, 83
contract of carriage 26, 27, 28, 31, 34, 51, 62, 124, 140, 144, 154
control of goods in transit 34, 52, 53–56
corruption 95
counterfeiting 9
criminal law and the master 140
Crown immunity 69
cryptocurrencies 3, 17, 40
cryptology 38
custody of goods 52
customary trade practices 26
Customs 103
C-WORKER 7 (ASV Global) 69, 79, 84
cyber insurance 184, 187
cyber resilience 86
cybercrime 101, 147
cybersecurity 77, 86, 111, 115, 122, 147, 154, 180, 184, 186, 187

damage to cargo 123–124, 140
damages 8, 125, 184
data connectivity 111, 115, 129
data management 98, 102–103
data protection 12, 180, 181
Data Sampling 168
data security 12, 18, 44, 45, 60, 103
data sharing 103, 166
decentralized networks 18
decryption keys 37–38, 45
defences 43–45, 46, 49–50, 120, 155
delivery of goods: bills of lading 33–34, 48, 49, 56–57, 118; carrier's obligation 33–34; definition of 'delivery' 53–56; delivery terms 49, 50, 52–53, 56–60, 61, 62; misdelivery 29, 61–62, 122; symbolic delivery 49, 53, 56
delivery orders 56–60, 61–62

deployed over side equipment 67
digital currencies 17, 40
digital payments 95
digital signatures 36–46
digitisation: Insurtech 178–190; legal technology 165–177; and product liability 116–120; smart ports 102–103
disabling want of knowledge 151
disclosure in shipping litigation 165–177
disposal of cargo in transit 29–30, 157, 158
dispute resolution 15–17, 165–177, 185–186
distress signals 136
distributed ledger technology (DLT) 5–7, 8, 9, 12, 18, 41, 117, 122
distrust, mutual 17
DNV GL 70
dockers 101–102
document, definition of 167–168, 173
document of title function 29, 31, 32, 117
door-to-door transactions 25, 33
double-spending 40–41
drones 14, 72, 94, 100, 101, 105, 180
drugs trade 101
due despatch 141
due diligence 42, 113, 149, 153, 154–155, 160
dumping (waste) at sea 81
duty of care 84, 121, 124, 128
duty to provide assistance 74, 135–137, 144

ECDIS (Electronic Chart Display and Information System) 98, 176
e-commerce 14, 16, 29
e-contracts 16
e-disclosure databases 167–168
e-documentation 117, 122, 165–177
e-freight forwarding 100
electronic certificates 43, 137, 146
Electronic Data Interchange (EDI) 29–30, 103, 117, 176
electronic disclosure 167–173
electronic messages 11
electronic monitoring systems 124
electronic release systems (ERS) 48, 49–50, 51
electronic signatures 7, 36–46
electronically stored information (ESI) 26, 27, 171
emails 48, 57, 60, 166, 169, 171, 172, 177
e-malfunctions 122
emergency situations 68, 92, 98, 110, 129, 153
e-navigation 98
encryption 11, 37–38, 41, 45, 122
enforceability of international contracts 15–17

entitlement to the cargo 40
environmental issues 86, 130
environmental standards 7
ESSDOCS 117
estoppel 49, 60–61
ethical dilemmas 108n15
evidential value of automatic detection systems 96

facilitation payments 95
facsimiles of signatures 36
fault liability 108, 109, 111, 119, 122, 160
ferries, autonomous 106
fines 137
Finferries 105–106
fireboats 69, 93
flag state jurisdiction 73–74, 79, 131–132
forgeries 44, 46
fraud 9, 185
freedom of contract 100
freight forwarders 100
functional equivalence 31
Fundamental Rights Agency (FRA) 187

gamification 178, 180, 181
GENCON 19, 143–144
genetic data 180, 181–182
geographical information systems (GIS) 182
Germany 71, 190
GIANO 69
giving way 134
global marketplace 17
global standardization 19
good faith defences 44
GPS (Global Positioning System) 86, 176
Greenhouse gas emissions 9, 70

hacking 60, 111, 122, 129, 145, 147, 154, 186
Hamburg 101
Harbour masters 94, 96–97
hardware failure 121, 127
hauliers 48
hazardous/toxic materials 82, 109, 125, 158
health insurance 180–181, 182
Himalaya clauses 8, 140
hold harmless provisions 85
holders of electronic records 33
holograms 105
Hull Fouling Clause 141
human error 86, 115, 116, 129, 150, 160, 189
hybrid autonomous-manned vessels 68, 74, 106, 149
hybrid blockchain 12, 15
hyperloops 101

INDEX

IBM 183
ice risk areas 143
IDEA 20
identity verification 36, 39, 41, 43, 45
ILO (International Labour Organization) 102, 138
IMDG Code 142
IMO (International Maritime Organization) 78, 87–88, 89, 91, 97, 98, 106, 113, 130, 132, 146, 147
imputation 50, 51
IMSBC Code 142
indemnity clauses 85
India 73
information asymmetries 9
infrastructure: digital signatures 41–42; electronic signatures 42–43; smart ports 94–95
inland destinations, carriage to 27
inland waterways 94, 129
insolvency 84
inspection regimes 96–97, 112, 113
insurance: and artificial intelligence 178–190; and autonomous ships 75, 83, 85–86, 137, 146; claims handling 184–185; document disclosure 167; fraud 185; Insurtech 178–190; product liability 118, 123; third-party liabilities 111, 112, 115; underwriting 178–184; Usage Based Insurance (UBI) 179–181
Inter-Club Agreement 120, 142
Interfishmarket 10
intermediaries: avoiding use of with blockchain 10; avoiding use of with smart contracts 13; in global marketplace 17; lawyers 13–14
internal waters 73
International Association of Marine Aids to Navigation and Lighthouse Authorities (IALA) 98, 99
international contracts, enforceability 15–17
international conventions: autonomous shipping 73–84, 130; carriage of goods by sea 23–25; definition of 'ship' 71; other modes of carriage 26–28; ports 91
International Group of P&I Clubs 85–86
International Monetary Fund (IMF) 75
International Ship and Port Facility Security (ISPS) Code 79–80
International Transport Forum, OECD 3
international waters 88
International Working Group for Maritime Law and Unmanned Craft (IWG) 87–88
Internet of Things (IoT) 9, 181, 182, 184
interoperability issues 18, 41–42

ISM (International Safety Management) Code 79
ISPS Code 79–80
IT managers and smart contracts 13; *see also* software producers and liability; voyage programmers

Japan 183
jettison 143–144, 157, 158
job losses 74, 101
jurisdiction issues 15, 16, 73, 85, 140

keys (physical) 54–55
knock-for-knock provisions 85
knowledge imputed 50, 51
Kongsberg 69, 129
KOTUG 69

labour laws 102, 138–139
lack of authority defence 44, 46
large vendors 14
legal technology, disclosure in shipping litigation 165–177
Lemonade Inc 184, 187
less container load (LCL) transport 10
liability: after discharge, before delivery 50; and artificial intelligence 188–189; and autonomous shipping 74–76, 88; blockchain 8; carrier liability 24, 50, 124, 148–161; channelling liability 112, 125–126; electronic signatures 42–43, 45; fault-based liability 108, 109, 111, 119, 122, 160; limited liability 74–75, 113–114, 119, 120, 124, 140; in the maritime transport industry generally 8; Nairobi Convention (Nairobi wreck removal convention 2007) 82–83; online intermediaries 100; pollution liability 125; product liability 116–128; Rotterdam Rules 28–29, 31; several liability 119; smart ports 95, 96; software producers and liability 155; strict liability 84, 88, 107–110, 121, 125, 126–128, 189; terminal operators 101
lie detector technology 185
limitation of liability 74–75, 113–114, 119, 120, 124, 140
liner transportation 10
linesmen 100
liquidation 54
Lloyd's Emerging Risks and Research 85
Lloyd's Open Form (LOF) 85
logistics sector 3
logs 141

194

look out, requirements for 76, 134; *see also* watch keeping requirements
loss of cargo 23–25, 28–29, 47–63, 123–124, 140

MAchine eXecutable Collision regulations for Marine Autonomous Systems research project (MAXCMAS) 77n21
machine learning 182, 187, 188
Maersk Line 147
maintenance 68, 70, 87, 113, 130, 141, 146–147, 158
malware 147, 184, 185
manning requirements 131–132
manoeuvring rules 76, 89, 93, 134–135
manufacturer, channelling liability to 112, 113, 117
marine diesel oil (MDO) 130
marine fuel purchasing 21
marine gas oil (MGO) 130
marine hull insurance 183
Marine Industries Alliance 88
Maritime and Coastguard Agency (MCA) 88
Maritime Autonomous Surface Ships (MASS) 67–89, 106, 130
Maritime Law Association 131, 132
maritime performing parties 101
Maritime Safety Committee (MSC) 87, 106, 130, 147
Maritime Single Windows 103
maritime tracking 103
maritime zones 73
Marsh 183
MASRWG Voluntary Code of Practice 84, 85, 88
master: care of cargo 157; MASRWG Voluntary Code of Practice 89; ship's delivery orders 58; smart contracts 21; UNCLOS 74; and unmanned vessels 74, 88, 129–147
mates' receipts 142
metadata 166, 169, 171
MIB (Motor Insurers' Bureau) 190
middlemen *see* intermediaries
misappropriation of cargo 47–49
misdelivery 29, 61–62, 122
mitigation 45, 181
monitoring systems 69, 86, 118, 124, 129, 133, 146, 158, 176
mooring men 100
mortgage 84
multimodal transactions 8, 25, 26–27
Mummery LJ 176n38

MUNIN (Maritime Unmanned Navigation through Intelligence Networks) 105, 109, 149

nationality of ships 73
native format documents 169–170, 175
nautical fault exception 158–161
navigation: and autonomous ships 76, 83, 86, 107, 110–111, 133; in the definition of a 'ship' 70; digitisation 118–119; e-navigation 98; nautical fault exception 160; navigation rights 73; navigation systems and document disclosure 176; product liability 124–126; role of the master 141; smart ports 92, 98; software producers and liability 141
negligence: and autonomous ships 76, 84, 107, 113, 134; electronic signatures 45; master 143, 144; nautical fault exception 159; product liability 116–117, 119, 121, 124–125; seaworthiness 150; and software 122–123
negotiability 29, 33, 50
neutral platforms 10
NKK 120
non-discrimination principle 91
non-permissioned DLT 6–7
non-vessel-operating carriers (NVOC) 27n28
Norway 39, 42, 44, 45, 71, 106
Norwegian Forum for Autonomous Ships (NFAS) 68n1
Norwegian Maritime Law Commission 42
Norwich Union 179
notify parties 48
NxtPort 103
NYPE (New York Produce Exchange Form) 141–143

off-hire 142
offshore sector 112
oil and gas contracts 85
oil pollution 82, 125, 137, 140
oil record books 137, 140
Optical Character Recognition (OCR) technology 101, 170, 175
oracles 7
original documents 39
owners *see* shipowners

P&I 49, 85, 118, 119, 123, 125, 128
paper documentation: audit trails on 19–20; benefits of pen-and-ink signatures 41–42; costs of 23, 34; e-documents with same

legal force as 11; holders of 33; security of 60; substitutability with electronic 32
paperless offices 165
paramount clauses 8
passphrases, security of 44, 45
patent applications 4n11, 6n16
pay as you drive (PAYD) insurance 179
pay how you drive (PHYD) insurance 179
PDF Advanced Electronic Signatures (PAdES) 39
peer-to-peer systems 9, 17
periodically unmanned bridge (PUB) 68, 74
periodically unmanned ships (PUS) 68, 74, 83
permissioned ledgers 7–8, 12, 15, 18
personal data 12, 180, 181, 182, 186
personal injury claims 75, 125, 127, 139, 184
pilotage assistance 99, 145–146
pilots 93, 99, 139, 143, 145–146
PIN codes 47–63, 101, 118, 122, 123
piracy 86, 142, 145, 157–158
pledges 55
pollution detection 94
pollution liability 125
pollution prevention 79, 80, 82, 108
'pooling' cargo 10
port agents 130, 141, 142, 147
port of refuge 143–144
port security officers 97
Port State Control 93, 96–97
Portable Pilot Units (PPUs) 99
ports: autonomous ships coming into 68, 73, 91, 99, 130, 145; crew's cargo duties 158; port management 94–96; port states 91, 131; security 96, 97; smart ports 90–104
port-to-port basis 33
port-to-port transactions 25, 26, 27
possession of goods 53–56
powers of attorney 45
powers of control 52
predictive coding 173
privacy issues 179–180, 185
product liability 116–128
property damage insurance 85
public blockchains 18
public keys 37, 38, 45–46
Purple Water 69

qualified signatures 40

radar 98, 103
radio communications 67, 74, 92, 98, 103, 129

real-time characteristics of smart contracts 14
real-time data and autonomous ships 77
real-time demand and supply matching 9
real-time tracking and insurance 180
reasonable care 113, 156
reasonableness test 73
reasonably suited standard 154
receipt for goods 31
recklessness 88, 114, 139
recourse action 113
reefers 118
registered owner, channelling liability to 112
reinsurance 183
release notes 48, 49, 50, 51, 52–53, 56–57, 62
relevance tests 166
Remote Operated Vehicles (ROVs) 67
remote operation of ships 67, 89, 99, 105, 106, 110, 130, 145, 149, 152–153, 159
rendering assistance to other ships 74, 135–137, 144
Report of the Working Group on International Legislation on Shipping 149n8
reverse engineering 15
revocations 52
right to be forgotten 12
right to demand delivery 33–34
right of disposal 29
risk profiles 86
robotic process automation (RPA) 182
robotics 101, 178, 182
Rolls Royce 69, 105, 118n18, 145
Rosetti Marino 69
Rotterdam 69, 90, 94, 100–101
routing recommendations 141

safe manning documents 138
sale and charter of vessel 7
sale of goods 44, 121
sale of services 121, 127
salvage 83, 85, 144
sandboxes, regulatory 190
SARUMS 149
satellite coverage 77
scrapping and recycling 7
seafaring 92, 138–139, 152
seals 39
seamanship 76–77, 78, 134
search, document 166–173, 174–175
search and rescue (SAR) 87
sea waybills 31, 32, 142, 144
seaworthiness 119, 141, 149–155
security, port 96, 97

INDEX

security alert systems 79
security risks 79–80, 110
self-mooring systems 100
sensitive data 12
sensors 77, 96, 97, 99, 112, 126, 127, 129, 182
servants of the carrier 144, 159, 160
several liability 119
ship to shore interfaces 86
shipowners: channelling liability to 112, 114; due diligence 153; in-house software development 160; insurance 137; product liability 117; and the role of the master 139, 143, 147
Shipowners' Club 86
ships, legal definition of 70–72, 73–84, 131n5
ship's delivery orders 50, 57–60, 144
ship's papers orders 167
shipwrecks 83
shopping agents 100
shore-based controllers: and autonomous ships 78, 92, 96, 97, 98; bills of lading 142, 143, 147; functional equivalent of master 140, 143, 144, 146; as master 133; multiple vessels at once 153; nautical fault exception 159; product liability 120; and proper manning requirements 152; and the role of the master 129, 130, 132, 138–140, 141–145; salvage 144; seaworthiness 143; and shipowners 153; training and certification 152–153
signatures 36–46
Singapore 100
slow steaming 141
smart cargo transportation 118, 158
smart containers 100–101, 158
smart contracts 4, 10, 12–15, 16, 18, 21, 178
smart ports 90–104
smart shipping 94; *see also* autonomous shipping
smart stowage 101
smart surveillance cameras 96
smart thermostats 182
SmartCon 20
smuggling 143
software maintenance standards 146
software malfunctions 109–110, 116, 119, 122, 126, 154–155, 185, 189
software producers and liability 108–109, 119, 121–122, 126, 127, 141, 160
sound systems 156, 158, 161
special trade passenger ship instruments 87
spoofing 86
standard disclosure 167
standard terms and conditions 47, 50, 100
standardized contracts 19–20, 85

states as trusted managers of blockchains 12
stevedores 142, 161
storage facilities 53
stowage 101, 118, 122, 156
streaming of data 77
strict liability 84, 88, 107–110, 121, 125, 126–128, 189
strike action 93, 143
sub-bailees 54, 55
sub-contracting 27
submarines 67, 105
submersibles 70
supercargo 143
supply chains 13, 14, 18, 181
surveillance 96, 105, 129

tackle-to-tackle basis 25, 33
tallymen 101
telematics 178, 179, 180–181, 182
temperature monitoring 118, 157
terminal operators 100–101
terms of carriage 49–50
terrorism 79, 81, 97
theft of cargo 48–49, 123
third parties, transfer of rights to 23, 34
third party authority 5
third party damage 85
third party losses 43
third-party liabilities 105–115, 120, 122, 125
third-party repairmen 154
tort 44–45, 76, 84, 107, 109–110, 113, 117, 139
towage 93
transfer of goods 53–56
transport sharing devices/apps 9
trigger events 18
trolley problem 108n15, 190
true records, establishing 5
trust: electronic versus pen-and-ink signatures 36; importance of 17; in the Internet 37; trusted actors 7, 12, 16; trusted clients 7; trusted managers 15
tube transportation 101
tugs, remote-controlled 69, 93–94, 118

UK Ship Register 69, 79, 83–84
ultra slow steaming 141
uncertainty 17, 20
UNCITRAL (UN Commission on International Trade Law) 29–34, 41
underwater vehicles 67, 70, 105
underwriting 178–184, 187
unmanned ships 14, 67–89; *see also* autonomous shipping
unpermissioned ledgers 6

unseaworthiness 119–120, 124, 143, 150–151, 153, 154–155
Usage Based Insurance (UBI) 179–181
user-points 41–42

variation of contract 61
verification 37
Vessel Traffic Service (VTS) 96, 97–99, 103
vessels not under command 134–135
virtual bridges 133
virtual watchkeeping 138
voice recognition 105
Voyage Data Recorders (VDRs) 103, 176
voyage programmers 130, 133, 142, 149–150, 160–161

waivers 62
walled gardens 20
war risk areas 142, 143
warehouses 101
warranties 141n31, 143
warships 82
waste management 81
watch keeping requirements 78, 137–138, 150
weight limits 80
wrecks 83

Yara Birkeland 69, 72–73, 92, 106, 129, 132